Korea Briefing, 1993

Korea Briefing, 1993

FESTIVAL OF KOREA

edited by
Donald N. Clark

Published in cooperation with
The Asia Society

Deborah Field Washburn,
Series Editor

Westview Press
BOULDER • SAN FRANCISCO • OXFORD

29393201

Copyright © 1993 by The Asia Society

Published in 1993 in the United States of America by Westview Press, Inc., 5500 Central Avenue, Boulder, Colorado 80301-2877, and in the United Kingdom by Westview Press, 36 Lonsdale Road, Summertown, Oxford OX2 7EW

Library of Congress ISSN: 1053-4806
  ISBN 0-8133-8770-1

Printed and bound in the United States of America

∞ The paper used in this publication meets the requirements of the American National Standard for Permanence of Paper for Printed Library Materials Z39.48-1984.

10   9   8   7   6   5   4   3   2

Contents

Preface

This edition of *Korea Briefing*, the fourth in the series, is issued in conjunction with The Asia Society's Festival of Korea, a yearlong, nationwide celebration of Korean history, culture, and contemporary life. A collaborative endeavor between The Asia Society and cultural institutions throughout the United States and Korea, the Festival begins in autumn 1993 and takes place in major U.S. cities including New York, Los Angeles, Washington, D.C., Houston, Atlanta, Chicago, and Seattle. Among its features are an art exhibition, an array of performances, a film festival, and a symposium series titled "Korea: Past and Present." *Korea Briefing, 1993* both stands on its own in a well-established series and serves as a companion to Festival events.

In addition to providing an overview of recent developments on the Korean peninsula—the precedent-setting election of Kim Young-sam as South Korea's first civilian president in more than three decades, changing security and economic relations between the United States and South Korea, the dramatic (though as yet unfulfilled) threat by North Korea to withdraw from the Nonproliferation Treaty regime—*Korea Briefing, 1993* supplies extensive historical background to these events. It traces South Korea's political and economic development from the time of Korea's liberation from Japanese colonial rule in 1945 to mid-1993. Likewise, it charts five decades of U.S. policy toward the Republic of Korea, beginning with an account of the birth of the Republic from postwar devastation in an atmosphere of growing U.S.-Soviet conflict, continuing with a description of the close military and economic relationship between the United States and South Korea, and winding up with a call for both sides to meet the opportunities and challenges of the new global strategic and economic environment.

This year's cultural chapters, on literature, dance, and music, explore the origins of these art forms and their evolution in modern times. Although the focus of the discussion of contemporary arts is on South Korea, sections on North Korean literature and music, as well as on the music of Korean communities outside of Korea, are included. The closely intertwined dance and music chapters are illustrated with photographs of performers and performances that complement Festival events.

A guiding purpose of the Korea Briefing series—and of the Festival of Korea—is to increase understanding by Americans of Korea and Koreans. To this end, *Korea Briefing, 1993* includes a chapter on Korean Americans—who they are, how they came to the United States, and what makes up the fabric of their lives today. The special challenges faced by the Korean American community in the wake of the 1992 Los Angeles riots are discussed in depth.

Two additional chapters, by a Korean and an American, are mirror images of one another. Drawing on personal experience and survey data, each author presents views of the other culture from the perspective of his own. By confronting areas of ambivalence and ignorance, both chapters puncture stereotypes and promote tolerance.

This special edition of *Korea Briefing* closes with a chronology of Korean history from the Choson dynasty (1392–1910) to the intensive negotiations between U.S. and North Korean officials over Pyongyang's nuclear program (July 1993). It includes a glossary of personalities and terms and a list of suggestions for further study that encompasses books, articles, sound recordings, and videotapes. We believe that this volume will both add an important dimension to classroom study and enrich individual exploration of Korea's past and present achievements.

Numerous dedicated individuals have worked together to bring this volume to completion. Editor, chapter author, and chronologer Donald N. Clark has been tireless in his commitment to the project. The high quality of the book is in large part the result of his efforts. We thank him and all of the other chapter authors, who fulfilled their assignments with proficiency and dispatch. At The Asia Society, Senior Editor Deborah Field Washburn shaped the chapters and oversaw all aspects of the project. Editorial Associate Sayu Bhojwani provided editorial assistance of a high quality, along with efficient management of all the details of publication. For the fourth straight year, Dawn Lawson copyedited the manuscript with great skill and thoroughness. Editorial intern Lisa Park made numerous helpful suggestions and proofread the chapters with care. Useful comments were also provided by Christine Kim, Gwi-Yeop Son, and Maria Tham. Finally, at Westview Press, Susan McEachern and her colleagues brought their high standards to bear on the volume's production.

Marshall M. Bouton
Executive Vice President
The Asia Society

August 1993

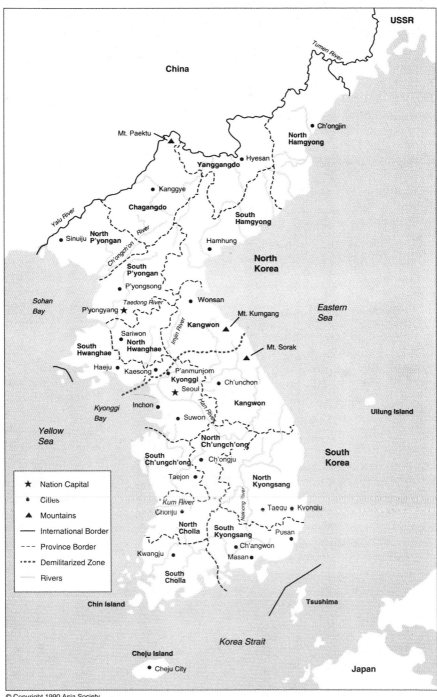

USSR

China

Tumen River

Mt. Paektu ▲
• Ch'ongjin

North
Hamgyong

• Hyesan
Yanggangdo

• Kanggye

South
Hamgyong

Yalu River

Chagangdo

River

North
P'yongan

• Sinuiju

• Hamhung

North
Korea

South
P'yongan

• P'yongsong

Sohan
Bay

Taedong River
• Wonsan

P'yongyang ★

Mt. Kumgang ▲

Eastern
Sea

Sariwon
•

Kangwon

Imjin River

Kangwon
Mt. Sorak ▲

South
Hwanghae

North
Hwanghae

Haeju •

Kaesong •

P'anmunjom
•
Kyonggi

★ Seoul
• Ch'unchon

Kyonggi
Bay

Inchon •

Kangwon

Ullung Island

Yellow
Sea

• Suwon

Han River

North
Ch'ungch'ong

South
Korea

South
Ch'ungch'ong

• Ch'ongju

North
Kyongsang

★ Nation Capital

• Taejon

• Cities

▲ Mountains

—— International Border

Kum River

North
Cholla

Chonju •

South
Kyongsang

Nakdong River

• Taegu
• Kyongju

- - - Province Border

• • • Demilitarized Zone

Rivers

South
Cholla

Kwangju •

• Ch'angwon
Masan •

• Pusan

Chin Island

Tsushima

Cheju Island

Korea Strait

• Cheju City

Japan

© Copyright 1990 Asia Society

Introduction

Donald N. Clark

Nineteen ninety-two was the final year of Roh Tae-woo's term as president of the Republic of Korea, following his dramatic Democratization Declaration of June 29, 1987. Roh did much to convert South Korean politics from the authoritarian habits of military-led rule to the freer—and riskier—atmosphere of plural politics. With election reform political participation expanded dramatically, and there was open competition for seats in the national legislature and local councils. The voters opened up the system and made the government deal with plural points of view on many levels. As Roh left office, nearly everyone gave him credit for that.

Roh's foreign policy successes were even more dramatic. After a steady increase in political contacts and trade arrangements with the nations of the former socialist bloc, in 1992 he established diplomatic relations with two old enemies, China and Vietnam. He even succeeded in cracking North Korea's shell and moving it toward a more tractable position when it came to inter-Korean relations. Beginning in 1990, Roh's prime minister began meeting with his North Korean counterpart in a series of talks that led to significant reconciliation—at least on paper—in December 1991.

The year 1992 began on a note of high hopes for further progress toward reunification. Unfortunately, however, the difficult problem of nuclear weapons intruded to stall the momentum later in the year, and questions about North Korea's suspected nuclear weapons program had grown into a major international confrontation by the spring of 1993.

Domestically, Roh delivered on increased prosperity, albeit at slower rates of growth. Rising wages outran increases in productivity; an intense effort to fulfil a campaign promise for 2 million housing units diverted too much money to the construction sector and created shortages; inflation and interest rates increased; and Korea once again began to run a trade deficit. But the Roh government managed to reestablish stability in 1992, with housing prices and real estate specula-

1

tion on the wane, inflation under control, and exports rising. Despite continuing concern over growing income disparities, the ongoing costs of maintaining a huge military establishment, and the disruptions that might accompany future unification with the North, most Koreans continued to believe in a brighter future.

In December 1992, the process of democratization in South Korea reached a new level when voters elected former opposition leader Kim Young-sam to the presidency. As Donald S. Macdonald explains in his chapter, the fact of Kim's election is eloquent testimony to how far South Korea's political culture has come in the more than 30 years since Korea had a civilian at the helm. Moreover, the public has shown enthusiasm for Kim's root-and-branch attack on corruption in the Korean system, something Kim referred to during his campaign as the "Korean disease." The new president has been fair but firm in dealing with people—even close associates—who have abused the system for profit. Such steps are necessary if people are to believe that Korea can function with an open democratic system. President Kim's unprecedented public approval ratings—over 80 percent—no doubt contributed to his strength as he delved into the secrets of past administrations and uncovered major scandals in the military and ruling-party establishments in 1993, and it is likely to sustain him for a good while to come.

In 1992 North Korea also passed some milestones. Kim Il-sung turned 80 in April, with crowds of cheering citizens wishing him "mansei"—"ten thousand years." His son and heir, Kim Jong-il, turned 50, beginning the year with an important new appointment as chief of the country's military forces. Yet for all the display of solidarity and passion for the North Korean system, the country's quandary was clear: how to maintain the rigid "Kimilsungist" system while opening the economy to much-needed foreign capital. It was the North Korean variation on a familiar theme in China and all the modernizing countries of East Asia: how to adapt outside influences to local needs without being corrupted in the process.

The leadership repeatedly exhorted North Koreans to work harder and consume less—with good reason. With few exports besides raw materials and weapons to offer the world economy, and with their former Russian and Chinese allies demanding cash for imports, the North Koreans were hard pressed to supply their needs for fuel and manufactured goods. North Korea's GNP shrank an estimated 5 percent in 1992, in the minus column for the third year in a row. Visitors—who were always on tightly controlled itineraries—reported that for the time being people seemed well enough fed and clothed; but it became increasingly difficult to see how the regime could continue to sustain the country without some major changes.

To compensate, Pyongyang sought new possibilities. Through most of the year there was reason to hope that relations with South Korea, Japan, and the United States would improve dramatically. But by Oc tober, the nuclear issue had come back to blight all hopes for progress. With the South and its allies demanding bilateral inspections of nuclear sites, in which South Koreans would actually see North Korean installations as part of the 1991 denuclearization agreement, the North balked. The South countered by going ahead with plans for the annual Team Spirit joint military exercises with the United States in March 1993, further estranging the North Koreans, who regard the exercises as a hostile provocation. Amid demands from the International Atomic Energy Agency for access to North Korean nuclear-waste dumps that were likely to prove it had a weapons program, and with the Team Spirit exercises proceeding in the South, the North Koreans took a surprising and dangerous step: they announced that they would pull out of the Nuclear Nonproliferation Treaty (NPT) on June 12, 1993.

With that, everything else was put on the back burner. The world community tried to pressure the Kim Il-sung regime to return to the fold, and on the very brink, two days before Pyongyang's NPT pullout was to take effect, the North Koreans agreed to stay for the time being. Many people marveled that a country with so few cards to play could cause such an upheaval and wondered glumly whether an accommodation could ever be found to settle the issue of Korean denuclearization once and for all.

This year's edition of *Korea Briefing* offers a trio of chapters intended to put recent developments in historical context. Donald S. Macdonald provides a concise overview of political development in the Republic of Korea since its founding in 1948, pointing to the historical significance of the Sixth Republic of President Roh Tae-woo and the election of Kim Young-sam. David I. Steinberg provides parallel treatment of the South Korean economy, highlighting the phases through which it has passed since the Korean War on the road to becoming one of the world's strongest trading economies. And Chae-Jin Lee charts the evolution of the U.S.-Korea military and economic relationship from a patron-client relationship to a more equal partnership.

And because this is the Festival of Korea volume of *Korea Briefing*, we offer three special chapters on Korean culture by outstanding specialists at the University of Hawaii at Manoa. Marshall R. Pihl, one of America's most lucid interpreters of Korean literature, tells us of the painful birth of modern Korean literary culture through periods of colonial oppression, war, and political censorship. Judy Van Zile introduces us to the world of dance in Korea, taking us from the formal styles of traditional court entertainment through the picturesque farmers' dances to the vibrant world of modern dance with its blending of Western and Korean motifs. In a related chapter, musicologist Byongwon Lee gives us the fundamentals of Korean music, some of which is rooted in the same upper- and common-class traditions mentioned by Judy Van Zile, and some of which is borrowed from neighboring peoples and the West. All three chapters are prime background material for audiences at The Asia Society's Festival of Korea events.

A third group of chapters offers insight into special features of the U.S.-Korea relationship. Eui-Young Yu reflects on the Los Angeles riots as they affected the Korean community in Southern California, using them as a springboard to discuss the history and way of life of the Korean immigrant community in the United States. Kim Kyong-Dong analyzes the ways in which Korean attitudes toward America and Americans have changed over the years, while Donald N. Clark looks at the relationship from the American point of view. The articles by Kim and Clark use survey data to highlight changes and problems that remain in the relationship, but they also provide personal vignettes that remind us of the human beings and feelings behind the dry statistics.

Acknowledgments

I would like to thank my fellow authors for their fine work on the chapters for *Korea Briefing, 1993*. They all accepted their assignments with grace, brought their considerable talents to bear on the difficult task of covering vast territory in limited space—and time—and patiently worked with the editors as the volume took shape. It is a privilege to work with such capable colleagues, and I am most grateful for their special effort. I am also thankful for the judgment of Senior Editor Deborah Field Washburn and Editorial Associate Sayu Bhojwani at The Asia Society, and for the mentoring shown by Senior Editor Susan McEachern at Westview Press. In the three years I have edited Korea Briefing I have acquired the greatest respect for their professional skills and standards and feel fortunate to have had their support.

1
South Korea's Politics Since Liberation

Donald S. Macdonald

The year 1992 may come to be viewed as a watershed in Korean history. The people of the southern half of Korea, who achieved an economic take-off a generation ago, have very likely reached their point of political take-off. To see how they got there, this chapter reviews not only the political events of the past year but the historical developments that led up to them. The focus on South Korea should not obscure the fact that the 65 million people on the Korean peninsula consider themselves to be inhabitants of one nation. All continue to hope for reunification of the politically incompatible North and South Korean states. How and when this will be accomplished remains the great question in Korea's future.

Introduction

During 1992, a series of political precedents were set in South Korea:

- On December 18, 81.9 percent of eligible voters went to the polls and elected a long-time political opposition leader and campaigner for political freedom, Kim Young-sam, as South Korea's first civilian president in 32 years (apart from a brief but portentous interregnum in 1980).
- Kim's victory, with a plurality of 42 percent, marked the first time in the history of the Republic of Korea (ROK) that a new president assumed office without a change in the constitution.
- The pragmatism that made it possible for Kim Young-sam to lead his party into a coalition with the government party in 1990, maintain the coalition, and ultimately become its standard-bearer was previously unknown in Korean politics.
- The principal challenger, Kim Dae-jung (also a long-time opposition leader), who received 34 percent of the vote, made a graceful

5

concession speech. That act was another "first" in Korean political history. As recently as 1987, the losers had cried foul in the face of evidence that the election had been reasonably fair.

These developments come after centuries of struggle by the Korean people against internal dynastic decay, the impact of Western industry and culture, foreign imperialist rivalries, colonial rule, and ideological division. Unlike many industrializing countries, Korea was a united state with a well-organized central government for hundreds of years before the modern era. The government, headed by a hereditary monarch and served by a sophisticated bureaucracy, was modeled on that of China. Though in decline in the 19th century, it functioned effectively in a basically static agricultural economy. As was the case in China, politics and society in Korea were guided by the Confucian classics, which looked back to an ancient golden age. The Confucian doctrine, as revised by the Sung dynasty (960–1279) sage Chu Hsi, was the measure of all people—even more so in Korea than in China.

In traditional Korea, the governmental and social structures were strongly hierarchical. Administration was in the hands of a meritocracy chosen by examinations that tested knowledge of the Confucian classics, but those who took the examinations were almost always the children of office-holders, thus creating a hereditary aristocracy. The officials monopolized governmental authority on the basis of their superior wisdom and benevolence; the people were bound to obey them.

But there were still pockets of political autonomy. In local farming villages, for example, the elders of the resident families were generally allowed to manage their own affairs. The patriarchal family, considered to extend as far as the eighth degree of blood relationship, commanded the loyalty of all its members, compelling them to subordinate their individual identity to its continuity and well-being. Family and small-group loyalties often superseded loyalty to the ruler or the state, and competition among rival leaders and factions for political power plagued Korea throughout its history.

So long as the physical and social environment of Korea remained reasonably constant, and so long as its rulers and ministers were alert to the needs of the polity, the Confucian system of government functioned well. The Korean political and social system never fully recovered from the Japanese invasion of 1592–98, however. This upset was compounded by internal dynastic decay. By the 19th century the impoverished Korean peasants, forced to support a swollen and parasitic aristocracy, had begun to manifest their discontent through popular uprisings.

As the West, both directly and through its modernization of Japan, came knocking at Korea's door, the Korean rulers sought to protect themselves through a policy of isolation and exclusion and the continuation of their traditional dependence upon China. This policy, together with the aristocrats' determination to resist social or political change, left Korea particularly vulnerable to foreign imperialism.

The Japanese, by their seizure of Korea in 1905 and subsequent colonial rule, denied the Koreans any opportunity for political development. With few exceptions, the population was encouraged to remain in its traditional agrarian mold, although it was mobilized in the 1930s and 1940s to work in Japanese-run industries and to support the Japanese war effort. Nonetheless, inspired by Woodrow Wilson's principles of self-determination, the Korean people rallied for independence in 1919. The Japanese promptly and forcibly put the uprising down, driving its leaders into exile.

With the defeat of Japan in 1945, Korea reemerged. Resentment at the oppression and poverty of the colonial era had sharpened the keen Korean sense of ethnic identity into a fierce nationalism. Despite this, however, the supposedly temporary division of the peninsula by Soviet and U.S. occupying forces, together with ideological differences among the Koreans themselves, interfered with the renascence of a united Korea and led instead to the emergence of two rival states, each representing itself as the sole legitimate expression of the Korean national destiny. This rivalry culminated in a tragic and costly war, diverting national energies from political and economic development to confrontation and military buildup, which were encouraged by the rivalry of the respective superpower patrons of North and South.

With help from their allies, both Korean states recovered from the war and achieved impressive records of economic development that would have been impossible without some measure of political stability. North Korea was far more successful than South Korea at first, because under its Stalinist political system, the economy could be more quickly built and its human and material resources mobilized more rapidly. In contrast, South Korea's political backwardness and economic stagnation were the despair of its international friends until the mid-1960s. By the mid-1970s, however, South Korea was rapidly gaining economic ground and the North was falling behind—although the South's gains were accompanied by political retrogression into quasi dictatorship.

In retrospect, it seems clear that while North Korea remained locked in its Stalinist mold, South Korea, through traumatic trial and error, was beginning to develop a modern and open political system —even as most Americans were criticizing its performance. Americans seemed to believe that the three-year U.S. military occupation of Korea should have created instant democracy; that this did not come about was variously judged to be the fault of the Americans, or the Korean leaders, or both.

In North Korea, communism could readily be imposed from above, as it was in Russia, because it did not require or expect true popular participation—only popular enthusiasm. Democracy, on the other hand, must come from the people and be imposed from below. Democratic development may well take three generations or more, as will probably be the case in the states of the former Soviet Union—and perhaps in North Korea as well.

It is still too early to conclude that the process of political development in South Korea has reached maturity. The new president, before his inauguration, laid out an ambitious policy agenda. Its themes faithfully reflected current public concerns: to achieve national reconciliation by easing conflicts among regions, socioeconomic classes, and generations; to "cure widespread social illnesses," including pervasive corruption and the "legacies of authoritarian rule"; to reduce government intervention in the economy; to work for economic justice and the public welfare; to strive for reunification; and to strengthen international relationships. To achieve these goals without the levers of authoritarian leadership and in the face of increasingly vocal expressions of divergent group interests constitutes a prodigious challenge.

1992: A Pretty Good Year

As 1992 began, the citizens of the Republic of Korea were looking forward to no fewer than four national elections. The 1987 constitution specified a four-year term for the National Assembly, the Republic's unicameral legislature; all of its seats would be up for election no later than April. At the end of the year, in anticipation of the close of President Roh Tae-woo's five-year term, an election was to be held for his successor. In the interim, according to a law passed in 1989, elections (the first of their kind since 1960) were to be held for the executives of all of Korea's cities and counties and then for those of the 14 provinces and special cities. (A first step toward restoring a local voice in administration—which had been suspended since 1961—had been taken in 1991, when elections for city, county, and provincial councils were held.)

In January 1992, however, the president announced that the provisions of the law notwithstanding, elections for provincial and local executives would be postponed at least until 1994. He reasoned that four elections in one year would overwhelm the energies and attention of the citizens and tax an already overheated economy by releasing large amounts of political campaign funds into the money supply.

The opposition forces strongly objected to the president's action; they had made the achievement of local autonomy a major political issue ever since the liberalization of 1987, not only because of its importance in the democratization process but also because it would give the opposition a power base—a possibility that doubtless contributed to the president's decision. This issue became the principal focus of confrontation between government and opposition during much of the year and blocked action by the legislature for four months. In the end, however, President Roh prevailed, and there were no local elections.

The Political Landscape

The legislative and presidential elections, and the preparations for them, dominated South Korean politics during 1992. They stimulated the competition both within and among the Republic's various contending political forces for control of government positions and policy. The National Assembly, the ROK's one-house legislature, had long been the principal arena for political competition, although for many years it had been little more than a sounding board for political oratory; political decisions were made by the president and supported by a captive legislative majority. However, the 1987 constitution reestablished the Assembly's original powers, and the opposition won more seats than the government in the 1988 election (although a three-party merger in January 1990 restored a government majority). Control of the Assembly was, therefore, a much more important political goal in 1992 than in the past. In addition, jockeying for position in the presidential race, theoretically almost a year away, was already in progress both among and between the parties.

At the beginning of 1992, the contending political forces were concentrated around the government's Democratic Liberal Party (DLP), headed by the president, and the principal opposition organization, the Democratic Party (DP), headed by the charismatic longtime opposition leader Kim Dae-jung. Neither party had a mass membership or following; to a greater extent than in the United States, they were small groups of politicians vying for power and prestige. A considerable number of politically active dissidents chose to remain outside the organized parties, acting through new or existing social organizations—particularly the Christian churches and student organizations—or forming small new political parties. On the other side of the political spectrum, another new political party, organized by the septuagenarian business tycoon Chung Ju-yung in late 1991, was beginning to attract considerable popular support.

To some extent, the components of the political landscape were reminiscent of those of previous years: a pro-government party, headed by the president and informally supported by the power of the state, with a majority of legislative seats; a principal conservative opposition party, with power only to obstruct and criticize, utilizing its legislative minority and the charismatic appeal of its leader to attract public anti-government support; several small parties, mostly organized around one person and his followers; and a largely unorganized pool of dissidents—particularly intellectuals, students, and Christian activists—often harassed or suppressed by the government on charges of anti-state activity or sympathy for the North.

In spite of numerous splits, reorganizations, and name changes, both major parties had significant links with their predecessors, and both were basically conservative, although the opposition endeavored to coopt the radical vote. There was no significant left-of-center party—a major void in South Korean politics that was rooted in the fear of communist North Korea. Questions remained in the public mind as to whether government policy could be significantly influenced by the parties or the electoral process: until recently power had been centered in the president, the executive bureaucracy, the armed forces, and the security agencies, all of which had largely crafted their own agendas and had contained or repressed dissent.

The situation in 1992 was nevertheless different—especially compared to the pre-1987 period. The armed forces had largely withdrawn from an active role in civilian politics, and awe of the government had diminished. In the much-freer political atmosphere, the government party did not enjoy the traditional degree of coercive support from officialdom, and the opposition party could take full advantage of increased public discontent, which was occasioned both by declining economic growth and by frequent revelations of corruption at high levels. Yet some of these revelations had touched the opposition as well. There was considerable public disenchantment with all of the traditional political parties, engendering popular cynicism and apathy.

At the start of 1992, the Democratic Liberal Party, headed by President Roh Tae-woo, held over two-thirds of the National Assembly seats and enjoyed the implicit support of the government bureaucracy and security agencies. Like the ruling Japanese Liberal Democratic Party, to which it was often compared, it had been formed through a merger, but because it had been in existence for only two years, it was still a somewhat uneasy coalition of factions. The largest of the three factions comprised members of the former Democratic Justice Party (DJP), among whom the most influential—including President Roh—were from the Southeast, particularly the city of Taegu and North Kyongsang province. Brought together by school ties and previous service in the military, the Assembly, or the government, they were divided ideologically to some extent by the degree of their identification with the previous Fifth Republic of Chun Doo-hwan, who had been discredited in the massive 1987 upheaval that created the Sixth Republic of President Roh. The factional head was Pak Tae-jun, who was also head of the giant Pohang Iron and Steel Corporation.

A second DLP faction was composed of people who had belonged to the opposition party of Kim Young-sam—many of them natives of Kim's home city of Pusan or of the surrounding South Kyongsang province who had accompanied him into the three-party merger that created the DLP in early 1990. The third faction comprised supporters of Kim Jong-pil, a large number of them from South and North Ch'ungch'ong provinces. Kim Jong-pil had been the architect of the 1961 military coup d'état, had organized a party to support Park Chung-hee as president, and, after a period of forced political inactivity, had reorganized the survivors of that party into an opposition force against President Roh.

As the National Assembly election approached, a new political force made itself felt in the form of the Unification People's Party (later renamed the United People's Party). This party was largely inspired and almost wholly financed by the oldest and richest among the heads of Korea's business combines, or *chaebol*, Chung Ju-yung, honorary chairman of the giant Hyundai Group. Chung's entry onto the political stage was another precedent-shattering event, since no businessperson had ever before sought the presidency. The party's main platform—apart from various proposals for improving the quality of life of the average citizen—was the reduction of the government's role in controlling business activities.

Chung's formation of a political party was a form of retaliation against government interference: a heavy tax burden had been imposed upon him in connection with the transfer of equity among the various companies in his business empire. His action dramatized the new political power of the private economic sector and epitomized individual ambition. He was joined by several leading political personalities, who saw his party as a means of advancing their own political fortunes. Most notable was Kim Tong-gil, an eminent scholar and longtime opposition figure, who had already organized his own small opposition group.

Since there was no important political party representing left-of-center views, some dissidents joined the opposition Democratic Party, among them Yi Pu-yong, a celebrated former student activist who had served time in prison for his views and had become an influential member of the DP. Others formed small parties, such as the Minjung (People's) Party and the Party for New Political Reform, but these parties suffered from public suspicions that they had links with subversives—suspicions that were subsequently reinforced, in the case of the Minjung Party, by the government's arrest of one of its members as a spy for North Korea. Still others outside the established parties formed an umbrella watchdog group supported by 420 social organizations to ensure that the coming elections would be fair.

The National Assembly Election

The official 18-day campaign for election to the National Assembly began in early March of 1992. Of the 299 legislative seats, 237 represented single-member constituencies with an average population of 200,000 each (the Assembly Election Law provided that the remaining 62 seats be distributed to the parties on the basis of total popular votes received). Altogether, 1,052 candidates registered to run for the popularly elective seats. The two major parties put up candidates for all of these seats; in doing so, amid furious infighting that involved personalities, questions of electability, and money, they dropped some leading members and added a few new faces but made no really sweeping changes. Some disgruntled former party members ran as independents; at over 21 percent of the total, the percentage of independent candidates was higher than in previous elections.

As always in Korean political campaigns, individual personalities, cliques, and regional and local loyalties played a large role in shaping voter preferences.[1] However, there were significant focal areas of public discontent to which all parties and candidates sought to respond: the slowdown of economic growth, inflation, the high cost of housing, corruption at high levels (often in connection with real estate speculation), increased crime, and disparities in income and wealth. The issue of political freedom was less prominent than usual because of progress in this area since 1987, but the opposition nevertheless pointed to the continued detention of a number—claimed to be in the

---

[1] A Korean Gallup poll in April found that 34.9 percent of the respondents said they voted primarily on the basis of the candidates' personalities; 13 percent voted for "national stability"—i.e., preserving the status quo; 12.6 percent voted according to party preference; 11.1 percent voted according to campaign pledges; and 6.8 percent voted for "changes in the establishment politics." *Korea Newsreview*, April 11, 1992.

hundreds—of political prisoners. Reunification of Korea, which had been a major issue in earlier years, was less important in this campaign because since 1990 the government had been far more aggressive in seeking agreement with the North and because the example of Germany had shown Koreans the economic costs of unification.

The duration and conduct of the election campaign were closely regulated by law and overseen by the government's Central Election Management Commission (a constitutionally ordained body) and its local counterparts. Advertising, door-to-door campaigning, meetings, and public appearances were all limited, as were campaign contributions and expenditures; nevertheless, large sums were spent by the candidates and their parties, and several candidates were disqualified because of illegal monetary contributions or other irregularities.

On election day, March 24, 1992, 71.9 percent of registered voters cast their ballots, compared with 75.8 percent in the 1988 Assembly election. The results surprised most observers. The enlarged government party, with President Roh Tae-woo as its president and Kim Young-sam as cochairman and campaign manager, got only 38.5 percent of the total vote (roughly comparable to the percentage won by the smaller Democratic Justice Party in 1988) and won 116 of the 237 popularly elective seats. Kim Dae-jung's opposition Democratic Party got 29.2 percent of the total vote, and 75 seats. Chung Ju-yung's new United People's Party, with 17.3 percent of the popular vote, won 24 seats. The Party for New Political Reform gained less than 3 percent of the vote, but its chairman, Park Chan-jong, won a seat. Independents won the remaining 21 seats, including all three seats representing Cheju province.

The Assembly Election Law provided that the 62 Assembly seats to be distributed to the parties in proportion to the total popular vote received be filled from national lists prepared by the parties in advance (a lucrative source of income for the parties, as a number of people were willing to pay large sums to have their names put high on the lists).[2] However, an additional stipulation of the Assembly Election Law was that the party with the largest popular vote receive half of the 62 seats. The government's Democratic Liberal Party accordingly got 33 "national constituency" seats, for a total of 149 out of 299. As in 1988, the government failed to gain a majority in the election, but the DLP was subsequently able to coopt several independents and thus eke out a thin majority. By August 1992, the relative Assembly

---

[2] The press reported that eight persons listed as candidates on the Democratic Party's national slate paid the party a total of 20.5 billion *won* (about $25 million). *Korea Newsreview*, March 14, 1992.

strengths were 159 for the DLP, 96 for the Democratic Party, and 32 for the redesignated United People's Party.

Not surprising, but disappointing, was the continuing regional division of the vote. Kim Dae-jung's opposition party won all but 2 of the 39 seats in North and South Cholla provinces and Kwangju, the two provinces and special city of his native southwestern region, and 25 of the 44 seats in the capital city of Seoul (to which many of his fellow natives had emigrated), but it won none of the 60 seats in the southeastern region, the stronghold of the government party. Kim Young-sam, who had entered the government party from the opposition in 1990 and who had been made chairman of the party's election campaign, was criticized for its failure to win a majority, but he resisted pressure to resign.

A Heated Political Climate

One of the principal factors in the government party's poor showing may have been an incident during the campaign in which four agents of the Agency for National Security Planning (ANSP, the renamed Korean Central Intelligence Agency) were caught distributing leaflets discrediting an opposition candidate. Late in the campaign, manipulation of the large military absentee vote was also charged. As a consequence, President Roh dismissed the ANSP director and the minister of home affairs, along with the agriculture, forestry, and fisheries and transportation ministers. Subsequently, in August, a former county magistrate announced that higher officials had given him large sums of money for use in helping the government party in the Assembly election. His story was played up by the opposition party, which kept him in its headquarters until police broke in to arrest him in September.

To offset growing public cynicism about the government's role in the election process, President Roh resigned the presidency of the ruling party in September and then withdrew from the party altogether. In October the entire State Council (cabinet) submitted their resignations, and a "neutral cabinet" was appointed, with a highly respected education scholar, Hyon Sun-jong, as prime minister; the home, justice, and information ministers were also changed, as was the ANSP director. All members of the new cabinet pledged noninterference in the presidential election. This move, which was made after consultation with political leaders, was widely approved, even by the opposition.

From the time of its election, the new National Assembly was paralyzed by the opposition's insistence on holding the scheduled elections of local government executives. A special session was finally scheduled for late June; it managed to elect the speaker and two vice-speakers but could not agree on standing committee chairs and memberships. Although the dispute did not reach the violent levels of previous years, it continued into September and threatened to prevent the passage of the annual budget. Finally, the need to deal with state business and the pressure of public opinion forced a compromise; the annual regular session convened in early October, organized its committees, and enacted essential legislation, including amendments to the Presidential Election Law.

Meanwhile, along with general public unhappiness about the sluggishness of the economy, several incidents had heated up the political temperature. In early March, the Supreme Court upheld the conviction of one DP and three DLP Assembly members for accepting large payments from a real estate developer to permit improper exploitation of limited-use land; the members were sentenced to three-to-six-years' imprisonment. In May a furor arose over press reports that the DLP had sold its Seoul training facility to a developer for 50 billion *won* (around $60 million) to be used as political funds, without reporting the transaction to anyone in the party except Kim Young-sam.

Backroom jockeying among aspirants for the presidency burst into the open with the party conventions in May. On the government side, President Roh had resisted pressure to designate his successor in the way that he himself had been anointed in 1987; instead, he insisted that the party's candidate be chosen in open competition and voting, and specified that none of his relatives, nor any career military officer, would be eligible. For his part, Kim Young-sam had hoped, if not for presidential designation, then at least for a party convention that would be held before the Assembly election, thus maximizing his chances for nomination. Other views prevailed, however, and the convention was held in May, with Kim handicapped by the party's poor showing in the Assembly elections.

The former DJP faction, while objecting to Kim's candidacy—ostensibly on the grounds that younger and fresher leaders were needed —had difficulty in choosing an alternative but finally designated Yi Jong-chan, a longtime party stalwart. (There were rumors of a backroom deal in which Yi was persuaded not to push his own candidacy.) Kim Jong-pil and his faction stood above the fray. In the voting, Kim Young-sam won the votes of two-thirds of the 6,713 delegates. Yi then withdrew from the party with several supporters, organized his own party, and announced his candidacy for president; Pak Tae-jun, who had headed the main faction within the Democratic Liberal Party, withdrew from politics.

On the opposition side, Kim Dae-jung was challenged by his co-chairman, Yi Ki-taek, a former Kim Young-sam supporter who with several others had refused to follow Kim Young-sam into the 1990 party merger and who had organized a separate party before merging with Kim Dae-jung's group to form the Democratic Party. Yi argued that as a native of Kyongsang province he could broaden the appeal of the party, which had its principal support in the Cholla provinces. In addition, some felt that the 67-year-old Kim Dae-jung, already twice a candidate for president (in 1971 and 1987, plus an aborted campaign in 1980) should retire in favor of a younger man. Kim, however, continued to dominate his party. In its convention, he won 60 percent of the delegates' 2,348 votes, thus becoming the official candidate. In consequence, the two Kims—rivals for many years—once again faced each other before the electorate, as they had in 1987; this time, however, Kim Young-sam was on the government side.

Chung Ju-yung's United People's Party continued to gain supporters on the basis of his anti-government message and promises to better the people's lot through such proposals as a 50 percent reduction in housing rents. Chung's criticism of government policies, his financial support of the party, and his unshakable self-confidence were strangely similar to those of Ross Perot in the United States, and the two were often compared—with Chung noting that he was many times richer than Perot. Despite the attempt of his supporters to put forward a younger and more attractive candidate, Chung insisted on running himself; because he was paying the party's bills and providing much of its staff from among executives of his business combine, he got his way.

In October a political bombshell exploded with the arrest of 62 people on charges of espionage and subversion for North Korea. They were alleged to have been recruited and directed by a female member of the North Korean Political Bureau who had managed to live in the South for ten years. Among those charged were a principal figure from the now-defunct radical Minjung Party and a secretary to Kim Dae-jung. A centerpiece of the alleged plot was the underground organization of a "central chapter" of the Korean Workers' Party—the ruling communist party of North Korea—in the South. Although the timing of the arrests was suspect, reminding observers of previous government arrests to underline the North Korean menace and silence the opposition, the case itself seemed well founded. The opposition did not attempt to challenge the merits of the government's action, and Kim Dae-jung apologized for the involvement of his secretary. The net effect, whether or not intended by the government, was to remind the public of the continuing threat from the North.

The Presidential Election

The presidential election campaign was officially limited to 30 days, beginning upon its announcement by the government on November 17. The major candidates and parties began stumping and trading derogatory comments long before the announcement, but stopped when reproached by the Central Election Management Commission. Possibly influenced in part by a citizen watchdog committee established earlier in the year, all of the candidates agreed to forgo the competitive mass meetings of previous years and pledged themselves to clean election tactics. To alleviate public concern that the vote counting might be rigged by manipulation of the computers, the commission announced that all counting would be done manually, by abacus.

Eight persons, including one woman, registered as presidential candidates, but one of them—Yi Jong-chan, the disappointed DLP rival of Kim Young-sam—withdrew in favor of Chung Ju-yung, and four others, independents or members of minor parties, were given no chance of election. A group of nonparty dissidents, the National Alliance for Democracy and Unification, entered into a "policy coalition" with the opposition Democratic Party to support Kim Dae-jung. Campaigning primarily took the form of television appearances, the distribution of leaflets, and rallies addressed both by the candidates themselves and by their party supporters; all of these activities were conducted more or less within the strict limits of the election law. Each of the three major candidates professed himself certain of victory.

On election day, 81.9 percent of the eligible voters cast ballots—slightly less than in 1987, but higher than in the legislative elections, demonstrating that voter apathy had been overestimated. The government candidate, Kim Young-sam, won the election with an unexpectedly large plurality of 42 percent; his archrival Kim Dae-jung drew 34 percent, largely from his traditional strongholds in the Southwest and in Seoul; and Chung Ju-yung, the tycoon-turned-politician, garnered only 16 percent. The basic fairness of the election was not challenged, as it had been in 1987; on the contrary, Kim Dae-jung made a graceful concession speech and announced his retirement from politics (which some believed might not last). Chung was clearly shocked by the small size of his vote and said he would retire from politics and return to his business interests.

Kim Young-sam's victory was probably due in large part to the popular desire for continuity at a time of economic uncertainty, to his reputation as a fighter for freedom, and to general recognition that he was a "clean" politician. Despite some gaffes, Kim ran a skillful campaign, emphasizing themes with broad public appeal: ending corruption, revitalizing the economy, reconciling political and regional differences, combatting crime, and maintaining good relations with the United States and other traditional international partners. Kim's party was well organized and well financed. Although attempts were made to smear his personal reputation (including one carried in an American syndicated column, alleging that Kim had secretly sent emissaries to North Korea), they gained little credence.

A Peaceful Outcome

Kim Young-sam was inaugurated on February 25, 1993, in a relatively modest ceremony. He moved quickly to name his cabinet, all of them apparently well-qualified people and almost all without ties to the armed forces or to the dominant elements of previous administrations. A few, including the deputy prime minister for unification, were former dissident activists. To underline the new president's anticorruption commitment, three of his appointees were subsequently dismissed because of relatively minor past transgressions. In a move unprecedented in Korea, President Kim published a statement of his personal worth and ordered his cabinet to do the same.

Soon, all the DLP assemblymen stated their assets publicly, putting the opposition on the defensive.[3] Insisting that the published figures were understated, the opposition temporized, but eventually it followed suit, showing that some of its leaders, too, were quite well off. The speaker of the National Assembly, amid criticism of the size of his personal fortune and allegations that he had gained it through real estate speculation, resigned his post, though he kept his Assembly seat. Three Assembly members resigned their seats, and others left the DLP or were subjected to party discipline. An Assembly member from the opposition Democratic Party was indicted for extorting political funds from the Pohang Iron and Steel Corporation.

President Kim took additional steps to carry out his campaign commitments. He promptly announced the general outlines of a 100-day plan to bolster the economy and called for a revision of the five-year plan set to begin later in the year. A sweeping amnesty released 2,000 people from prison, including prominent dissidents; one of these,

---

[3] On March 19, 1993, the *Korea Times* published a table showing the assets of all cabinet members, ranging from $2.74 million for the foreign minister, Han Sung-joo, to $360,000 for the agriculture minister, Ho Shin-haeng. On March 23, the same paper published a table listing the assets of 161 DLP Assembly members; the richest was Kim Jin-Jae, worth about $30 million, and the poorest was Kim Ko-il, with $16,200.

Reverend Moon Ik-hwan, who had been jailed for an illegal visit to North Korea in 1989, was quoted as saying that President Kim "should be given a chance." Senior military officers were arrested for the alleged sale of promotions, and others, including the army chief of staff and two key army component commanders, were reassigned in an assertion of the president's control. Education officials were arrested for the sale of student admissions, and a number of traffic policemen were dismissed or disciplined for fixing tickets—a long-standing and widespread abuse. Thus Kim Young-sam's administration made a strong start.

Korean Political Development

South Korean political behavior in 1992 presented a vivid contrast to the traditional agrarian polity of the 19th century, which continued to be the principal Korean political model until after the country's liberation from Japanese colonial rule in 1945. To appreciate the magnitude of the changes that have taken place since Liberation, and how they came about, one must examine South Korean political history during the intervening half-century.[4]

The Situation in 1945

As of 1945 the Korean people had had virtually no experience of participation in modern politics. The Japanese, responding to international pressures after the national popular uprising in Korea on March 1, 1919, had introduced local elections in 1921, but property requirements limited voting eligibility chiefly to the Japanese themselves and the wealthy. The Christian churches had encouraged membership participation in congregational affairs; however, Christians at the time were but a small minority, albeit an influential one. There was some semblance of Korean participation in the Japanese-sponsored agricultural cooperatives, but basic decisions were made at the top. The Koreans were mostly hewers of wood and drawers of water in a colony run by and for the Japanese.

---

[4] More detailed discussions of Korean political development during the postwar period are presented in Joungwon A. Kim, *Divided Korea: The Politics of Development, 1945–1972* (Cambridge: Harvard University Press, 1975); Young Whan Kihl, *Politics and Policies in Divided Korea: Regimes in Contest* (Boulder: Westview Press, 1985); *Korean Politics in Transition*, ed. Edward R. Wright (Seattle: University of Washington Press, 1975); and Koon Woo Nam, *South Korean Politics; The Search for Political Consensus and Stability* (Lanham, Md.: University Press of America, 1989).

Although the 1919 uprising was put down with ruthless efficiency, some of its leaders escaped to China, where they established a provisional government in exile in the form of a Western-style parliamentary democracy. The provisional government continued a tenuous existence until 1945, with some support from the Chinese, but contacts with the homeland were severely obstructed by the Japanese authorities.

The provisional government was also handicapped by the split among Korean nationalists between "rightists"—those who looked to Western Europe and the United States as models—and "leftists"—those who saw Soviet-style communism as the means of their national salvation. The leftists, who were also divided among themselves, had their own headquarters in China and the Soviet Union; their partisans fought with the Chinese communists against the Japanese, and a few were active within Korea.

A few days before the end of World War II, the Japanese governor-general, fearful of Korean revenge, called on a leftist nationalist leader named Yo Un-hyong to maintain law and order until the arrival of the victorious Allied forces. Following Yo's lead, local notables organized "people's committees" in many parts of the country, with associated volunteer peacekeeping forces. Communists in the people's committees were influential and perhaps better organized than other members but by no means monopolized the committees, which displaced the Japanese authorities in varying degrees. Two thousand or so representatives of the people's committees attended a national convention in Seoul on September 7, 1945, at which Yo Un-hyong and his associates proclaimed the People's Republic of Korea.

U.S.-USSR Military Occupation, 1945–1948

U.S. forces entered Korea on September 9, 1945, two days after the proclamation of the People's Republic. They were ill prepared for their responsibility and had only two basic guidelines: to preserve law and order and not to recognize any Korean group until the Korean people had had an opportunity for self-determination. These instructions meant the rejection of both the People's Republic—which was forced to reconstitute as a political party in the American zone—and the provisional government in China, members of which were allowed to return to Korea as individuals. The local people's committees, suspected by the Americans as communist, were gradually forced to disband.

In the absence of any Korean group they regarded as legitimate, the Americans used the structure and the Korean personnel of the former

Japanese government-general to govern their zone. The Japanese were repatriated, and a search was made for qualified and respected Koreans to take over senior government posts. However, the Americans generally chose conservative, propertied Koreans who knew how to deal with Westerners. These people, sincere and qualified though they might have been, were often regarded by the general public as collaborators with the hated Japanese.

A few noted Korean leaders were free of the collaborationist taint. The more conservative among them included Syngman Rhee, who returned to Korea in October 1945 after 40 years of exile in the United States, Kim Ku, the president of the provisional government in China, and Kim Kyu-sik, the chair of the provisional government's shadow legislature. Others, such as Pak Hon-yong, an avowed communist, and Yo Un-hyong, the left-leaning organizer of the People's Republic, were suspect in American eyes. Rhee was initially welcomed by the Americans, but his construction of an independent political power base, his stubbornness, and his support of a separate state in South Korea led to near-enmity between him and the American commander, General John R. Hodge.

During World War II, the preferred U.S. solution for the problems of dependent territories was international trusteeship. This policy was announced for Korea at a foreign ministers' conference in Moscow on December 27, 1945. The Koreans, who had had no share in formulating the plan and had not been informed of it in advance, strongly opposed it as a further postponement of their desired independence. The trusteeship debate became the primary stumbling block in two years of U.S.-Soviet discussions about a unified Korean administration, reflecting the intense ideological gulf between both the two occupying powers and Korean nationalists of left and right.

The forces of the Soviet Union, fighting their way into Korea against the Japanese in the last week of World War II, confirmed the political control of the people's committees. By the spring of 1946, a five-province people's committee had been established as the central authority for the Soviet zone. Committee members who resisted communization were purged. The Soviets brought in a young anti-Japanese guerrilla leader named Kim Il-sung as their chosen instrument, supporting him as the principal leader in preference to older and better-known nationalist figures.

Acting through Kim Il-sung and his administration, the Soviet authorities set up a communist regime modeled on the Stalinist Soviet structure. They redistributed farmland to tillers without compensation to landlords and nationalized large industry. The result in the South was political stabilization and, in the North, economic progress. The

Americans, while repealing undemocratic Japanese legislation by decree and trying to provide a free political atmosphere, postponed major reforms; they sought both to avoid any obstruction to the establishment of a unified administration for all of Korea and to respect Anglo-Saxon concepts of property rights. The result was political confusion and economic instability, which climaxed in demonstrations and bloody riots in the autumn of 1946.

In response to growing popular discontent in their zone, the Americans held elections for an interim zonal legislature in 1946 and established a Koreanized South Korean Interim Government in 1947. They also sought to establish a moderate third force through a coalition committee headed by Yo Un-hyong and Kim Kyu-sik; but that effort, uncertain at best, ended with Yo's assassination by rightist forces in 1947. Syngman Rhee, meanwhile, campaigned for a separate anticommunist South Korean state.

When the U.S.-USSR Joint Commission disbanded in failure in October 1947, the United States—eager to end its involvement and withdraw—referred the Korean question to the United Nations. The result was elections under U.N. supervision in the southern zone only (the U.N. representatives having been refused admittance to the Soviet zone) for a constituent assembly, which launched the Republic of Korea on August 15, 1948, with Syngman Rhee as its elected president. The northern zone held elections in August, in which it speciously claimed 80 percent South Korean participation, leading to the proclamation of the Democratic People's Republic of Korea on September 9, 1948.[5]

The Rhee Years, 1948–1960

The new Republic of Korea in the South faced severe challenges from the outset. Senior officers of the South Korean Interim Government were, understandably, dismissed immediately, and they took their administrative experience with them. Their replacements had had little previous experience; many of them put their traditional obligations to family and friends above the national interest. Much of the population was disaffected, both because many Korean employees of the Japanese government-general, particularly members of the police force, remained in office and because of the lack of economic improvement, especially in contrast to the rapid progress rumored to be occurring in the North. Communist leaders from both South Korea

---

[5] For a review of the occupation period in Korea, see George M. McCune, *Korea Today* (Cambridge: Harvard University Press, 1950).

and the North had a receptive audience for subversion, which Rhee countered with increasing repression. A regiment of the new army mutinied in October 1945, setting off a protracted guerrilla war that took more than a year to put down. The Americans had little economic aid to offer, and their military aid was deliberately limited out of fear that Syngman Rhee would carry out his threat to "march north." U.S. soldiers (except for a 500-person advisory group) were withdrawn by July 1949. There were constant threats of North Korean invasion, some of them caused by South Korean military adventures along the 38th parallel.

By the spring of 1950, both political stabilization and economic progress were evident in the South, but the populace remained disaffected, and some of Rhee's conservative supporters turned against him. Rhee endeavored to postpone scheduled legislative elections, but American pressure forced him to hold them in May, resulting in considerable loss of his parliamentary support. The new Assembly had no sooner organized itself, however, when North Korea—well equipped by the Soviet Union—invaded the South on June 25, 1950, with the expectation of a prompt takeover.

After three years of fighting, which involved forces of the United States and 15 other members of the United Nations supporting the South and Chinese "volunteers" supporting the North, an armistice was signed that still remains in effect. The result was a dividing line between the two Koreas in almost the same place as before the war, the loss of perhaps 2 million or more military and civilian lives, millions of permanently injured, an enormous disruption of society, and the destruction of a large part of the housing and industrial capacity of both states. Because of American bombing, the devastation in the North was far greater than in the South.

In the midst of the war, Syngman Rhee had struggled with his conservative rivals to keep his grip on power, forcing through a constitutional amendment in 1952 to secure his reelection by direct popular vote and organizing a political party to subdue the legislature. Another constitutional amendment in 1955 removed a two-term limitation on his reelection.

The brief and draconian North Korean occupation of virtually all of South Korea had destroyed most of the goodwill felt by southerners toward the northern regime, replacing it with a deep fear of renewed attack and a dependence upon the remaining U.S. military forces for protection. The war also left the Republic of Korea with an enormous military establishment, composed primarily of very young and ambitious men, and a distorted and impoverished economy. With massive foreign economic aid, mostly from the United States, the prewar standard of living and some stability had been restored by 1957, but the direction of future political development was uncertain.

After Rhee gained firm control of his legislature, a semblance of a two-party political system emerged, with some degree of freedom for those who were not too "progressive" in their ideas. This freedom was sufficient to permit the election of the opposition vice-presidential candidate in 1956, although for the next four years he was given nothing to do and an attempt was made to assassinate him.

In 1958 the opposition gained significantly in legislative elections. A hard-line group of supporters of the aging President Rhee commenced a program of tightening repression to ensure his (and their own) continuation in office. The leading "progressive" (leftist) figure, Cho Pong-am, was executed in 1959. The presidential election of March 1960 was blatantly rigged, and masses of students marched upon the president's residence in April to protest. Nearly 200 of them were killed by police. The populace supported the students, the army stood aloof, Syngman Rhee resigned, and the new Second Republic appeared, organized as a free parliamentary democracy.[6]

Parliamentary Democracy, 1960–1961

Unfortunately, the short-lived Second Republic demonstrated that the Korean people were not ready for so much democracy. The conservative opposition, which now came to power for the first time, split in two over differences in personality and policy, including the question of which of its leaders would be the figurehead president (a Korean aristocrat named Yun Po-son was installed) and which the governing prime minister (a leading Catholic layman, Chang Myon, was chosen). The government was perceived as unable to cope with the republic's economic and political problems and unable to control the crowds that demonstrated almost daily for the fulfillment of their various demands. When Major General Park Chung-hee and 3,600 military supporters seized power in the predawn hours of May 16, 1961, the prevailing popular attitude was one of relief.[7]

---

[6] The events of the Rhee years, and an explanation of the First Republic's demise, are presented by John Kie-chiang Oh in his *Korea: Democracy on Trial* (Ithaca, N.Y.: Cornell University Press, 1968).

[7] The failure of the Second Republic is analyzed by Han Sung-joo (now the ROK foreign minister) in his *The Failure of Democracy in South Korea* (Berkeley: University of California Press, 1974). The "military revolution" is described in Se-jin Kim's *The Politics of Military Revolution in Korea* (Durham: University of North Carolina Press, 1971).

The Years of Military Hegemony, 1961–1987

General Park suspended the constitution and all political activity, governing for two years through a Supreme Council for National Reconstruction composed of military men. His regime nonetheless pledged from the outset to restore civilian rule after cleansing the nation of corruption and dirty politics, and in 1963, with considerable nudging from the United States and despite opposition from some of his own hard-line supporters, he did so. A new constitution, similar to that of the First Republic, was adopted by referendum; Park resigned his military rank and was elected president by a bare plurality of 46.6 percent over his nearest rival, former president Yun (who received 46.1 percent).

President Park recognized that he could achieve legitimacy only by meeting popular demands for economic progress. With continuing U.S. economic support conditioned on performance, he brought qualified economic experts into his government, placed military men in key civil government posts, and developed a five-year economic development plan for 1962 to 1966 that was fulfilled ahead of schedule. He tolerated some degree of political freedom, although an omnipresent Central Intelligence Agency kept rivals and subversives in check and legislative and judicial independence was limited. In 1967 he was reelected by a substantial margin (51.5 percent, against 40.9 percent for Yun Po-son), reflecting popular satisfaction with rapid economic progress, but the legislative elections that year were rigged to favor his supporters.

In 1969 President Park, like Rhee before him, sought to ensure his continuance in power with a constitutional amendment to remove the two-term limitation. The opposition, unable to defeat the amendment, nonetheless seized upon this and other issues in the 1971 presidential election campaign. Park's principal opponent, the charismatic opposition leader Kim Dae-jung, gained 45 percent of the officially counted votes—probably more in actuality—and the opposition gained seats in the Assembly elections. These events were accompanied on the international scene by the American failure in Vietnam and the related Guam Doctrine, under which one of the two remaining U.S. divisions in Korea was withdrawn.

Park, never a convinced democrat, now sought to strengthen his state's capacity for self-defense against the North. He accelerated the development of the heavy and defense industries and undertook secret negotiations with the North which, while leading to a joint declaration in July 1972 supporting peaceful unification, also apparently increased his fear and respect for North Korean mobilization and war capability. Accordingly, he mounted a "coup d'état from within," leading to a new and highly repressive regime—the Fourth Republic, also known as "Yushin," which translates as "revitalizing reform." He had now gained sweeping powers to rule by decree and suppress any opposition or criticism. In 1973 intelligence operatives endeavored to liquidate Kim Dae-jung, but he was imprisoned instead.

The opposition was not entirely silenced, however. On March 1, 1976, its leaders published a manifesto, read at the Myong-dong Catholic cathedral, protesting suppression and economic injustice. The leaders, both political and religious, were arrested. Although Park was dutifully reelected in 1978, the opposition again gained seats in the legislature. Public discontent mounted, fueled both by political repression and by the distortion of the economy caused by the emphasis on heavy industry. The principal expression of discontent was by college students, whose leading role in the "student revolution" of 1960 had reinforced their status as the nation's conscience and whose views and actions became increasingly radical as the government's repression of them continued.

In 1979, as strikes and demonstrations mounted, Park's hard-line advisers urged a crackdown; Kim Young-sam, the opposition spokesman in the National Assembly, was expelled for criticizing the regime. This triggered more demonstrations. On October 26, 1979, the chief of Korea's Central Intelligence Agency, apparently despairing of the trend of affairs, shot the president at dinner.[8]

The unintended consequences of this act were a brief relaxation of the oppressive political atmosphere, as the civilian prime minister, Ch'oe Kyu-ha, assumed the presidency in accordance with a constitutional provision. However, Major General Chun Doo-hwan made a power grab within the armed forces in December 1979. In the "Seoul Spring" of 1980, rivalry among contending politicians threatened a renewal of the confusion of 1960, and General Chun sought to reenact Park Chung-hee's 1961 seizure of power. Like Park, he suspended the constitution and suppressed all political activity, but, unlike Park, he encountered sullen civilian opposition and student demonstrations.

Chun apparently decided to make an example of the student opposition in Kwangju, a major city in the traditional opposition stronghold of the southwest Cholla provinces. The special forces sent to subdue the students brutalized them, killing 200 or more. The result was a general citizen uprising that seized control of the city for ten

---

[8] For a good discussion of politics during the Fourth Republic, see Hak-kyu Sohn, *Authoritarianism and Opposition in South Korea* (London: Routledge, 1989).

days; negotiations with city leaders failed, and additional military forces were sent to reestablish government control. This macabre event lost General Chun any goodwill that he might otherwise have had and greatly intensified the existing regional split between the Chollas and the southeast Kyongsang provinces, whence Park, Chun, and most of their principal lieutenants had come.

Chun attempted to legitimate his power by arranging his election as president by a new electoral college, which had been institutionalized in the constitution of the Fifth Republic adopted by referendum in 1980; by promising to democratize the regime gradually; and by pledging to step down after a single seven-year term of office. After a recession in 1980, he restored rapid economic growth. His regime was never accepted as Park's had been, however. Students and dissidents kept up the pressure on him by constantly staging strikes and demonstrations, which he firmly put down. Activist leaders were arrested by the hundreds. Although many of them were released, others were imprisoned, and the death of one student by torture gave further ammunition to the opposition.

In keeping with his commitment to liberalization, Chun eventually restored the political rights of most of the opposition politicians banned prior to the 1985 legislative elections. In those elections, a new opposition party organized only a few months previously by opposition leaders Kim Dae-jung and Kim Young-sam won more popular votes than the government party. It mounted a vigorous campaign to liberalize politics with a new constitutional amendment that provided, among other things, for direct popular election of the president. Chun at first insisted that the next presidential election be carried out under the existing constitution, then considered amendment, then again opposed it. In 1987 he handpicked his successor, former general Roh Tae-woo, who had supported him in his seizure of power, and had Roh nominated by a rubber-stamp government party convention. This sequence of events angered the public to the point that half a million demonstrators—led by students as well as by both party and nonparty opposition groups—were in the streets in June, demanding political change.

On June 29, 1987, came one of the most dramatic moments in Korean political history. Roh Tae-woo, as presidential candidate, publicly accepted the principal demands made by the opposition, including those for direct presidential elections, release of political prisoners, freedom of the press, protection of human rights, and university autonomy. This act greatly reduced public tension and set the stage for another constitutional revision, establishing the Sixth Republic.[9]

The Sixth Republic: Korea's Political Take-off?

The December 1987 presidential election, conducted by direct popular vote under the new system, gave the opposition nearly five-eighths of the vote under conditions that were considered by most foreign observers to be reasonably free of manipulation. The principal opposition leaders, Kim Dae-jung and Kim Young-sam, together with Kim Jong-pil, architect of the 1961 coup d'état, split the opposition vote among them. Roh won the election with a plurality of 36 percent. There were shrill cries of fraud from the disappointed candidates, but fraud could not be proved to have affected the outcome, and Roh duly assumed office.

The ensuing legislative election reflected the presidential election almost exactly: the three opposition parties won a majority of the Assembly seats, but they had difficulty in maintaining a united position. The situation was unprecedented; no previous Korean administration had had to contend with a legislative minority. The surprise solution, achieved in January 1990 to the amazement of nearly all observers, was the merging of the government party with the opposition parties of Kim Young-sam and Kim Jong-pil to form the Democratic Liberal Party (somewhat consciously modeled on Japan's governing Liberal Democratic Party, itself composed of several factions), thus establishing a government majority of more than two-thirds of the legislative seats. This merger held together, despite severe internal stresses, through the presidential election of December 1992, which put Kim Young-sam in office as Roh's successor.[10]

As of June 1993, the 1987 constitutional framework remains firmly in place, although most of the senior office-holders have changed. The Democratic Liberal Party has survived a purge of some of its major factional leaders in the anti-corruption campaign and commands a small majority in the National Assembly.[11] The principal opposition party, the Democratic Party (which also absorbed a smaller opposition

---

[9] The text of the June 29, 1987, declaration is contained in the second of two volumes of Roh Tae-woo's presidential speeches: Roh Tae-woo, *Korea in the Pacific Century* (Lanham, Md.: University Press of America, 1992), appendix 1, pp. 293–97.

[10] Manwoo Lee discusses the politics of the Sixth Republic in his *The Odyssey of Korean Democracy* (New York: Praeger, 1990).

[11] For a summary discussion of the Democratic Liberal Party purge, see Shin Yong-bae, "DLP Faces Shake-up After Wealth Disclosures," *Korea Newsreview*, April 3, 1993, p. 7.

party in 1991), has survived its defeat both in the presidential election and in three significant April by-elections to the National Assembly. At its annual convention in spring 1993, its retired longtime standard-bearer and hero of the southwest Cholla provinces, Kim Dae-jung, was replaced in an open election by Yi Ki-taek, native of the south-eastern Kyongsang region.[12] Dissident voices are still heard, but their tone is muted for the time being (although in late May thousands of students held an anti-government rally, and in June attempted a march for unification), and some dissidents are expressing support for Kim Young-sam and his reforms.

Conclusion

Certain salient trends characterize South Korea's political history over the past 47 years.

- The Korean people have recognized the power of the vote in a score of general elections and have used it to register a variety of discontents.
- Until Roh Tae-woo's statement of June 29, 1987, however, South Korean political leaders responded to popular discontent by sup-pressing it. This tendency was the most pronounced in the late 1950s and late 1970s.
- South Korean political leaders have been able to repress political freedom to their own advantage by playing up the threat from the North—real though it unquestionably has been.
- Until recently, the Korean people, lacking real experience in de-mocracy, have not been ready for the responsibilities that accom-pany representative and participatory government. They have been more interested in security and economic benefit than in po-litical freedom. However, the resistance to the military seizure of power in 1980, together with the great popular outcry of the mid-1980s, suggests that a growing readiness and desire for democracy have brought Korea to a point where the people cannot accept retrogression to the ways of the past.
- Nevertheless, as recent public opinion polls make clear, the con-version of the Korean people to a total support of democracy is by no means complete.[13] Severe and protracted economic recession, particularly if accompanied by the rise of a charismatic political

---

[12] For a discussion of Democratic Party problems, see Kim Kyung-ho, "DP Facing Identity Crisis After Losing By-Elections," *Korea Newsreview*, May 8, 1993, pp. 6–7.

[13] See Myung Chey and Doh Chull Shin, "Democratization in Korea as Perceived by Its Mass Public," paper prepared for presentation to the 1993 annual meeting of the As-sociation for Asian Studies, Los Angeles, March 24–27, 1993.

figure, could bring about at least a temporary reversal in political progress.

American critics of South Korean political behavior expected too much political progress too soon. At the same time, however, it may well be that American and other foreign criticism, when not too shrill, too public, or too unrealistic, has served to encourage Korean political modernizers and reinforce their efforts.

President Kim Young-sam's accession to office brings with it a multitude of challenges and political tests. In a climate soured by diminished economic growth and public disenchantment with the traditional political parties and their games, the new president's rivals—some of whom were targets of his anti-corruption campaign —will be harsh critics of his performance as he attempts to solve the many problems that he himself has identified. They will be quick to seize upon his shortcomings in an effort to position themselves as his challengers in 1998. To gain political control, they may raise yet again the idea of amending the constitution to provide for a parliamentary system of government, thus reducing the presidency to a figurehead. For the new Korean political style to succeed and become permanent, the people must be patient, and the leaders must put the good of the state above their own.

2
The Transformation of the South Korean Economy

David I. Steinberg

When Koreans and foreigners alike surveyed the state of the South Korean economy and its future three and one-half decades ago, they might well have silently invoked the classic characterization of economics as the dismal science. South Korea was widely regarded as an economic disaster, informally known in assistance circles as a "basket case" requiring foreign largesse for an indefinite period to survive. Most observers predicted that it could never be economically self-sufficient. The military was an intolerable economic burden, insupportable without external assistance. In 1953 an officially sponsored U.S. study calculated that Korea could export only agricultural commodities.

Koreans were also characterized as having a "mendicant mentality," continuously seeking foreign aid and dependent on it. But the nation's economic crutch, the United States, had determined that assistance would have to be reduced. Grant aid for food was to be transformed into loans, and overall economic support diminished. The Stalinist regime in North Korea, even though virtually destroyed by the Korean War, seemed to have a higher standard of living and was growing at rates far in excess of the South's, thus intensifying this frustration. Probably half the people of the Republic of Korea (ROK) lived below the absolute poverty line.

If observers at that time had attempted to predict long-term economic growth in Asia by comparing Burma, Thailand, and South Korea, all of which had per capita incomes in the $60–80 range and populations within about 10 percent of each other, Burma would likely have been their first choice and South Korea their last. Yet today South Korea's per capita income is some 6 times that of Thailand and some 32 times that of Burma, while its GDP is 3 times that of Thailand. In 1962, Burma's exports were 6 times greater than South Korea's; in 1990, South Korea's were 85 times those of Burma. South Korea's total annual exports in 1962 would have equaled about eight hours of its exports in 1990; in 1990, 95 percent of its exports were manufactured goods, while in 1962 they were primary products (as are Burma's today).

These economic changes won international acclaim. South Korea has become a "model" developmental success. Its methods are widely studied, its policies emulated, and its economic experts in wide international demand as advisers, managers, and consultants on how to replicate Korea abroad.

Economic development, however, is not only an increase in GNP or growth rates; it is also the distribution of the fruits of those changes and the involvement of people in its processes and products. Who pays, who benefits, how, and how much for how long, are thus critical questions in any assessment of the process.

As many benefited from this growth, South Koreans shared the world's enthusiasm for their economic success—until the late 1980s. Since that time, many Koreans have had second thoughts. Although foreigners still remark upon the relatively robust growth rates—4.7 percent in 1992, 8.4 percent in 1991—which were two or three times those of Japan and the United States, these fall far below the double-digit economic expansion that characterized most of the previous decade (an average annual growth of 10.1 percent, 1982–91). Koreans in the early 1990s became dissatisfied with their economy, with the political leadership directing it, and with what they perceived to be growing disparities of wealth. The purported South Korean economic phoenix rising from the ashes of the Korean War as the "miracle on the Han" seemed stricken. Indeed, it is ironic that as the political optimism associated with the liberalization, pluralism, and free elections instituted in 1987 spread, a corresponding malaise developed with regard to economic matters. The people may be better off: some two-thirds characterize their status as middle class. But the new beneficiaries of Korea's rapid progress began to worry when the strong managerial leadership that they had excoriated under Chun Doo-hwan and Park Chung-hee gave way to the less repressive and less dirigiste leadership of Roh Tae-woo, who appeared less able to keep up the economic pace. Labor and other groups, however, welcomed these changes. Many Koreans, it seems, wanted political conciliation and strong economic performance at the same time, a combination hitherto unknown in South Korea and difficult anywhere.

The Economic Development of the Republic

To understand the present and explore the future of the South Korean economy, we must first review the conditions that made Korea's phenomenal growth possible and the extent to which they can be duplicated elsewhere. To economists, the reasons for South Korea's economic successes may seem obvious—concentration on export promotion rather than import substitution, effective exchange rates, a vibrant private sector and healthy market forces, foreign investment and new technologies, and prudent fiscal policies. No doubt these generic economic desiderata were critical to success, but alone they explain neither the process of growth in Korea nor its causes, for other states have followed these policies and not done so well.

The ROK has managed to link these universalistic prescriptions for growth with elements from its cultural heritage. Korea has been both cursed and blessed by geography and history. Placed at the nexus of great regional power relationships, most recently during the cold war, it may have surpassed Poland in its suffering at foreign hands and in multiple invasions. But it has also had unique advantages for an Asian society. It has no significant minorities, is bound by a common culture and language, and has maintained a strong sense of ethnic identity that has enabled its culture to survive in the face of colonialism and military exploitation. Korea does not suffer from an alien, dominant economic class, such as the Chinese in Southeast Asia or the Indians in Burma or East Africa. It has no low castes mired in poverty retarding the better distribution of economic assets. The liberation from Japan, land reform, the destruction during the Korean War, and the breakdown of the economic (if not the social) influence of the former *yangban* (aristocratic) class created more equal income distribution—shared deprivation, to be sure, but that has since been overcome. As Korea has expanded its international economic and political roles, cultural and linguistic homogeneity and growing social mobility have allowed more rapid and thorough economic and political mobilization and emphasized a sense of ethnic, and thus national, purpose.

A strong sense of ethnic nationalism combined with shame and revulsion over the Japanese colonial experience has spurred Korean accomplishments. Japan is a constant presence in the Korean psyche, and nowhere is this more evident than in economics. In the 1960s, many Koreans compared the way they were profiting from the American offshore procurement of goods and services for the Vietnam War with the way Japan's postwar recovery was stimulated by American purchasing during the Korean War. In the 1980s, many Koreans stressed that the 1988 Seoul Olympics would do for South Korea what the 1964 Tokyo Olympics had done for Japan in terms of world recognition. So too Japanese economic accomplishments and technology have given Korea palpable goals to surpass, even as the ROK cautiously refrains from becoming too dependent on Japanese investment, technology, and capital. An important South Korean political goal of the mid-1970s was to exceed Japan in per-hectare rice production. Korea triumphed for a short period, becoming the world's leading rice producer. Korea has won considerable attention by excelling at Japan's economic game; and yet, the essential motivating factors—pride and political legitimacy—have always been internal.

Korea has often been described as the Confucian state *par excellence*. But the Korean cultural heritage transcends Confucianism. Traditionally more hierarchical than China and not feudal like Japan, Korea grafted Confucian paternalistic and political values onto a strong, vertically oriented indigenous social system. The result is visible, for example, in the way its military command structure gave South Korea a unique capacity to implement development programs after 1961. Other states may also have adopted sound economic policies, but they often lacked the means to put them in effective motion.

Furthermore, Korea is a society in which the Confucian concept of the importance of education in combination with the stress on a bureaucratic meritocracy has encouraged the rise of talented individuals who understand personal efficiency and know how to use the levers of government. Until a generation ago, Western theory and even some Asian views held that Confucianism was an obstacle to progress and economic development because it fostered reverence for a mythic golden age and the status quo. Reality has demonstrated, however, that those states sharing the Confucian tradition have done exceedingly well in economic terms. For this reason, Singapore even introduced the teaching of Confucianism into its state school system.

Confucian values alone, however, are not sufficient to create the conditions needed for sustained growth, one of which is an economic base on which to build. South Korea's economic growth and export economy are generally regarded as having begun following the military coup of 1961, although such Cartesian clarity is not completely justified. There were preconditions for this growth, dating from the infrastructure constructed during the Japanese colonial era (1910–45), the expansion of education following Liberation in 1945 and reconstruction after the Korean War, the foreign assistance of the 1950s, and the advanced training of development specialists abroad.

Another factor was political will. Park Chung-hee was different from many leaders of the newly independent states emerging from the colonial chrysalis. Syngman Rhee in South Korea and Kim Il-sung in North Korea received political legitimacy from their anti-colonial struggles. Park, however, had been in the Japanese army. He came from a poor rural background and could not claim leadership from the traditional *yangban* literati. He was a soldier, and according to the old Confucian concept, good men did not become soldiers. Further, Park overthrew a popularly elected government supported by the United States at a period when U.S. approval was important in Korea, and he was suspected early on of having communist leanings.

Park Chung-hee thus needed political legitimacy, and to acquire it he focused the state's and his own personal attention on the economic development process. He exploited two important traditions: the old dirigiste concepts of the Confucian state, in which the leader is the father and knows what is best for the people, his children; and a powerful military command system. He centralized virtually all institutions and organizations and by nationalizing the banks created a monopoly on all institutional credit in the society. He rigidly controlled labor and its unions. He unified economic planning and budgeting in an Economic Planning Board under a deputy prime minister. He eliminated elected local government, placing military officers in key provincial positions and ensuring that local administration was intimately associated with the centrally controlled police. He instituted a far-reaching, often autonomous, and ubiquitous intelligence system. He owed no economic or political debts and could plug the loopholes and destroy the favoritism by which earlier regimes had allowed money to be made in the private sector through means other than production. He could, in essence, start afresh. The result was what has sometimes been called a "bureaucratic authoritarian" state. Perhaps no other noncommunist society has experienced such pervasive economic control, reaching down even into the villages.

This element of centralization, which Park used so effectively, would not have produced such spectacular results without sound policies, and it might well have proved disastrous. Park generally listened to professional Korean economists (and to foreigners insofar as they enabled him to go in directions he had already determined) and even established an institution—the Korea Development Institute, now a model for many Asian states—to further that process.

Internationally, political and economic relations were closely intertwined and dominated by links with two countries: the United States and Japan. A close security alliance between Korea and the United States characterized the Park Chung-hee period, concealing considerable political and economic tension with profound economic consequences. The tensions today are over trade issues—rivalries for markets, charges of dumping, intellectual property rights, and others.

Then, however, the issues were connected with economic stabilization and aid, because the two countries were involved in a patron-client association characteristic of many of the donor-recipient economic relationships of the 1950s.

The early U.S. skepticism following the coup of 1961 gave way to economic cooperation, but the United States did not trust the authoritarian tendencies of Park in his various political incarnations as junta leader, president, and finally, ruler-by-decree. It attempted to mitigate the regime's excesses and ameliorate problems privately rather than publicly castigating the government.

The distrust, however, was mutual; Park Chung-hee came to question the United States as well. Unable to distance himself in security terms, he tried to do so economically; the United States, which found it increasingly difficult to provide support at the previous high levels, encouraged him in this. In 1962, soon after the coup, he found alternative sources of foreign aid in West Germany and the World Bank. He began the process of normalizing relations with Japan, long advocated by the United States, which in 1965 resulted in economic agreements for some $800 million in aid over ten years. At the request of the United States, he negotiated Korean troop and civilian participation in the Vietnam War and as a consequence received close to $1 billion in foreign exchange earnings. The Vietnam War experience also trained a Korean construction industry that soon developed worldwide scope and power. During the 1970s, especially during the oil crises, Park pursued an independent Middle East policy to ensure oil supplies and garner foreign exchange through that Vietnam-trained construction industry.

The Guam (Nixon) Doctrine of 1969, which stipulated that the United States would no longer fight Asian ground wars, further spurred Korean independence from Washington. Although primarily focused on Vietnam, in Park's eyes the Guam doctrine cast grave doubt upon the U.S. commitment to the 1953 U.S.-ROK Mutual Security Treaty. Park thus became determined to build up the industrial and defense capacities of the state to meet his national priorities, both economic and security-related. He subsidized the heavy, defense, and chemical industries with credit. To do this, Park turned to the *chaebol*—the large, family-owned business conglomerates that have become the dominant feature of the South Korean private sector—and helped to make them strong, granting loans of up to four times their assets. The process, complicated by the oil crises of that era, led to inflation, labor shortages and thus higher wages (even though labor was controlled), a greater debt burden, underutilized industrial capacity, increased pollution, and the need for major structural adjustment following Park's assassination in 1979. Although that early period was one of considerable economic waste, the effort nevertheless set the stage for Korea's later steel, automobile, defense, and chemical exports—in short, for much of what Korea has become in the world economy.

Although close ties with the United States were at that time required for political legitimacy, legitimacy also required that the Park regime collaborate with Japan economically while maintaining political distance. Korea needed Japanese economic aid and capital and, later, components for Korean exports and other technological advancements. But no Korean regime could allow itself to appear subservient to Japan, and the normalization of relations between the two states (promoted by the United States, which considered Japan its primary Asian strategic partner and knew that initial economic growth in Korea would in large part be dependent on Japan) was accomplished only with much acrimony and popular demonstrations in South Korea.

Although Japan moved many of its polluting and labor-intensive industries to South Korea after normalization, Korea went to great pains to keep Japanese foreign investment balanced against that of the United States, Europe, and the multinational corporations. South Korea is still dependent on Japan for various sophisticated components of its exports, and Korea's major corporations have formalized relationships with many of Japan's premier industries. Because of this and Japanese protectionism, South Korea had run up a cumulative trade deficit with Japan of some $66 billion by 1992. But as a result of limiting the Japanese presence, Korea has far less foreign investment for the size of its economy than most comparable countries. From 1962 through 1990, total direct foreign investment amounted to $6.6 billion, of which about half came from Japan.

Internal and external politics and political will were important factors in Korean growth, and Park supplemented them with his personal attention to economic affairs. He met monthly with key industrialists and his economic team, and he resolved issues personally. He rewarded good economic performers with additional, often subsidized, credit, prizes, and public recognition but denied such largesse to nonperformers or those who did not play the economic game according to the government's rules. Forced onto the curb (informal) credit market with interest rates three or four times those provided by the state, they could not compete. Later, in the early 1970s, when Park founded the *Saemaul* ("New Village" or "New Community") movement, to which he was particularly attached because of his rural background, he gave it the same personal attention.

Korea was fortunate to have launched its export drive in the 1960s with virtually no external debt, for U.S. support had been almost exclusively in grant form. At this time international protectionism was quite limited. Foreign aid had been essential to national survival, most critically during and immediately following the Korean War. Later, as Korea's export drive succeeded and the state appeared creditworthy, internal savings were mobilized and foreign commercial credits became accessible. Foreign aid thus became peripheral. Overall, though, from after the Korean War through 1975, when the U.S. economic aid program was terminated, the United States supplied some $13 billion, of which about half was economic and half military assistance.

The economic policies instituted by Park Chung-hee were continued by his successor, Chun Doo-hwan (1979–88). The latter, coming to power through a coup in December 1979 but elected in 1980, had a more difficult time dealing with the political economy. He inherited from the Park government a high economic plateau but was forced at the outset to deal with three difficult situations: the political crisis of Kwangju in May 1980, the need for a structural adjustment to halt inflation from the too-rapid expansion of heavy industry, and the 1980 rice crop failure. He attempted to exert stringent control over society, repressing the labor force, among other sectors. His policies, which were largely successful, called for economic stability, though even this stability could not give him the political legitimacy he sought.

In retrospect, one of the most profound changes brought by these three decades of economic progress has been attitudinal. In the early 1960s, a pessimism about the future pervaded economics, politics, and social life and was reflected in art and literature. This gradually subsided, and although the "fragility" of the Korean economy (because of its dependence on exports and related imported components) is still a recurring theme in Korea, malaise has long since given way to pride and a sense of national achievement.

Thus, a unique combination of Korean cultural practices, political needs and will, generally sound economic policies, effective implementation, propitious timing, business subsidization, and imposed hierarchical discipline produced the startling results that have transformed the lives of South Koreans and the role of South Korea on the world political and economic scene.

The Economy of the Roh Administration

The first administration of the Sixth Republic (1988–93), a product of the forces that culminated in substantial political liberalization in

Vital Economic Statistics for South Korea

Year	%Growth of GNP	GNP per Capita ($)	GNP (Billion $)	Gross Savings (Share of GNP)	Gross Investment (Share of GNP)	Trade Account (Billion $)	Total Foreign Debt (Billion $)
1972	5.1	319	10.7	—	—	—	—
1986	12.9	2,505	102.8	32.8	28.9	4.2	44.5
1987	13.0	3,110	128.9	36.2	29.6	7.7	35.6
1988	12.4	4,127	172.8	38.1	30.7	11.4	31.2
1989	6.8	4,994	211.2	35.3	33.5	4.6	29.4
1990	9.3	5,659	242.2	36.0	37.1	-2.0	31.7
1991	8.4	6,498	280.8	36.1	39.3	-7.0	39.2
1992 est.	4.8	6,685	297.0	NA	NA	-1.4	42.6[1]

[1] Figure calculated through the end of August.

Sources: *Korea Herald* (Seoul), July 3, 1993; *Korea's Economy 1993*, Vol. 9 (Washington, D.C.: Korea Economic Institute of America, 1993); and Il Sakong, *Korea in the World Economy* (Washington, D.C.: Institute for International Economics, 1993).

1987, will be remembered for both the domestic political changes it solidified and its diplomatic successes abroad. Its economic accomplishments, however extensive the contemporaneous internal dissatisfaction, were also significant. The Roh administration was marked by four major dynamic economic tensions and actions, none of which can be separated from domestic politics: conflict between government and business over which would dominate economic policy formulation and execution; confrontations between labor and management and labor and government over the problem of wages and benefits; trade friction between Korea and the United States; and *Nordpolitik* —Korea's economic and diplomatic advances to the former communist states. Much of Korea's emerging international reputation for success was based on the Fifth Republic's heavy investment in the infrastructure associated with the Olympics, from roads and subways to housing. Although the world tended to judge South Korea positively, internally there was a strong undercurrent of disquiet remaining from the Chun Doo-hwan years that was only partly attributable to the economic statistics of the period.

The Sixth Republic began almost simultaneously with the Sixth Five Year Plan (1987–91). That plan surpassed expectations. The average annual growth of the economy over the five-year period reached 9.9 percent, instead of the anticipated 8.2 percent. Total GNP grew from $102.8 billion in 1986 to $280.8 billion in 1991, with per capita GNP rising from $2,505 to $6,498 over the same period. (As late as 1985, the Korea Development Institute had estimated that per capita income in Korea would not reach $5,100—in constant 1984 U.S. dollars—until the year 2000.) At the same time, exports increased from $34.7 billion to $72 billion, although imports grew even more substantially, from $31.6 billion to $81 billion. It is ironic that in spite of this overall stellar performance by international standards, considerable anxiety existed among South Koreans concerning the recent economic past and the state's economic future. These doubts were fueled by both inflation and the current account deficit. Inflation, according to official statistics, was 9.7 percent in 1991, although many observers thought that imaginative bookkeeping was being used to keep the rate below the politically troublesome double-digit figure. The current account dropped from a surplus of about $5 billion in 1989 to a deficit of $2.2 billion in 1990, $8.7 billion in 1991, and $4.5 billion in 1992.

The State and the Chaebol

Although many non-Koreans have held that South Korean economic growth was essentially attributable to a vigorous private sector, a statement that is perhaps half true, Korea is more accurately characterized as having had a strong centrally managed economy in which the private sector was effectively subordinated to the state. Market forces played a decisive international role, but internally businesses and the market were subject to stringent state regulations. State controls over credit and institutional relationships and the authoritarian nature of the regime forced private-sector compliance with the government. If during the 1970s there was, in addition to the "Japan, Inc." noted in studies by the Harvard Institute for International Development and the Korea Development Institute, a "Korea, Inc.," in Japan it was a partnership between the state and business while in Korea the government was chairman of the board. The balance of this lopsided relationship has shifted considerably over the past decade, with business becoming more important. Yet business and government keep a certain distance from one another in Korea. It is significant, for example, that few Koreans who are primarily known as business leaders have entered legislative politics. The Korean National Assembly has always been the agora of the literati, journalists, professional politicians, and the former military.

As the economy grew more complex, as the private sector expanded and began to develop the independent capacity to seek markets and compete internationally detached from the state, and as the *chaebol* came to dominate economic life, these corporations began to demand more autonomy. The Sixth Five Year Plan recognized these changes and stipulated that the state should release control over much of the economy and interfere less in the markets. However, the government had difficulty veering away from its established interventionist path.

The political reforms that began on June 29, 1987, were a product of the growing institutional pluralism, which was in part a product of urbanization and the state's diminished control over political processes. That pluralism was reflected in the growing autonomy of the business community, which itself contributed to pluralism and which sought a probably unattainable milieu—a combination of freedom, government support, and politically strong but economically pliant leadership. The administration of Roh Tae-woo was characterized as *mul* (literally, "watery"; i.e., spineless). Many Koreans felt that it lacked direction and could not control labor, strikes, U.S. pressures for market opening, and the price increases that were a part of the ebullient aftermath of political liberalization. At the same time, world economic conditions had caused a slowdown in export growth, on which the state was dependent, and foreign sentiment for protectionism had become apparent.

The year 1992 was in a sense a watershed both for politics and for the economy. Growth was the lowest (4.8 percent) since the disastrous year of 1980, when the economy had actually declined by 3.7 percent with the failure of the rice crop. Even more important, 1992 was the first time in Korean history that the business community had vied directly with the government for political power, both institutionally, in the National Assembly, and personally, for the presidency, with the candidacy of former Hyundai chairman Chung Ju-yung.

Chung Ju-yung had been elected to the National Assembly in 1988 as an independent. He was the first representative of a *chaebol* ever to sit in the Assembly. Railing against the policies of the government and its leaders, he then formed a political party that won 11 percent of the National Assembly seats in the March 1992 elections. He lost his presidential bid in the election of December 1992 and then retired from politics, but he did garner a significant 16 percent of the vote. Although the electorate returned the ruling party to power explicitly along the Japanese political model that the government had overtly emulated in January 1990, economic disquiet was manifest everywhere. It seemed evident that business would no longer be reluctant to engage and challenge the state in politics—and this in itself may be the most significant change in recent Korean economic history.

The Question of Labor

No group welcomed the political liberalization of 1987 more openly than did labor. Korea's economic successes since 1961 had partly been due to the use of its "comparative advantage," namely, low-cost labor. Labor was controlled and exploited, unions infiltrated and regulated by the government, women paid less than half of male wages, leaders occasionally arrested, intellectuals kept apart from laborers to prevent ideological "pollution," and most strikes declared illegal. The problem intensified with the introduction of new, more stringent labor legislation after the transition from the Fourth to the Fifth Republic in 1980. The government, in league with business management, was in command.

Upon liberalization this changed. Labor's pent-up demands exploded and were pursued through extensive strikes. There were 3,749 strikes in 1987, 1,873 in 1988, and 1,616 in 1989, after which the numbers dropped to 322 in 1990 and 234 in 1991. More than $2.5 billion was lost in exports during those first three years alone. Management was hard-pressed, and it generally capitulated along with the government. The costs of labor doubled in a few years as a result of the annual spring labor drives, and in the first few years government guide-lines limiting wage increases were not effectively enforced. In 1990 the government's attempts to regulate increases were unsuccessful because wages were only one part of a complex package that included bonuses and benefits. This drove down profits in many industries and made many labor-intensive Korean products less competitive on the world market.

The problem was exacerbated because the United States had put great pressure on Korea to revalue its currency, the *won*, upward to relieve pressure on imports into the United States by making them more expensive. As a result, the value of the *won* to the U.S. dollar changed from W890 in 1985 to a low of W667 in July 1989 (it was W790 in March 1993). Korean firms in such labor-intensive fields as footwear and textiles began to invest abroad, in countries where labor costs were much lower. Capital flowed out of Korea, encouraged and subsidized by government, to ensure continued growth but also to take advantage of the export quotas of the countries, such as Indonesia, in which Korean firms invested. By 1990, Korean overseas investment was greater than foreign direct investment (FDI) in Korea; in 1991 it was $1.6 billion compared to $1.4 billion of FDI. The most important area for overseas investment was North America (about 40 percent), in high-technology products, but by 1990 Korea had also invested about $2 billion in Southeast Asia, and it continued channeling about 38 percent of its overseas investment there. In Indonesia alone, Korean firms employed more than 260,000 workers. At the close of the Roh administration, labor's demands had eased somewhat (wage increases were 17.4 percent in 1992) because productivity had not kept pace with rising wages, the government was taking a stronger position on wage increases, and the populace feared heightened inflation. Nevertheless, labor's expectations of increased income and status in Korea's political and economic future have significant implications, which are examined below.

The United States as Trading Partner

By 1990, Korea's two-way trade with the United States was between $33 and $36 billion, with the United States dominating Korean exports; in 1991 it absorbed a quarter of them. Korea had become the seventh largest trading partner of the United States. From the inception of the Republic until the early 1980s, Korea had been in a trade deficit with the United States. But in 1982, Korea registered its first trade surplus, $0.8 billion. It grew, and at its height in 1987 the surplus with the United States was $9.6 billion. Protectionism became an

American political issue just before the U.S. presidential election of 1988. Trade between the two nations then achieved a fragile balance. By 1991, however, Korea was once again in deficit ($-0.3 billion) with the United States.

The political liberalization of 1987 had in a sense made U.S.-ROK trade relations more difficult. The United States had continuously held democratization of Korea as an important foreign policy goal, along with security of the peninsula and a more open Korean market. With democratization, however, business and the populace could make their views public. The National Assembly no longer gave a rubber stamp to presidential policies; even the government party took positions different from those of the executive branch. Market openings, acerbic negotiations, quotas, charges of dumping, and all the detritus of trade relations were debated and aired fully in the now-free press. The result was considerable consternation over some of the U.S. demands, especially with regard to the tobacco market, and the overt, and in Korean eyes excessive, pressures the United States applied to open up Korean markets.

Korea had been accustomed to a strong governmental hand in planning and guiding the execution of economic policies and achieving economic objectives. The economy was exceptionally dependent on exports (37 percent of GNP in 1982, double that in Japan), especially to the United States, and in the early stages of export growth Korea could not have succeeded without the U.S. market. It was dependent on Japan for imports of components that eventually would be exported (some 40 percent of imports were later exported in finished form). Yet the United States was exerting heavy pressure on the Korean administration not only to revalue the *won*, but also for more open markets, the "level playing field" from which, the Koreans warned, the Japanese, not the Americans, would finally and essentially benefit.

The Korean markets about which the United States was most concerned were agricultural products, services, and luxury goods. Each had its special attributes.

Agricultural Products. The United States was the major supplier of Korean agricultural imports, and Korea was the second largest customer for American wheat. It had become uneconomic to grow wheat in Korea, but as the country urbanized, wheat consumption increased, and Korean self-sufficiency dropped from some 22 percent to 2 percent. The United States also supplied cattle feed and soybeans. Two major areas of agricultural dispute emerged: beef imports, and more important, rice imports. Both were major internal political issues because they struck at the small holders, who were ubiquitous since farms were limited to three hectares and most farmers had just a few head of cattle.

At various times farmers have demonstrated extensively against import liberalization. The National Assembly, created on the Japanese model, is heavily weighted toward rural constituencies, which make up approximately 50 percent of it even though the rural population constitutes less than 20 percent of the Korean population overall. Although compromises were reached on beef after acerbic debates and demonstrations led by the livestock cooperatives, the cardinal problem, rice, remains unresolved at this writing. The issue of rice played a part in the 1992 presidential campaign, with both major South Korean parties promising some form of protectionism. The South Korean government, together with the urban Korean consumer, subsidizes the paddy price to the farmers by some 500 percent over the world market, essentially duplicating the Japanese practice. Also in keeping with the Japanese model, it is likely that Korea will eventually allow the import of rice, resorting to very high, but slowly shrinking, tariffs.

Korea and Japan have both maintained that rice self-sufficiency is a matter of security, not economics, and that on principle the state should not be dependent on imports for its basic foodstuff. Significantly, Korea has more than twice as many agricultural workers (16.7 percent in 1991) as Japan, and the contribution of rice to the income of Korean farm households (23.5 percent) is more than five times that in Japan. The Korean urban population, having evolved more recently than Japan's, has closer links to the rural community. Thus, the issue is more important in Korea than in Japan.

Koreans drew contrasts between the mass of South Korean farmers who depend largely on rice for a major share (over 60 percent) of their farm income, and the very small number of California growers who are the only Americans who produce the variety (*japonica*) acceptable to Korean and Japanese tastes. The U.S. government was thus seen as a captive of a small but influential special interest group.

Services. Services were an expanding field in which the United States excelled and to which its businesses wanted more access. Banking and financial institutions were a preliminary focus, then the insurance industry, and more recently the stock market. The American Chamber of Commerce in Korea, a staunch advocate of market openings, considered financial liberalization to be the key to foreign business success in Korea. In 1991, the rules for establishing branch foreign securities companies and regulations on local currency and foreign exchange transactions were liberalized. In January 1992, foreigners were given limited direct access to the stock market, and a few foreign securities firms were allowed to operate in Korea. As services expand in Korea, there will be further pressures to open other aspects of what, with increased Korean personal income, is becoming a lucrative market.

Luxury Goods.   The issue of consumer goods illustrates a major difference between the South Korean and U.S. import regimes. Consumer goods now represent only about 10 percent of Korean imports. Many of those items shipped to Korea are considered "luxury" goods. Most prominent have been American automobiles and wines, both of which command premium prices and are very heavily taxed. These and other American products were "voluntarily" withdrawn from shops after a merchant boycott that many felt was government inspired. Those who bought American automobiles were sometimes subject to tax investigations. The problem has since eased, but tensions remain. Korea claims that it cannot afford the "excessive" Korean consumption levels (consumption grew faster than GNP in 1989–91—some 10 percent annually), and the government has sought to enforce (with marginal success) "traditional" Korean frugality, although Koreans remain highly brand conscious and interested in foreign "name" brands.

Although Korea has lowered tariffs (and has scheduled more reductions) and opened many new avenues for direct investment, the United States has been stymied by the Korean government's perceived need to deny access to Japanese products (such as automobiles) and shield its all-important private sector, which would like protection at home and access to U.S. markets at the same time.

But Korea has proceeded cautiously. Not wishing to be considered a "second Japan" by the United States, which was becoming increasingly concerned over Japanese and Korean trade surpluses during the 1988 U.S. presidential election campaign, the state liberalized imports, lowered some tariffs, regulated the flow of some of its exports to the United States, sent "buying missions" there, and sought alternative foreign markets, including those in the (at that time) centrally planned economies. Korean rhetoric about the rapid opening of its markets, however, was somewhat at variance with its slow, bureaucratic reality, which caused great frustration in U.S. trade circles.

Nordpolitik

Prior to the 1988 Olympics, Korea inaugurated a combined political and economic policy known as *Nordpolitik* (Northern Policy). That policy had a dual purpose: the diplomatic one of establishing friendly relations with the centrally planned economies—and in its initial stage, of isolating North Korea from its former friends and allies—and the economic one of diversifying exports and investment as alternatives to ties with the United States, which were seen to be more vulnerable as a result of the U.S. political process.

At first, trade delegations were sent to Eastern Europe and the Soviet Union, and later to China and Vietnam. Then trade offices were established. With the political changes in the former communist world, trade soon led to diplomatic recognition. China offered the major trading and investment opportunities: two-way trade, which had been a trickle through Hong Kong at the beginning of the Sixth Republic, reached $10 billion in 1992. Although political problems in Russia and its associated republics prevented large-scale investments, Korea promised to provide the former Soviet Union with $3 billion in investment and credits, ensuring a major role for the ROK in any Russian economic recovery and leapfrogging over Japan, which kept its distance from Russia because of the dispute about sovereignty over the Kurile Islands and perhaps also because of historical fears dating from the 19th century. South Koreans became economic advisers to some of the former Soviet republics. *Nordpolitik* was a major diplomatic success that changed South Korean international relations and paved the way for the two Koreas to enter the United Nations in September 1991. At the close of 1992, Korea and Vietnam established diplomatic ties, thereby completing the policy.

Challenges for the Roh Administration

Rising living standards in Korea created a demand for foreign labor to perform the menial jobs Koreans no longer considered desirable. Illegal "guest workers" began to enter Korea, especially ethnic Koreans from Manchuria. In late 1992 the total number was estimated at some 80,000. The structure of employment and technology has begun to change and will ultimately develop into a problem that Kim Youngsam's administration will have to face. Although unemployment was a low 2.4 percent in 1990, growing pressure was evident on the educated working elite, who were having difficulty finding appropriate employment.

Unemployment in 1991 was only 1.1 percent for those with less than a junior high school education but more than three times that figure for those with some college. In addition, labor-shortage ratios (unfilled vacancies to current employees) were becoming more pronounced because of a successful family planning program, the lack of a surplus rural population, and the expansion of secondary education.

In fact there was a 20 percent labor shortage among unskilled workers in 1991.

The Roh administration was scarred by a number of scandals, despite its effort to channel investments into production, not speculation. The power of the business community was evident in its ability to prevent passage of an act supported by the government requiring "real name" bank accounts, which would have forced increased adherence to tax regulations. In turn, on political or policy grounds, the government could and did use the tax audit system to try to control, regulate, and punish the *chaebol* in a selective manner, indicating that the confrontations between them were not yet over and in fact may have entered a new phase. In summary, the first administration of the Sixth Republic was perceived to be wounded—floundering in its policies, unable to control labor, and marred by scandals.

At the same time, the quality of life seemed to deteriorate even as incomes rose. Inflation was higher than it had been for many years. Crime, especially violent crime, was rising. Environmental problems became of increasing concern. Pollution pervaded all urban areas. Seoul, with a quarter of the nation's population and exponential increases in automobiles, was frequently in a state of gridlock. There were 5.25 million vehicles in Korea in 1992, one for every nine persons. Although a series of environmental regulations was enacted beginning in the late 1970s, progress has been slow. For example, though sulphur dioxide levels in Seoul have lessened over the past five years, Seoul has still violated the World Health Organization standard for "days in excess" by a multiple of 11. If that city has improved slightly in a number of environmental aspects, other cities have deteriorated.

To many Koreans, there appeared to be growing disparities in income and wealth distribution, although critical differences exist between the two. Absolute poverty has declined from about 40 percent to perhaps 5 percent since the early 1960s (it is now less than in the United States). Income disparities, measurements that are both difficult to make and politically charged, remained roughly constant between 1965 and 1985 and are comparable to those in the United States, Japan, and Taiwan (and far less marked than in the Philippines, for example). During this period, the top 20 percent of the population received about 47 percent of the national income. Yet overall wealth is even more concentrated because of real estate holdings. The top 5 percent of the population has 31 percent and the top 1 percent, 14 percent of the national wealth. Ten percent of landowners own 66 percent of the land, and capital gains from real estate exceeded the GNP in 1989. Land prices increased by more than 100 percent between 1987 and 1991. Thus land and related housing costs loom as major economic and social issues.

These circumstances seemed like a prescription for political change, but it was not to be. The ruling party managed to forge a controlling coalition after the National Assembly elections in March and to hold on to the presidency with a 42 percent plurality in December. The public was clearly concerned about the economy in 1992, but economic conservatism and safety turned out to be a greater motivation.

The New Administration and Beyond

As Kim Young-sam and his new administration continue to evolve in 1993 and beyond, the president will have to address the issues and goals formulated under the Seventh Five Year Plan (1992–96). The plan was devised by Roh Tae-woo and his Democratic Liberal Party (DLP), and as heir to Roh's administration, Kim Young-sam will likely keep to the goals of the party's economic plan. He will also have to confront a set of broader issues that have both political and diplomatic aspects. President Kim will need to expend considerable political capital to control the DLP, and he will have to deal with the economic and social expectations of the middle class: education and employment, housing, the functioning of the rural sector, and income distribution. Abroad, he will have to handle Japan, continue to negotiate with North Korea for reunification—a problem that concerns Koreans even more now that they have witnessed the German experience—consider Korea's new and important economic relations with China, continue to negotiate with the United States to assure that the North America Free Trade Agreement (NAFTA) does not undercut Korea's markets, and move into the European Community markets. These tasks will be difficult and require strong leadership.

The targets for the Five Year Plan are ambitious but attainable. By 1996, GNP is expected to total $492.6 billion, with an annual growth of 7.5 percent. Per capita income is expected to be $10,908, placing Korea in the ranks of the economically advanced states and ahead of many of the European nations. Korea is planning to join the Organization for Economic and Cooperative Development. Exports and imports will balance at $140 billion each. Unemployment is to be kept to 2.4 percent, and some 54 percent of students of college age will be in school, compared to 38 percent in 1991. Women will make up a larger proportion of the labor force. Greater emphasis will be placed on the social infrastructure, and there is to be continued liberalization of government controls over the private sector.

Korea has continuously defied the expectations of internal and external skeptics, performing better than virtually anyone anticipated. Although the seventh plan is based on various international assumptions (regarding energy prices and the rate of growth of the industrialized nations, for example), most of the projections are reasonable. Should a German model of reunification (a collapse of the North Korean regime) take place in that plan period, however, the massive costs of unification, variously estimated at $141 billion a year for several years, or perhaps $1 trillion over ten years, would require the rethinking of all goals. A more likely early scenario would be the increasing of direct trade and investment between two independent but less confrontational regimes.

Internally, Korea will have to deal with its labor force, which increasingly identifies with the middle class. To believe in such status is, essentially, to have hope for a better life for the next generation. But to have such hope requires expectations of increases in wages and living standards and access to higher levels of education, and, if Korea is to remain competitive, increases in productivity as well. This means more advanced technology if Korea is to compete with Taiwan, Singapore, and other such states and eventually challenge Japan for new high-technology markets. Korea invested about 2.02 percent of its GNP in research and development in 1991, while Japan invests almost double the same percentage of a much larger base. Korea would like to expand its investment level to 3–4 percent of GNP to ensure that it remains current with or ahead of the world technological curve.

Like most countries, Korea has acquired its technology by example, by aid, by sales, through direct investment, and through pirating (which is now under more stringent control). From 1962 through 1991, Korea spent $6.1 billion in purchasing technology and an additional $359 million in acquiring technological services, and received $315 million in technological aid. Yet, as Korea raises its technological sights, it causes potential competitors, such as Japan and the United States, to begin to restrict Korean access to the most sophisticated processes. For Korea to succeed, it needs to invest more in research and development. Although Korean technological successes have been impressive, there has been a deterioration of quality in exports —the rejection rate rose from 3.0 percent in 1988 to 5.3 percent in 1991, more than double that of Taiwan and triple that of Japan.

In its democratic incarnation, Korea will have to address a set of economically and politically important social issues. In 1987 housing was the major perceived need, and although some 2 million units have since been built, the issue still looms large and is difficult to resolve because of land prices. By the completion of the seventh plan, an estimated 50 percent of women will be in the labor force, but discrimination in salaries and promotions is likely to continue despite legislation against such practices. The government plans to increase the size of allowable agricultural land holdings from 3 to 20 hectares to rationalize farming, but this is likely to exacerbate income and wealth differentials both among the rural population and between urban and rural areas. The growing perception that income and wealth disparities are increasing will have to be countered with real working-level gains.

How to deal with the concentration of wealth in the *chaebol* is yet another critical issue. One solution, which may be difficult to put into practice, could be to make the *chaebol* public through sales of stock, break up the complex web of interlocking relationships of firms within each *chaebol* structure, and seek the gradual replacement of family ownership with professional managers. The *chaebol* leadership will no doubt resist (even though Chung Ju-yung publicly advocated these changes), and this may be a major element in the future struggle between the state and the private sector. The internal agenda for the new government under the economic plan is thus extensive.

The external agenda is equally challenging. With a rising sense of Korean nationalism in a new generation that does not subscribe to previous stereotypes of Korea's Confucian "younger brother" international role, external relations must be deftly handled by all concerned. Japan and the United States must tread warily and negotiate their inevitable disputes with a new degree of sensitivity. As South Korea invests more overseas, it must learn to respect other peoples and confront the fact that its factory managers abroad are perhaps even more insensitive to local customs and needs than are many foreigners investing in Korea.

How much South Korea should, or could, invest in labor-intensive jobs overseas, how much in high technology, and where, are all salient issues as well. In 1993, China was the most obvious and the preferred site for investment, and with diplomatic relations with Vietnam newly established, that country will likely follow. Both China and Vietnam are strong states with literate and disciplined labor forces. Koreans feel more culturally attuned to those countries than to the non-Confucian states of Southeast Asia. Korean companies may consider investing in Guangdong province, where Chinese growth is most rapid, in Shandong province, now linked with Korea by ferry service, or in Manchuria in the Yanbian (Korean) Autonomous Region, which is home to over 1 million ethnic Koreans. We may in the next decade witness the development of a major new growth pole in

Asia—South Korea, North Korea, parts of Manchuria, the Korean population of Japan, and the Maritime Province of Russia—the ethnic Korean industrial complex.

NAFTA poses an important challenge for South Korea and for U.S.-ROK relations. Korea views NAFTA as an indication of increasing protectionism on the part of the United States and will attempt to counter it. It will likely invest in Mexico, where low wages within NAFTA may give Korean firms broader market access. Korea is also concerned that the Democratic administration in the United States will tend to be more protectionist than a Republican one.

Eight or more years ago, some had suggested that Korea and the United States enter into a free trade agreement (like that between the United States and Israel). At that time, there were few constituencies for it in either country. From a Korean perspective, that approach might now be helpful. Korea hopes for a U.S.-Korea "industrial alliance" that would wed American technology and Korean productivity. From a long-range American vantage point, a relationship that does not force Korea into greater dependency on the Japanese market should be important for the United States and for the balance of economic power in East Asia. How Japan, Korea, and China relate to each other in terms of investments, labor, technology, and trading blocs is of the utmost significance to the United States. The United States should not inadvertently push these groups together into bloc relationships.

For self-protection, diplomatic reasons, and access to markets, Korea has for years been an advocate of regional cooperation rather than regional economic blocs. It has an ongoing annual dialogue with the ASEAN states and is a participant at their ministerial meetings, and it has been a strong supporter and host of APEC (Asia-Pacific Economic Cooperation).

For South Korea, the most emotional and potentially important external issue will be relations with North Korea. Whether unification comes quickly or slowly, there will in all probability be closer economic relations between the two states under the new administration. This will likely take the form of the South's investing in the North, assuming that the doubts about North Korea's development of nuclear weapons can be resolved. Some of the major *chaebol* have already indicated their desire to invest in the North and to "make Korea more internationally competitive," that is, take advantage of the cheap labor there. In 1992 direct two-way trade between North and South Korea reached $210 million. As these issues unfold, regional interest is growing in the Tumen River Free Trade Zone, an area along the North Korean, Chinese, and Russian border that would engage in production and service the region as far as Mongolia. Spurred by the United Nations Development Program, the complex is being planned to attract South Korean and Japanese investment. It will require some $30 billion in infrastructure.

As Kim Young-sam took command in 1993, his economic actions were both strong and impressive. He called for the people to "share the [economic] pains together." He stressed wage and price restraints, froze civil service salaries, forced the declaration of economic assets, cut the Blue House budget, engaged in an anti-corruption campaign, fired some early appointees, indicated that he intended to push for "real name" bank accounts (which to be effective would have to include real estate holdings), and even called for a reduction in golfing —an elite preoccupation.

The tasks facing the new administration are in a sense daunting, but in the past the Koreans have shown both resilience and flexibility in responding to new challenges. If modern history is any indication, they are likely to continue to do so.

Peninsular Lessons

The South Korean economic experience is instructive. Although Korea should not be considered a development model, the World Bank and the Japanese regard it as a model user of foreign assistance and industrialization policies. To be sure, its experiences cannot simply be mimicked by other developing economies. There are, however, generic aspects of its path to economic success from which lessons may be drawn.

The conventional wisdom about economic development, as fostered by the international aid agencies, includes a number of critical exhortations: export; stress the private sector and markets, keeping the government as far removed from the process as possible; avoid subsidies that distort economic relations; invest first in the rural sector and then use those surpluses to invest in industry; "get the prices right"; and ensure that fiscal and monetary policies are sound.

South Korea effectively violated some of these exhortations. It did export and "get the prices right," but it also ensured a strong, even commanding role for government and the public sector in these processes. It subsidized both industry and agriculture for state purposes. It also invested first in industry and then later in the agricultural sector. The Korean example illustrates that there are various paths to developmental success and that universalistic answers tend to be both simplistic and, sometimes, unsuited to individual national circumstances.

The Korean example also demonstrates that investments in human resources, education, and training at all levels are major elements in sustained economic growth. It was the training begun in the 1950s, when policies were not conducive to continuous economic expansion and those trained could not yet be effectively employed, that allowed Korea to move ahead when the political will was in place and flexibility was possible in policy formulation.

Political will is itself a critical component of economic success. To paraphrase, economic planning is too important to be left only to economists. The role of political leadership is an understated element among economists, but the Korean experience amply demonstrates the centrality of politics as an "unindicted co-conspirator" in the process. An example of this is the political will necessary to curb speculation, the acquisition of land purely for future sale at a profit, or the search for money-making opportunities that are not productive. The state needs to promote productive investments rather than manipulation of exchange rates, abuse of personal and family ties, and schemes designed for quick profit.

It will be difficult for another country to duplicate the South Korean experience because the development process has become more difficult. The debt burden on most states is onerous, there is heightened protectionism, and newly industrialized states must compete with the economic "tigers" of the world as well as with the more industrialized societies. More pluralistic political systems tend to demand more social investments and environmental controls by their governments along with policies that redistribute the fruits of growth, thereby preventing the concentration of attention on the growth process alone.

The South Korean experience puts to rest the stereotypical and ethnocentric prejudices that denigrate the capacities of non-Western societies to mature. Korea has exceeded all foreign, and indeed internal, expectations. For the past 30 years in South Korea, economics has not been the "dismal science"; the next 20 years look equally promising.

3
U.S. Policy Toward South Korea

Chae-Jin Lee

Our two nations share a history written in the blood of our people. The bonds forged in the cold war, at the brink of Korea's mortal danger, have grown stronger through the years.

—George Bush in January 1992

The Korean peninsula remains a vital American interest. . . . Our troops will stay here as long as the Korean people want and need us here.

—Bill Clinton in July 1993

For the last five decades the United States has had an extraordinarily intimate and complex relationship with the Korean peninsula—a unique situation for U.S. foreign policy in the non-Western world. After World War II ended Japan's 35-year colonial rule in Korea in 1945, the U.S. military government administered the southern half of Korea for three years. The United States then sponsored the inauguration of the Republic of Korea (ROK) as a rival regime to the Democratic People's Republic of Korea (DPRK) to the north, which was established by the Soviet Union in 1948. Hence from the outset inter-Korean relations were inevitably linked to growing U.S. Soviet conflicts. When the Korean War (1950–53) broke out, the Truman administration assumed that the North Korean attack was part of a global strategic conspiracy by the Soviet Union and intervened decisively to repel the invaders. In the process the United States became engaged in a costly military confrontation with the People's Republic of China.

America's vested interest in South Korea thus began as a legacy of the Korean War. Even after the United States brought about a negotiated settlement of the war, it continued to protect South Korea by promptly concluding a mutual defense treaty with that nation and agreeing to provide it with significant military and economic assistance. The United States, recognizing the value of South Korea as a vital bulwark for its anti-communist struggles in the cold war era, embraced it as one of its closest client-states in the Asia-Pacific region. This general framework, in which the United States played a preeminent, benevolent, and unilateral role in South Korea, continued throughout the 1950s and 1960s.

As South Korea achieved rapid economic development and sought to increase its self-defense capabilities and adopt a more assertive diplomatic posture during the 1970s and 1980s, the United States accepted a gradual, but unmistakable, change in its relations with South Korea—the transition from an essentially unequal and hierarchical alliance to a reciprocal and interdependent partnership. The United States no longer regarded South Korea as a mere instrument of its global cold war policy but rather valued it as an increasingly important and confident participant in regional economic and military affairs.

This structural transformation of U.S.-ROK relations has been accompanied by perceptual differences and policy conflicts on a number of bilateral and multilateral issues. With the erosion of the cold war system has come a critical reappraisal of the traditional assumptions underlying U.S. policy toward South Korea. The two allies must now cooperate in the face of the various conflicts that arise in their intricate linkages, and chart a new direction for their relations amid a rapidly shifting international environment. Now that both countries have new presidents, it is useful to review recent developments in U.S.-ROK military and economic relations and consider the Clinton administration's emerging policy toward the Korean peninsula.

Military Affairs

It is remarkable that, in spite of dramatic changes in the international strategic environment, the United States has never deviated from its legally binding commitment to protect South Korea's security interests. This commitment was initially spelled out in the Mutual Security Treaty signed by the two nations on October 1, 1953.

> Each Party recognizes that an armed attack in the Pacific area on either of the Parties in territories now under their respective administrative control, or hereafter recognized by one or the other, would be dangerous to its own peace and safety and declares that it would act to meet the common danger in accordance with its constitutional processes.[1]

---

[1] As quoted in Chae-Jin Lee and Hideo Sato, *U.S. Policy Toward Japan and Korea* (New York: Praeger, 1982), p. 20.

The treaty also stipulated that "the United States accepts the right to dispose United States land, air and sea forces in and about the territory of the Republic of Korea as determined by mutual agreement."

The United States made full and effective use of its right to deploy armed forces in South Korea as a deterrent against North Korea's military ambitions. The continuing U.S. military presence also served a number of other purposes—to allow the United States to exercise political influence in South Korea, to support South Korea's diplomatic and economic activities, and to provide a training ground for U.S. combat troops. In the context of the cold war conflicts, the United States viewed the presence of its military forces in South Korea as a means to counterbalance Soviet and Chinese military expansionism and as a buffer to safeguard Japan's security and political interests. The U.S.-ROK alliance was an integral part of the worldwide anticommunist containment system.

Guided by the Guam Doctrine, which envisaged an indigenous solution to military conflicts in Asia, however, presidents Richard M. Nixon and Jimmy Carter both attempted to withdraw the U.S. ground forces from South Korea in the 1970s. They believed that the reduction or pullout of the U.S. military presence in South Korea would increase U.S. strategic flexibility, lessen the U.S. financial burden, and mollify domestic critics of U.S. military policy abroad. President Nixon was successful in withdrawing the Seventh Infantry Division (about 20,000 troops) from South Korea by March 1971, but President Carter was unable to implement his decision to withdraw almost all U.S. combat troops from South Korea over a period of four or five years. He had failed to persuade either his allies (South Korea and Japan) or his domestic constituencies, especially those in Congress and the military establishment, who argued that U.S. military disengagement from South Korea would lead to another Korean War.

The military decisions made by Nixon and Carter greatly distressed the South Koreans and severely strained the U.S.-ROK alliance. Nixon and Carter had rationalized their decisions on Korea both in terms of U.S. global strategic calculations and domestic political considerations, but their South Korean counterparts perceived their nation's security ties with the United States almost exclusively in the context of the inter-Korean military rivalry. This marked disparity in perceptions and policy priorities became apparent in the reactions of the South Koreans to the Nixon and Carter decisions. They felt betrayed and insulted because both presidents had announced their decisions without prior consultation with the South Korean government and because they appeared to downgrade the importance of the special security relationship between the two countries. More important, the South Koreans resented what seemed to be insensitive and arrogant U.S. behavior and seriously questioned the reliability of U.S. security commitments.

When Ronald Reagan, a staunch advocate of cold war measures, assumed the presidency in 1981, he reversed the premises of Nixon's and Carter's military policies toward South Korea and gave a semblance of stability to the U.S.-ROK alliance system. In a series of summit meetings with President Chun Doo-hwan, President Reagan made it clear that the United States, as a Pacific power, would continue its active role in ensuring the peace and security of the region and that it had no plans to withdraw U.S. ground combat forces from the Korean peninsula.[2] He enthusiastically assisted South Korea's force-modernization programs and carried out joint military exercises and other strategic cooperative activities with South Korea.

It is ironic that while the South Korean government welcomed Reagan's hard-line military policy toward Korea during the 1980s, an increasing number of radical students, political dissidents, religious leaders, and nationalistic intellectuals in South Korea openly voiced criticism of U.S. military policy. They argued that the U.S. military presence supported the continuation of military-led regimes in South Korea, condoned armed suppression during the popular uprising at Kwangju in 1980, and obstructed inter-Korean reconciliation. They contended that the Agreement on the Status of United States Armed Forces in the Republic of Korea, which had gone into effect in 1966, was detrimental to the legitimate exercise of South Korea's sovereign independence and that the U.S. nuclear weapons deployed in South Korea increased the danger of nuclear warfare on the peninsula. They also claimed that U.S. operational control over the South Korean armed forces was a national disgrace. Even though the governments of the United States and South Korea rejected these criticisms, they failed to thwart the rising anti-American movement in South Korea.

As an extension of President Reagan's military policy toward South Korea, President George Bush wished to reiterate the U.S. security guarantee for South Korea and quell anti-American sentiment there. Speaking before the National Assembly in February 1989, Bush reaffirmed "America's support, friendship, and respect for the Republic of Korea and its people," and America's commitment "for your right to determine your own future." He added that "the American people share your goal of peaceful unification on terms acceptable to the Korean people." He went on to say:

---

[2] For the Reagan-Chun summit meeting, see *Department of State Bulletin*, March 1981, pp. 14–15.

As President, I am committed to maintaining American forces in Korea, and I am committed to support our mutual defense treaty. There are no plans to reduce U.S. forces in Korea. Our soldiers and airmen are here at the request of the Republic of Korea to deter aggression from the North, and their presence contributes to the peace and stability of Northeast Asia. They will remain in the Republic of Korea as long as they are needed and as long as we believe it is in the interest of peace to keep them there.[3]

President Bush's strong pledge was short-lived, however. Three main factors soon led him to revise U.S. military policy toward South Korea. First, the reduction in cold war confrontations, the decline of the Soviet Union, and China's open-door policy undermined the earlier argument that a U.S. military presence in South Korea was required to contain the outward expansion of the Soviet and Chinese military forces. The United States was more interested in seeking arms control and confidence-building measures with the Soviet Union and China than in escalating the endless arms race and military hostilities. Second, many U.S. senators and representatives asked the Bush administration to scale down its overseas military activities and reap a "peace dividend" from the cessation of the cold war, and Bush had no choice but to accommodate this type of mounting legislative pressure. Third, South Korea's successful *Nordpolitik* (Northern Policy) had weakened the political basis of North Korea's alliance with the Soviet Union and China and increased the possibility of an easing of tensions on the Korean peninsula. The Soviet Union and China were no longer suspected of supporting or encouraging North Korean armed aggression against South Korea and instead were now urged to exercise a moderating influence over North Korea. Moreover, the United States recognized the far-reaching military implications of South Korea's economic and technological superiority over North Korea and concluded that South Korea would soon be capable of defending itself against North Korea.

In response to the changing military situation in the Asia-Pacific region and on the Korean peninsula, the Bush administration issued a programmatic report, "A Strategic Framework for the Asian Pacific Rim: Looking Toward the 21st Century." The report indicated that the United States, as a Pacific power, would continue to keep its forward-deployed forces, overseas bases, nuclear umbrella, and bilateral security arrangements in the Asia-Pacific for an indefinite period, but that

---

[3] George Bush, "Continuity and Change in U.S.-Korean Relations," *Current Policy*, No. 1155.

it would incrementally reduce the number of U.S. forces stationed in South Korea, Japan, and the Philippines. In addition, the Bush administration also maintained that U.S. military policy was not merely motivated by altruism but also functioned to set the stage for U.S. economic involvement in the region.

The report described the danger posed by North Korea:

> The Korean Peninsula will remain one of the world's potential military flashpoints. The North has retained its reunification objectives, devoting an extraordinary percentage of its national wealth and maintaining a favorable military balance with over a million men under arms, at the expense of the welfare of its citizens. It belligerently defies the international trend towards freedom and democracy witnessed elsewhere.[4]

It identified U.S. security objectives in South Korea as (1) deterring North Korean aggression or defeating it if deterrence were to fail, (2) reducing political and military tensions on the Korean peninsula by encouraging North-South talks and instituting a confidence-building-measures regime, and (3) converting U.S. forces in South Korea from a leading to a supporting role, including force reductions.

The report spelled out a gradual and conditional phased reduction of the U.S. forces stationed in South Korea. In the first phase (from one to three years), the United States planned to cut administrative overhead and undertake a modest reduction of about 7,000 personnel—2,000 Air Force personnel and 5,000 ground force personnel—and promised to assist South Korea in its force-improvement program, including the acquisition of sophisticated U.S. weapons and aircraft. In the second phase (from three to five years), the United States intended to reassess the North Korean threat and the status of North-South relations and restructure the Second Infantry Division. Assuming successful completion of the earlier phases, the third phase (from five to ten years) envisioned South Korea assuming a leading role in its own defense and the presence of fewer U.S. forces on the Korean peninsula. This was a purposeful, but cautious, scenario for U.S. military disengagement from South Korea by the year 2000.

In order to pave the way for South Korea's assumption of a leading role in its own defense, the United States agreed to appoint one

---

[4] "A Strategic Framework for the Asian Pacific Rim: Looking Toward the 21st Century," in U.S. Senate Committee on Armed Services, *The President's Report on the U.S. Military Presence in East Asia* (Washington, D.C.: U.S. Government Printing Office, 1990), p. 6.

South Korean general as the senior member of the Military Armistice Commission at Panmunjom and another as commander of the Ground Component Command of the Combined Forces Command, which was set up in 1978 to coordinate and integrate military operations between the United States and South Korea. The United States also deactivated the 12-year-old Combined Field Army headed by an American general, removed the U.S. Eighth Army from the Demilitarized Zone, and made plans to relocate the headquarters of the U.S. forces away from Seoul. Hence the profile and functions of the U.S. forces in South Korea were lowered considerably. The South Korean side agreed to increase its annual share of the *won*-based local costs of the U.S. forces in Korea and to assume one-third of those costs (estimated at $900 million) by 1995.[5] Most important of all, the United States and South Korea announced in October 1992 that operational control over the ROK forces would be transferred to South Korea no later than December 31, 1994.[6] The North Koreans have long argued that since the United States has operational control over the South Korean forces, they do not want to discuss the most important military issues with South Korea but rather with its American "master." As a result of its achieving of operational control, then, South Korea is expected to become able to exercise a bona fide sovereign role in managing its own defense as well as negotiate a wide range of military issues with North Korea on an equal basis.

The United States agrees with South Korean estimates that North Korea enjoys a quantitative superiority over South Korea in such critical categories as ground troops, jet fighters, bombers, tanks, artillery, armored personnel carriers, attack submarines, amphibious craft, and commando forces. The two allies also share the assessment that North Korea, by deploying its forces offensively near the Demilitarized Zone and developing nonconventional weapons of mass destruction and SCUD-type long-range missiles, poses a serious threat to South Korea. At the Senate Armed Services Committee in March 1992, General Robert W. RisCassi, commander of the U.S. forces in South Korea, pointed out that North Korea had impressively increased the speed, pace, and lethality of its offensive ground forces, and he argued that "our military presence in Korea remains an irreplaceable investment, both for resolving the potentially volatile struggle within a divided

---

[5] The South Korean government contributed $40 million for the U.S. military presence in 1989, $70 million in 1990, $150 million in 1991, and $180 million in 1992.

[6] For the agreement, see *Korea Herald*, October 9, 1992.

Korea, and for sustaining peace and stability in one of the world's most dynamic and powerful regions."[7]

In an attempt to encourage North Korea to adopt a peaceful stance toward South Korea and also to explore the possibility of improving its own relations with North Korea, the United States has held almost 30 low-level diplomatic talks with the DPRK in Beijing since December 1988. During these meetings the United States has rejected DPRK proposals that the armistice agreement be changed to a bilateral peace treaty, U.S. forces be withdrawn from South Korea, U.S.-ROK joint military exercises be stopped, and a nuclear-free zone be established on the Korean peninsula. The United States has requested that North Korea reduce tensions with South Korea, accept military confidence-building measures, account for about 8,200 U.S. soldiers listed as missing in action during the Korean War, and stop exporting ballistic missiles to the Middle East. In the Beijing talks, the United States has also made it clear that North Korea must not only submit its nuclear facilities to full-scope inspections by the International Atomic Energy Agency (IAEA) but also implement the bilateral nuclear inspection regime agreed upon in the Joint Declaration for a Nonnuclear Korean Peninsula signed by the two Korean prime ministers on December 31, 1991. Since President Bush announced the withdrawal of all tactical nuclear weapons from South Korea in September 1991, the United States has viewed the nuclear issue as a litmus test of whether North Korea really intends to become a responsible participant in the international community and improve its relations with the United States and Japan.

It is unlikely that the Clinton administration will significantly change the basic framework of U.S. military policy toward South Korea. In his campaign speeches and documents, Bill Clinton expressed his intention to maintain a U.S. military presence in Korea as long as North Korea threatens South Korea's security. He argued:

> America is the world's strongest military power, and we must remain so. A post–cold war restructuring of American forces will produce substantial savings beyond those promised by the Bush administration, but that restructuring must be achieved without undermining our ability to meet future threats to our security.[8]

In his Inaugural Address, President Clinton declared that "as an old order passes, the new world is more free but less stable" and that

---

[7] See "Briefing Remarks by Gen. Robert W. RisCassi" before the Senate Committee on Armed Services, March 4, 1992.

[8] See *Congressional Quarterly*, July 18, 1992, p. 2111.

"when our vital interests are challenged, or the will and conscience of the international community defied, we will act—with peaceful diplomacy when possible, with force when necessary."[9] While promising to restructure the U.S. forces and reduce defense expenditures, the new U.S. president also planned to enhance his country's rapid deployment capabilities and military technology to meet regional crises. Secretary of Defense Les Aspin added that regional threats to U.S. interests in places like North Korea, Iraq, and Africa would replace the former Soviet Union as a major focus of U.S. military policy and that a new position, assistant secretary of defense, would be established to oversee policies toward those areas.[10]

President Clinton attaches high priority to halting the spread of nuclear and other weapons of mass destruction by strengthening the IAEA's authority and enforcing strong sanctions against governments that violate the Nuclear Nonproliferation Treaty (NPT), a stance that was tested by the DPRK early in 1993. In February the North Koreans rejected the IAEA's request for a "special inspection" of their suspected nuclear facilities at Yongbyon, 90 kilometers north of Pyongyang. The IAEA wanted access to two sites where North Korea stores waste from its nuclear energy and research program so that it could search for evidence of a suspected nuclear weapons program. North Korea had already permitted IAEA inspection of its operational power and research reactors and a nearby facility under construction which it calls a "radiochemical laboratory" but which international authorities suspect is actually a production facility for weapons-grade plutonium. The two sites on the IAEA's February inspection list, however, were deemed by the North Koreans to be "military" and therefore out of bounds. North Korea insisted that it had already revealed everything and that the IAEA was encroaching on its sovereignty. Its refusal to permit the inspection was followed by the resumption of the annual U.S.-ROK Team Spirit military maneuvers, and on March 12 the North Koreans announced that they were pulling out of the NPT regime.

North Korea's decision to divest itself of the obligation to live up to the terms of the NPT caused consternation around the world. Though nearly everyone in the international community thought it imperative to persuade the North Koreans to return to the fold before June 12, 1993, when their withdrawal was scheduled to take effect, there was little consensus on how to do so. Hard-liners and soft-liners within the governments most closely involved, namely the United States,

---

[9] For the text of Clinton's Inaugural Address, see *Los Angeles Times*, January 21, 1993.
[10] *Los Angeles Times*, January 23, 1993.

South Korea, and Japan, argued over "carrots" and "sticks," while the North Koreans themselves adamantly stuck to their decision, at least in public. Their demands continued to be that the IAEA drop its demand to inspect "military" sites; that the entire peninsula be made "nuclear-free" (meaning that an end be brought to the U.S. nuclear umbrella over South Korea, a pledge be made by the United States that nuclear weapons would never be used against North Korea, and the DPRK be given access to U.S. military bases in the South to verify the absence of tactical nuclear weapons); that the annual U.S.-ROK Team Spirit maneuvers be ended; that the remaining 36,000 U.S. military personnel in South Korea be withdrawn; and that improvements be made in intergovernmental relations between the United States and North Korea.

In early June, Robert L. Gallucci (assistant secretary of state for political-military affairs) and Kang Sok-ju (North Korean vice-minister of foreign affairs) held a series of meetings in New York amid published reports that the United States was about to ask the United Nations Security Council to bring economic sanctions against North Korea. On June 11, at the end of these meetings, Kang announced that North Korea would unilaterally "suspend" its decision to withdraw from the NPT, in effect taking a step back from the brink. Both sides hinted that the United States had offered no concessions; however, their joint statement gave "assurances against the threat and use of force, including nuclear weapons" and declared their commitment to a "nuclear-free Korean peninsula."[11] It remained to be seen whether the United States was attaching a qualification to its pledge to defend the South, but at least it seemed that North Korea had thought twice about becoming the first country ever to renounce the NPT.

The Clinton administration now faces a major challenge: it must coordinate its policy with South Korea in a way that will persuade North Korea to remain in the NPT and accept the IAEA's "special inspections" as well as a bilateral inspection regime between North and South Korea. Though the United States would like to solve the question of North Korea's nuclear weapons potential once and for all, no long-term solution is in sight. Meanwhile, as Assistant Secretary of State Winston Lord stated in his confirmation hearings, the United States "will continue to support fully the IAEA and other international bodies to eliminate the North Korean threat."[12]

---

[11] See *Los Angeles Times*, June 12, 1993.

[12] See Winston Lord's opening statement, entitled "A New Pacific Community: Ten Goals for American Policy" (March 31, 1993).

If this issue is satisfactorily resolved, it is conceivable that the Clinton administration may revise "A Strategic Framework for the Asian Pacific Rim" in accordance with the new requirements of the post–cold war era, expedite the phased reduction of the U.S. forces stationed in South Korea, and ask South Korea to share more than one-third of the *won*-based costs of maintaining the U.S. forces in South Korea. Yet, at the same time, President Clinton is expected to uphold the U.S.-ROK Mutual Security Treaty and sustain America's demonstrable, albeit reduced, military presence in South Korea during his tenure.

Economic Relations

It is indisputable that the continuing U.S. military presence has created a secure and stable environment in South Korea, thus making possible its postwar reconstruction and subsequent economic development. The United States provided significant economic and military assistance for South Korea throughout the 1950s and 1960s. For the 1953–61 period, U.S. direct assistance to South Korea exceeded $4 billion—$2.6 billion in economic aid and $1.8 billion in military aid. Because the South Korean economy was too weak to withstand the burden of loan repayment, almost all U.S. assistance was in the form of grants-in-aid. As measured by the amount of aid per capita, South Korea ranked as one of the largest recipients of U.S. assistance programs. For the 1962–73 period, U.S. direct assistance to South Korea amounted to $6.9 billion—$2.4 billion in economic aid and $4.5 billion in military aid. As its economic conditions improved, South Korea prepared to receive more loans than grants-in-aid from the United States and to shift its emphasis to the receipt of military, rather than economic, assistance. Throughout, the United States practiced a strict policy that required South Korea to buy U.S. goods and join the international economic order controlled by the U.S. hegemony. The United States Operations Mission played an important role in guiding South Korea's domestic and foreign economic activities and in assisting South Korea's first two five-year economic plans (1962–66 and 1967–71).

Even after South Korea successfully launched its ambitious developmental programs and outgrew the need for U.S. grants-in-aid in the mid-1970s, the United States continued to provide technology transfer, capital investments, managerial advice, and scientific cooperation for South Korea's export-led growth programs. Most important, the United States made its vast domestic market easily accessible to imports of such labor-intensive South Korean products as textiles, in part because the United States wished to strengthen South Korea's economy and security in the context of the cold war conflicts. South Korean exports increased from $50 million in 1961 to $72 billion in 1991, and its gross national product grew at an average rate of 10 percent per year during the same period. The per capita GNP increased from $88 in 1961 to $6,500 in 1991.

As an early economic patron of South Korea, the United States was immensely pleased with its client's success story, referred to as the "miracle on the Han." In the relatively short span of three decades, the United States and South Korea had shifted their economic relationship from one of vertical dependency to a mutually beneficial and interdependent partnership. The United States conducts more trade with South Korea than with many of its traditional European trading partners. The United States is South Korea's largest trading partner after Japan; in 1991 the United States provided 23.5 percent of South Korea's total imports and absorbed 25.5 percent of South Korea's total exports. South Korea is the seventh largest trading partner of the United States and the fifth largest market for American agricultural products. Hyundai cars and Samsung electronics are as well known in the United States as Boeing, Coca-Cola, and McDonald's are in South Korea.

As a consequence of this intimate economic relationship, however, the United States and South Korea have had a series of conflicts and disputes over trade issues. In a larger sense, the U.S.-ROK trade disputes can be seen as a function of the relative decline of the United States in the international economic order, especially vis-à-vis Japan and the European Community. The U.S. share of the worldwide GNP aggregates declined from 25.9 percent in 1960 to 21.5 percent in 1980. The U.S. GNP, expressed as a percentage of the GNP of the United States, Japan, and the EC combined, decreased from 61.6 percent to 40.5 percent during the same period.[13] U.S. trade, expressed as a percentage of total trade of the United States, Japan, and the EC combined, fell from 27.0 percent to 22.1 percent during the same two decades, while the deficits in U.S. global trade increased from $25 billion in 1960 to $170 billion in 1980. In short, the U.S. economic hegemony once manifested in the Bretton Woods system collapsed during the 1970s.

In order to avoid a further slide in its position in the international economic order, the United States initiated an attempt to protect its major domestic industries, such as textiles and electrical appliances,

---

[13] See Robert O. Keohane, *After Hegemony* (Princeton: Princeton University Press, 1984), pp. 197–99.

against the rapid influx of inexpensive South Korean products. To do so it employed a variety of methods, such as the Orderly Marketing Agreements and the Voluntary Export Restraints, to limit South Korean exports to the vulnerable U.S. market. Bilateral trade negotiations were often acrimonious and difficult during the 1970s. One study shows that the United States and South Korea negotiated 13 cases of significant trade conflicts between 1960 and 1981—9 cases in textiles and apparel, 2 in color television sets, and 2 in footwear.[14] In the early 1970s the South Koreans frequently misunderstood U.S. intentions and priorities in trade matters and hence adopted an unsuccessful negotiating approach. For its part, the United States refused to accept the usual South Korean argument that any measure that harmed the ROK economy would also weaken its self-defense capability and thus undermine a key U.S. foreign policy objective. In some cases, however, the South Koreans were successful because they had accumulated experience and expertise in their trade negotiations with the United States and because they held out longer than did other Asian countries. Moreover, the United States tended to refrain from pushing South Korea too hard in trade disputes, largely because its trade imbalance with South Korea was not significant in the 1970s and early 1980s.

After experiencing a growing deficit (as much as $9 billion per year) in its trade with South Korea during the second half of the 1980s, however, the United States intensified its pressure, not only to restrict South Korea's exports to the U.S. market but also to remove tariff and nontariff barriers against U.S. exports to South Korea. The United States used the General Agreement on Tariffs and Trade (GATT) Committee on Balance-of-Payments Restrictions to challenge South Korea's position that its quantitative import restrictions were justified because of its balance-of-payment problems. In 1989 the ROK government agreed to phase out or bring into conformity with GATT more than 270 agricultural restrictions over a seven-and-one-half-year period. The United States trade representative claimed that "this landmark agreement resulted almost entirely from patient and consistent U.S. pressure."[15] Even though presidents Ronald Reagan and George Bush advocated the goal of a liberal international trade regime and resisted any excessive form of protectionist agitation in Congress, the

[14] John S. Odell, "The Outcome of International Trade Conflicts: The U.S. and South Korea, 1960–1981," *International Studies Quarterly*, September 1985, pp. 263–86.

[15] *1990 Trade Policy Agenda and 1989 Annual Report of the President of the United States on the Trade Agreements Program* (Washington, D.C.: U.S. Government Printing Office, 1990), p. 33.

United States used Section 301 of the 1974 Trade Act and the 1988 Omnibus Trade and Competitiveness Act as a lever to gain access to the South Korean market. Section 301, usually referred to as the "Super 301" provision, mandated that the U.S. government adopt retaliatory measures against a country engaged in unfair trading practices against its economic interests. In particular, the United States pressed South Korea to liberalize its trading practices, to import American cigarettes, wine, and beef and other agricultural products, to honor intellectual property rights, and to allow U.S. participation in service industries ranging from stock markets and insurance to advertising, telecommunications, and government procurement.[16]

In response to U.S. pressure, South Korea advocated a gradual and incremental approach to the long-range goal of complete trade liberalization and offered a number of limited concessions to the United States in the late 1980s and early 1990s. The South Koreans typically argued that their fragile industries were not yet ready to face the sudden challenge of open international competition and that they had the enormous burden of increasing their defense capabilities against the persistent threat from North Korea. They pointed out that South Korea experienced a double-digit increase in labor wages per year, had a large foreign debt, needed imports of crude oil and other expensive raw materials, and suffered from a chronic trade deficit with Japan. Moreover, they contended that the appearance of submitting to the well-publicized and high-handed pressure tactics of the United States would fuel anti-American sentiment in South Korea and thus weaken the friendly alliance between the two countries. Although the U.S. government was sympathetic to such arguments, it still demanded a tangible breakthrough in its trade negotiations with South Korea.

In the case of U.S. cigarette exports, in September 1986 the ROK government offered an initial concession by opening the door to foreign cigarettes, but imposed high prices on them. In 1987 imported cigarettes had only a 0.27 percent share of South Korea's domestic tobacco market. The state-run Korean Monopoly Corporation (KOMOCO), which was assigned the exclusive right to import and distribute foreign cigarettes, had no interest in increasing imports of American cigarettes because it wanted to maintain its virtual monopoly over South Korea's tobacco market. Dissatisfied with this situation, the U.S. government pressed its demands for complete market access in South Korea by pointing out that foreign cigarettes amounted to about 10 percent of tobacco consumption in Japan and

---

[16] For U.S.-South Korea financial relations, see *Korean-U.S. Financial Issues* (Washington, D.C.: Korea Economic Institute of America, 1992).

Taiwan. The South Koreans argued that unrestricted imports of American cigarettes would jeopardize their own tobacco growers and cigarette companies. This resistance was buttressed by a broad coalition of tobacco growers, religious organizations (such as the South Korean YMCA), radical students, and opposition political parties, who organized a campaign to boycott American cigarettes. They assailed the "hypocrisy" and "immorality" of U.S. trade policy by pointing out that while the U.S. surgeon general warns that cigarette smoking is harmful to public health, the U.S. government champions cigarette exports to other countries. Moreover, a former ROK finance minister suggested that American cigarettes had come to represent many of the social evils that had existed in South Korea during the Korean War—smuggling, illegal activity, conspicuous consumption, and so forth.[17]

Sensing that no further concessions would come from the ROK government, which was constrained by the rising campaign against American tobacco, the U.S. Cigarette Export Association used Section 301 of the Trade Act to file a petition against the ROK government and KOMOCO in January 1988. The association estimated that if the South Korean market were completely open and prejudicial pricing removed, American cigarettes would account for as much as 25 percent ($500 million) of South Korean tobacco consumption per year. A group of powerful legislators from the tobacco-growing southern states were mobilized to draft a protectionist bill against South Korea. In anticipation of this legislation and possible U.S. retaliation, ROK Ambassador Park Tong-jin and U.S. Trade Representative Clayton Yeutter signed an agreement in May 1988 to open the South Korean market to the importing, distributing, and advertising of American cigarettes. The agreement stipulated that American cigarettes would be subject to the same amount of excise tax levied on quality South Korean cigarettes but that importers of American cigarettes had to be approved by KOMOCO.

The agreement led to an increase in the sales of American cigarettes in South Korea. It was reported that "some Koreans became two-pack smokers—puffing away at domestic cigarettes in public but keeping a pack of foreign cigarettes to inhale in private."[18] This report illustrated both the outward effectiveness of the South Korean boycott campaign and its real limits. The share of South Korean tobacco consumption attributed to foreign cigarettes grew to 5.2 percent in quan-

---

[17] See Il Sakong, *Korea in the World Economy* (Washington, D.C.: Institute for International Economics, 1993), p. 133.

[18] *Los Angeles Times*, July 24, 1988.

tity (or 7.4 percent in value) in 1991, with Marlboro and Virginia Slims especially popular among South Korean smokers. Yet U.S. cigarette companies accused KOMOCO of encouraging the anti-American boycott movement, while KOMOCO complained that U.S. cigarette exporters organized unfair advertising tactics and committed illegal marketing practices in South Korea. The continuing controversy over U.S. cigarette exports to South Korea strained the cooperative atmosphere of bilateral economic transactions.

An equally contentious case involved U.S. efforts to export beef to South Korea. The ROK government had restricted beef imports since 1967 and imposed a total ban since 1985. When the Reagan administration, which was sensitive to the cattle industry in the midwestern states and its political sponsors in Congress, asked South Korea to open its domestic market to American beef and other agricultural products in 1987, the South Korean Ministry of Agriculture, Forestry, and Fisheries categorically responded, "We are not in a position to allow U.S. farm products at this time when Korean farmers are beset with difficulties." The Korean Dairy and Beef Farmers Association, the National Livestock Cooperatives Federation, and other interest groups organized mass rallies and protest activities against the United States and urged their own government not to capitulate to U.S. pressure. After the American Meat Institute filed a Section 301 petition against South Korea, and the United States, along with Australia and New Zealand, asked for a GATT investigation of South Korea's beef-import restrictions, the Ministry of Foreign Affairs and the Ministry of Trade and Industry overcame their interbureaucratic policy differences and advocated a partial concession to the United States. In the summer of 1988 the South Korean government agreed to import 14,500 tons of high-quality American beef (equivalent to 100,000 head of cattle) during the second half of 1988 for use by tourist hotels and restaurants.[19] The government explained to South Korea's angry beef breeders that if it had defied the GATT rule, it would have faced legal retaliation, not only from the United States but also from other GATT members. It also argued that beef imports were needed to control rising beef prices and accommodate unhappy consumers in South Korea. In November 1988 the South Korean government agreed to import 39,000 tons of foreign beef (equivalent to 260,000 head of cattle) during 1989, which amounted to about 25 percent of South Korea's annual beef consumption.

In an attempt to contain the growing protectionist mood among American legislators, President Roh Tae-woo stated at a Joint Session of

---

[19] *1990 Trade Policy Agenda,* p. 41.

the U.S. Congress in October 1989 that South Korea "is moving vigorously toward a more open, liberalized and self-regulating economy" and that in the next four or five years South Korea would achieve "the same degree of openness as is found in the OECD [Organization for Economic and Cooperative Development] countries."[20] However, following a GATT panel review that found South Korea's quantitative restrictions on beef imports inconsistent with GATT provisions, in April 1990 the United States and South Korea signed a bilateral beef agreement that, in effect, required South Korea to liberalize beef imports completely by July 1997. The U.S. government assumed that South Korea would increase its beef-import quota significantly each year until the 1997 deadline, but the South Korean government refused to raise the annual quota drastically and indicated that it was willing to increase it by only 7 to 8 percent yearly. South Korea explained that more significant increases in beef imports would destroy its fragile livestock industry and increase its trade deficit during a business recession. In the summer of 1992 a petition drive against beef imports, sponsored by the National Livestock Cooperatives Federation and other livestock-producers' organizations, collected more than 4 million signatures. In view of the forthcoming South Korean presidential election and transfer of power, President Roh found it difficult to ignore the strong domestic pressure to resist demands from the United States that South Korea allow beef and rice imports. For its part, the United States preferred to resolve the politically sensitive and highly emotional question of rice exports to South Korea at GATT's Uruguay Round negotiations.

As the U.S. trade deficit with South Korea decreased appreciably in the early 1990s, the United States expressed general satisfaction with the implementation of South Korea's market liberalization measures, except in the case of agricultural imports. During his visit to Seoul in January 1992, President Bush stated:

The world recognizes Korea as an economic powerhouse. We are pleased that over the past few years, we've narrowed our current account imbalance from about $9 billion to about $1 billion and that U.S. exports to Korea have increased at a pace of more than 7 percent over the last 2 years. . . . America is not only Korea's largest market but a leading source of the technology and capital that helps fuel your economic growth.[21]

---

[20] See the text of his speech in Roh Tae-woo, *Korea: A Nation Transformed* (Elmsford, N.Y.: Pergamon Press, 1990), pp. 11–17.

[21] George Bush, "The U.S. and Korea: Entering a New World," *U.S. Department of State Dispatch*, January 13, 1992, p. 24.

He also urged South Korea to fight the forces of protectionism and tip the world balance in favor of free and fair trade policies.

Meanwhile, the Bush administration continued to crack down on what it regarded as South Korea's unfair trade practices in the U.S. semiconductor market. As a relative newcomer to the semiconductor industry, South Korea invested heavily in this lucrative market and dramatically expanded its exports from $860 million in 1983 to $5.7 billion in 1991; the latter amount accounted for 28 percent of South Korea's electronic exports and 8 percent of South Korea's total exports in 1991. That year the U.S. market absorbed $2.2 billion worth of South Korean semiconductor exports, which included $612 million in dynamic random access memory (DRAM) chips.[22] Alarmed by South Korea's phenomenal success in the U.S. DRAM market, Micron Technology Inc., a leading American chipmaker, filed an anti-dumping petition with the government in April 1992, alleging that South Korean semiconductor companies were selling memory chips in the United States at prices below production costs. After a preliminary investigation, in October 1992 the U.S. Department of Commerce issued a ruling in favor of the Micron petition and determined that three South Korean exporters of DRAM chips had sold their products in the United States at prices between 5.99 percent and 87.4 percent lower than fair value. This decision shocked both the South Korean government and the country's semiconductor companies. The South Koreans made a concerted effort to persuade the U.S. government to determine that the dumping margin was below 10 percent in its final ruling. They argued that a higher dumping margin would further solidify Japanese dominance in the U.S. DRAM chip market and undermine those U.S. semiconductor companies that export over $600 million worth of semiconductor-manufacturing equipment to South Korea, thereby earning some $100 million in royalties from South Korea each year. This argument was persuasive to the U.S. Department of Commerce, which decided in March 1993 to set the anti-dumping margins between 0.74 percent and 7.19 percent (an average rate of 3.96 percent) against South Korean DRAM makers.[23] This took the pressure off the South Korean government for the time being. This case illustrates both the limits of South Korea's aggressive export programs and the complexity of economic interdependence between the United States and South Korea.

It is anticipated that because President Clinton's electoral victory was based on a mandate for change in U.S. economic policies, he will

---

[22] See *Korea Newsreview*, October 31, 1992.
[23] *Hanguk Ilbo*, March 18, 1993.

energetically pursue the goal of "American renewal," invest in economic infrastructure, and sharpen the U.S. competitive edge in the new international economic order. Clinton stated that "the United States cannot be strong abroad if it is weak at home" and that "restoring America's global economic leadership must become a central element of our national security policies." As to U.S. trade policy, he declared:

> Our government must work to expand trade while insisting that the conduct of world trade is fair. It must fight to uphold American interests—promoting exports, expanding trade in agricultural and other products, opening markets in major product and service sectors with our principal competitors, achieving reciprocal access. This should include renewed authority to use America's trading leverage against the most serious problems. The U.S. government also must firmly enforce U.S. laws against unfair trade.[24]

This tough and sweeping declaration suggests that the Clinton administration may aggressively carry out its policy commitment to gain access to the South Korean market in the agricultural and service sectors, eradicate unfair trade practices in the United States, and strengthen Section 301 of the Trade Act and other retaliatory instruments. It may cooperate with the Democratic Party majority in the U.S. Congress to enact a set of potentially protectionist measures. It may also view diplomacy as a means to enhance U.S. economic security. In his confirmation hearings before the Senate Committee on Foreign Relations, Secretary of State Warren Christopher stated that market opening in East Asia was a priority of U.S. foreign policy. Pointing out that "economic competition is eclipsing ideological rivalry" after the cold war, he declared: "We'll not be bashful about linking our high diplomatic goals with our economic goals."[25] He also cited China, Japan, and South Korea as countries that had put up trade barriers against the United States.

The Clinton administration's decision on steel imports illustrates that there is a distinct possibility of further disputes and tensions in U.S.-ROK economic relations. On January 27, 1993, the U.S. Department of Commerce issued a stiff anti-dumping decision against 19 major steel-exporting countries.[26] This decision signified the failure of multilateral negotiations to conclude a "multi-steel agreement" and ig-

---

[24] *Congressional Quarterly*, July 18, 1992, p. 2112.

[25] As quoted in *Far Eastern Economic Review*, January 29, 1993, p. 15.

[26] *New York Times*, January 28, 1993.

nited a serious global trade war over steel. The United States imposed import duties ranging from a low of 3.28 percent to a high of 30 percent on South Korean steel companies, which would apply to about 60 percent ($400 million) of South Korea's total annual steel exports to the United States. The 30 percent anti-dumping tariff, plus a 5.51 percent countervailing duty levied on the hot-rolled coils that the Pohang Iron and Steel Corporation sold to UPI in Pittsburg, California, the firm involved in its joint venture with the USX Corporation, dealt a particularly severe blow to the concept of U.S.-ROK joint ventures. While Secretary of Commerce Ronald Brown called the anti-dumping approach "fair and effective," the South Koreans expressed "deep disappointment and concern" and mounted an aggressive lobbying campaign to reverse the U.S. decision. This conflict not only undermined U.S.-ROK cooperation in the area of steel manufacturing but also threatened to disrupt efforts to liberalize the international trading regime.

Yet it is important to point out that despite continuing bilateral disputes over U.S. exports of beef, tobacco, rice, automobiles, and other products to South Korea, and U.S. imports of semiconductor chips, steel, and other industrial goods from South Korea, the two countries recognize that they have a common stake in the nurturing of essentially cooperative and mutually beneficial economic relations. Gone are the days when the United States regarded South Korea as an economic burden or attached a "special" designation to its economic activities, especially in connection with cold war politics; it now has an intrinsic interest in conducting "normal" trade with South Korea. Moreover, the Clinton administration may realize that at a time when a number of Asian countries propose to form regional trading blocs (for example, the East Asia Economic Caucus) as a counterweight to the European Community and the North American Free Trade Agreement, South Korea can play a pivotal role in supporting U.S. participation and leadership in APEC (Asia-Pacific Economic Cooperation) and other multilateral economic organizations in the Pacific Rim. The scope of U.S.-ROK economic linkages is no longer confined to bilateral trade issues but extends to a wide range of regional and global issues that are vital to their respective domestic and foreign policies. It has even been suggested that the United States and South Korea transcend their conflicts over bilateral trade issues and form an "industrial alliance," using a combination of advanced American technology and

South Korean manufacturing and engineering skills to enhance the competitive positions of both countries.[27]

Meanwhile, it is unlikely that in the absence of meaningful concessions from North Korea, particularly with regard to nuclear weapons development, the Clinton administration, notwithstanding its primary emphasis on economic interests, will significantly ease the strict U.S. economic sanctions against the DPRK. Despite the flexibility it has shown in diplomatic talks and cultural exchanges, the United States continues to ban almost all types of economic transaction with North Korea, allowing exports or donations of humanitarian goods (medicine, food, and clothing) only with an export license issued by the Treasury Department. The United States does not welcome North Korea's admission to international financial institutions such as the World Bank and the Asian Development Bank. Nor does it support North Korea's embryonic open-door economic policy. It is not enthusiastic about multilateral development programs such as the Tumen River project. The U.S. economic policy toward North Korea is more conservative and rigid than that of South Korea, which is willing to promote inter-Korean economic cooperation in accordance with the Agreement on Reconciliation, Nonaggression, and Exchanges and Cooperation Between the South and the North signed by the two Korean prime ministers in December 1991. There is, however, no insurmountable conflict between the United States and South Korea about their respective economic relations with North Korea.

Conclusion

The preceding discussion suggests that the United States has, by and large, been successful in achieving its twin policy goals toward South Korea—namely, to protect South Korea's national security and assist its economic development. While preventing another Korean War, the United States has gradually lowered its military profile on the Korean peninsula and has articulated a long-term plan to change its direct and leading role in South Korea's defense preparedness to an indirect and supportive one. The South Koreans have sometimes misunderstood U.S. intentions, but they have gradually gained a degree of confidence in their military relations with the United States and North Korea. The United States has effectively transcended its earlier position of economic tutelage over South Korea and developed

---

[27] For example, South Korea's minister of trade, industry, and energy, Kim Chul-su, articulated a proposal for "industrial alliance" during his visit to the United States in April 1993.

a mutually beneficial and interdependent economic association with it. As far as military and economic affairs are concerned, the United States now appreciates South Korea's intrinsic importance to vital U.S. interests and recognizes South Korea's pivotal status in the Asia-Pacific region. Yet the evolution of U.S. policy toward South Korea has generated a wide range of difficult problems that have at times resulted in mutual misperceptions and uncomfortable situations.

As was graphically demonstrated in the decisions of presidents Nixon and Carter to withdraw U.S. forces from South Korea, the United States has tended to perceive and pursue its military policy toward Korea in the broad context of its global and regional strategic calculations and to disregard South Korea's legitimate security interests and procedural sensitivities. The same tendency was shown in President Bush's decision to remove U.S. tactical nuclear weapons from South Korea. The end of the cold war raises the further possibility that the United States may be tempted to underestimate the inherent instability of inter-Korean military relations and extend the relaxation of global confrontations to the Korean peninsula.

On the other hand, the South Koreans have tended to view U.S. military policy primarily in connection with their hostility toward North Korea. They consider the continuing U.S. military presence to be an indispensable deterrent to armed attack by North Korea. They have expanded their economic capabilities, launched an ambitious northern diplomacy, modernized their military forces, and agreed to the U.S. plan for gradual troop reductions in South Korea. In spite of the manifest anti-American agitation in South Korea, however, it appears that a large majority of South Koreans prefer to continue to have U.S. forces stationed in their country. Hence there is an element of ambivalence in South Korea's attitude toward the United States—a complacent inertia that would continue dependence upon U.S. military protection while at the same time asserting a nationalistic desire for sovereign independence.

This assertiveness is frequently evident in U.S.-ROK economic relations. Even when the United States follows an internationally accepted procedure in asking South Korea to adopt a fair trade policy and open its market to U.S. products, the request often prompts a rapid spread of anti-American sentiment, as exemplified in the boycott campaign against American cigarettes. A 1991 report by the U.S. trade representative detailed other manifestations of this tendency:

> Since March 1990 the U.S. government has received numerous reports of discriminatory treatment of U.S. consumer products in Korea. A government-inspired campaign to curb "excessive consumption" and to

promote "austerity" led to the removal of imported products from store shelves, limitations on promotional activities, and threats of tax audits on Korean purchasers of imported automobiles. U.S. firms also reported increased delays in port clearances of imported consumer products. The anti-import bias associated with the campaign against "excessive consumption" probably contributed to the Korean government's initial reluctance to address problems surrounding implementation of the wine, cigarette, and beef agreements.[28]

When the issue of frugality resurfaced in September 1991 in the form of the South Korean New Life/New Order campaign, the United States again voiced its objection to any policy that could unfairly limit U.S. exports to South Korea.[29] Furthermore, in his address before the South Korean National Assembly in January 1992, President Bush openly complained that the frugality campaign was a form of protectionism.

The South Koreans contended that the U.S. reaction to the New Life/New Order campaign and Bush's subsequent complaint reflected a complete misunderstanding of their economic system and culture and that the traditional Confucian culture of frugality supported a social movement against the consumption of luxury goods.[30] They explained that the campaign was intended to discourage the extravagant purchase of fancy foreign cars and clothes by South Korea's *nouveaux riches* and reduce the explosive consequences of income disparity in South Korea. This combination of cultural differences and specific policy disputes has intensified the perceptual dissonance between the United States and South Korea. The notion of "fairness," too, is subject to different interpretations by the two countries. While the United States holds a relatively simple and empirical view that South Korea is unfair because its domestic market is not as accessible to American products as the U.S. market is to South Korean products, the South Koreans feel that the United States, a big and powerful brother, is abusive to its younger, weaker brother. This dissonance suggests that both the United States and South Korea need to make a greater effort to understand each other and be particularly aware of the cultural and psychological milieu in which their relations take place, for economic interdependence breeds mutual vulnerability.

---

[28] See *1991 National Trade Estimate Report on Foreign Trade Barriers* (Washington, D.C.: U.S. Government Printing Office, 1991), p. 149.

[29] See *1992 National Trade Estimate Report on Foreign Trade Barriers* (Washington, D.C.: U.S. Government Printing Office, 1992), p. 167.

[30] *Los Angeles Times*, December 31, 1990.

Viewed from a long-range historical perspective, the tensions, disputes, and misperceptions that the United States and South Korea have experienced in recent years are a function of their extraordinary intimacy as well as a transitional by-product of the structural transformation in their relationship. It has indeed been difficult for both countries to adjust to the unmistakable change from a patron-client relationship to a reciprocal partnership, from "special" relations to "normal" relations, from instrumental value to intrinsic importance, and from unilateral alliance to competitive cooperation. The difficulties have been further compounded by a dramatic change—both military and economic—in the global and regional landscape. The Clinton administration now has a challenging opportunity to reaffirm a policy of military and economic cooperation with South Korea, transcend the vestiges of the cold war in its relations with Korea, and play an active role in promoting inter-Korean reconciliation.

4
Contemporary Literature in a Divided Land

Marshall R. Pihl

For more than a century, modern Korean literature has been searching for a wholeness and identity that have been denied the Korean people by history. The nativist Tonghak Movement of the late 19th century, which called compatriots to arms through the poetry of its leader, was suppressed by a degraded Korean monarchy and finished off by its Japanese successors. An early expression of indigenous dramatic ideas, seen in experimental performances of lengthy oral narrative songs staged as operas, was quashed in the early 1900s by Korean leaders who, with Japanese tutelage, were denying their own heritage in search of a modernized national salvation. A longing for nationhood—which demands a national language as its first condition—sought a voice in the modern fiction and poetry of the 1920s and 1930s but was overwhelmed by the political, economic, and cultural *tsunami* of Japanese imperialism, which sought the literal obliteration of Korean cultural identity.

Therefore, many Koreans saw the 1945 Liberation as the first opportunity in history to be truly Korean in their own land. The pent-up fervor of a people long denied, of a people at war with themselves, poured through the chaotic gates of Liberation. Of this moment, literary critic Kwon Youngmin says, "The conviction that all anti-national, colonial cultural vestiges had to be liquidated and that a nationalist literature had to be established along with the new national state reflects that time when issues of national self-awareness and of literary form were raised with exceeding fervor."[1] As political struggle gave way to armed conflict in the Korean War, Korean literature was stifled for another decade by historical realities. There is still no one body of

---

[1] Kwon Youngmin [Kwon Yong-min], "The Logic and Practice of Literary Nationalism," trans. Marshall R. Pihl, *Korean Studies*, Vol. 16 (1992), p. 63.

modern *Korean* literature, but rather North Korean and South Korean literatures.

A Century of Modern Korean Literature

Barely one century has passed since the first serialized fiction began to appear in late-19th-century Korean newspapers, heralding the emergence of a literature sufficiently unlike what had preceded it and new enough in content to be called "modern" in the Western European sense. The unfolding of Korean literature over this reach of time is commonly divided into three main stages, each linked to certain distinct changes in social conditions. The literature of the period from the end of the 19th century through the early years of the 20th century, frequently called "enlightenment literature," constitutes the first of these stages. The second stage is the literature of the Japanese colonial period, running from the early to the middle 20th century. Post-Liberation literature, divided into that of the North and that of the South and coinciding with the second half of this century, makes up the third stage.

Some critics, trying to set the boundaries of modern literature, designate the insurrectionary political poetry of Ch'oe Che-u in the 1860s as a starting point, while others hark back even farther, to the literary reflections of 18th-century social change. Most, however, tend to settle upon the Kabo Reform Movement of 1894–96, which unleashed modernizing intellectual forces, as a marker for the beginning of the modern literature of enlightenment.

The most dramatic changes in modern Korean literature took place over a comparatively short period—the quarter century between the Kabo Reforms and the independence demonstrations of 1919. These changes were undertaken mostly by a small, elite, and homogeneous class of early modern intellectuals and, for that very reason, could proceed apace.

Enlightenment Literature

In the early years of the 20th century, much material was translated from Chinese, Japanese, and other foreign languages into Korean and published in Korea.[2] But, at the same time, modernized expression was also evolving in original Korean composition, as shown in early

---

[2] The earliest translations consisted mainly of Western history, biography, and literature, much of which was retranslated from Chinese and Japanese versions, largely abridgements and summaries. Chon Kwang-yong, *Shin sosol yon'gu* (Studies in new fiction), Seoul: Saemun sa, 1986, pp. 41–48.

newspapers, magazines, and books. This was the heyday of the "new novel," a vehicle for such progressive ideas as equal education for both boys and girls, free choice in marriage, national pride, and the importance of widespread literacy to a developed nation. For all their enthusiasm, the didactic works that emerged seem quite dated to the modern eye.

The first era of modern newspaper publishing in the Korean language in Korea covered a stretch of 25 years dating from January 25, 1886 (with the first edition of the *Hansong Chubo*), to the general newspaper shutdown by the Japanese in late 1910. In that quarter century well over 100 newspapers came and went—about half of them written in Korean, the others in Chinese and other languages. Poetry and narrative fiction became regular fare in many of the Korean newspapers and, between late 1896 and the shutdown of 1910, some 120 narratives were serialized. At the same time, Korean publishing was also promoting the growth and spread of modern literature by other means. Between 1906 and 1909, some 15 magazines printed nearly 60 works of narrative fiction and, in roughly the same period of time, about 30 book-length literary works were also published.[3]

When all Korean-language newspapers but one were shut down in 1910, publication in book form became the principal outlet for Korean writers until 1920. During that decade, more than 300 literary works of varying lengths were published, mostly by private publishers and coterie magazines.

Colonial Literature

Enlightenment literature gave way to colonial literature in the early 1920s after the tumultuous anti-Japanese March First Movement of 1919 had altered the consciousness of the Korean people and Japan's new Cultural Policy had permitted the opening of several private Korean-language newspapers and magazines for the first time in more than a decade.

While the modern fiction of the 1920s has been widely recognized for its epoch-marking break with the traditional and early modern themes that had dominated previous decades, the maturity in technique that sets the 1930s apart as unique in the history of modern Korean literature is only now beginning to be appreciated.

---

[3] Han Won-yong, *Han'guk kaehwagi shinmun yonjae sosol yon'gu* (A Study of Short Fiction Serialized in Korean Enlightenment Period Newspapers), Seoul: Ilji sa, 1990.

In addition to the realism introduced in 1919 by the coterie maga-zine *Creation* (Ch'angjo), edited by the pioneer Kim Tong-in and his friends, there emerged the socialistic writing of a generation of young Korean students who had been educated in Japan, where they en-countered a wave of European thought that was not well known back home. In 1925 they formed the Korea Artista Proleta Federatio (KAPF), and until May 1935, when KAPF was closed down by the au-thorities, socialist writers added a fresh intellectual edge to Korean writing, although they ultimately failed to contribute many works of lasting importance to literary history.

The 1930s introduced a growing Japanese suppression that drove many writers away from the here-and-now as a subject. This decade witnessed a maturation in modern Korean literature within which the giants of the post-Liberation literary establishment, such as Ch'ae Man-shik, Kim Tong-ni, and Hwang Sun-won, served their appren-ticeships.

Literature in an Age of Division

The most ironic formative experience of the 20th century for Korean literature began with Liberation on August 15, 1945. Koreans regained a country that had been lost to Japanese imperialism, only to lose it again to Russian and American imperialism. What has remained are two distortions of Korea—a "North" and a "South"—which have been further deformed by war and industrialization. In Korean, the 1945 Liberation is called *Kwangbok*, "Glorious Recovery," but it was neither glorious nor a recovery and, worse, it was capped by an in-ternecine war of horrifically compressed violence that spared no cor-ner of the country. Of the Koreans who survived, 10 million remain separated from members of their families by the impassable truce line. These events have so informed contemporary Korean literature in one way or another that some critics define literature since 1945 as the "Literature of an Age of Division."[4]

Three Stages of Contemporary Literature

The half-century of literature since Liberation can itself be grouped into three stages according to the thrust of its ideas. The brief five-year span from Liberation in 1945 to the outbreak of war on June 25,

---

[4] Notable is Kwon Youngmin, "Haebang sashimyon ui munhak" (Literature of Forty Years since Liberation), *Han'guk munhak*, Vol. 13, no. 1 (January 1985), pp. 406–20.

1950—a period that was focused on the task of redefining and rebuilding a national literature—comprises the first stage. The second stage spans the immediate postwar era between the early 1950s and the mid-1960s, during which South Korean literature was generally estranged from its surrounding reality. The third stage dates from the late 1960s through the early 1990s, a time of self-discovery and social awareness by South Korean writers in the midst of breakneck industrialization.

In the period from Liberation to the Korean War, the questions of a new awareness and the establishment of a national literature were widely discussed in literary circles. New newspapers and literary magazines devoted space to laying a foundation for a national litera ture and to a self-cleansing effort frequently referred to as the "liqui dation of the remnants of colonial culture." As critics debated the nature and direction of the national literature, some literary works began to appear, but owing to the division of land and people, that literature was little better than a deformity incapable of expressing the wholeness of the Korean experience.

The literature of the 1950s was fraught with a sense of estrangement, reflecting the barrenness of the aftermath of the Korean War. Although efforts were made to grapple with questions of existence, works of this period emphasized conflicts between the individual and the world and fell short of offering a general perception of life. Critics decried Korea's denial of its own traditions and the tendency toward existential darkness that stressed the insecurity, loneliness, and irrevocability of individual human experience. But the many questions of national identity and existence left simmering since the Korean War were not faced until after the 1960 student uprising, which brought in its wake a new receptivity to change.

Young writers of the generation that emerged in the mid-1960s investigated the life and inner consciousness of the petty bourgeoisie. More important, their writing gave evidence of a search for value in life through exploration of the experience of the individual. As this new awareness began to extend from the self to social reality, the social involvement of literature became a matter of debate in literary circles. In the context of the political changes and rapid industrialization of the 1970s, this issue provoked a sharp confrontation between proponents of pure literature, on the one hand, and those who believed that literature must engage with society, on the other. The literature of the 1970s spawned widespread interest in what was called "literary nationalism," a trend that gave rise to "literary populism" in the 1980s.

Confrontation and Exodus

The immediate post-Liberation period—the literary void of 1945–50—was an ordeal for Korean writers. Pro-Japanese collaborators were being singled out and ostracized, while the decades-old division between left and right—quiescent during the latter days of colonial suppression—asserted itself again as literary groups formed, split, and merged. The rightist administrations of the U.S. Army Military Government in Korea and, later, of Syngman Rhee, contributed to an increasingly hostile environment for the left. Ideological strife tore the literary world apart, and its ranks were significantly thinned as about one-third of Korea's writers—more than 100—migrated to the North by the early 1950s. At the same time some writers also moved to the South, but it appears that, for each writer who went South, three southerners went North. "Questions about the literary people who went North—Who? Why? How?—inevitably produce an acute allergic reaction in people who talk about them because of the ideological questions that are entailed," says Kwon Youngmin of Seoul National University.[5]

The first writers to leave the South were Yi Ki-yong and Han Sor-ya, who went North in December 1945 when they lost their leadership positions after the merger of two writers' organizations—the Headquarters for the Construction of Choson Literature and the Choson Proletarian Literature Alliance—into the Choson Writers' Alliance. In Pyongyang, Yi and Han joined forces with northern writers to form a literary organization that further arrivals from the South later joined. This first group movement of writers to the North, which started late in 1945 and continued into 1946, was led mainly by members of the defunct Choson Proletarian Literature Alliance. Generally speaking, the members of this first group went on to form the main body of the new northern literary establishment.

The second group movement of writers from South to North began in 1947 and extended to the 1948 establishment of the Republic of Korea (ROK) government in the South under President Syngman Rhee. The U.S. military authorities, convinced that such social disorders as the counterfeiting incident of May 1946 and the railroad strike that September were products of Communist Party agitation, began to tighten their control over that party's political activity with the issuance of a warrant for the arrest of Pak Hon-yong, an important communist leader since the 1920s. With this shift in conditions, the leadership of the southern Labor Party went North, followed by leaders of

---

[5] *Wolbuk munin yon'gu* (Studies on Writers Who Went North), ed. Kwon Youngmin, Seoul: Munhak sasangsa, 1989.

the Choson Writers' Alliance and many other writers of whom little has been heard since.

The members of the Choson Writers' Alliance who remained in the South after the establishment of the ROK government in 1948 dissolved the alliance and pledged their ideological conversion. But with the outbreak of war on June 25, 1950, the literary scene was again in chaos, and these converts soon dropped out of sight, some voluntarily going North and others taken there against their will. Since the war, little has been learned of the activities of writers who went North, and the silence has deepened as southern government policies have prevented open discussion of northern writers and writing. (Well into the 1960s, printed references to their names in the South were restricted to the family name with the characters of the personal name represented only by small circles.) By the 1970s fuller studies were allowed, but only if sensitive issues were carefully skirted, among them the 1945–50 literary scene, the literature and thought of left-wing leaders, and the massive movement of writers to the North. As recently as 1983, a book by Kwon Youngmin, *Recent Korean Literature and the Spirit of the Times*, was impounded by the authorities because of its chapter on 1945–50, "Korean Literature and Ideology."[6] Only after the 1987 liberalization was freer discussion allowed, making possible such books as Kwon's 1989 work on writers who went North (see footnote 5).

Although materials published in the North were not available in the South for many years and the exchange of writers and scholars is still prohibited, we have managed to learn something of the fate of literature in the North through official publications issued in Pyongyang and available outside the Korean peninsula. A discussion of North Korean literature appears below.

Estrangement and Denial

Although no literature worthy of note was produced in the South during the hectic five years of political confrontation between left and right that followed Liberation, the terrible experience of the 1950–53 war demanded, and got, a response from the literary establishment. While many writers, retreating from ugly reality, resurrected the pastoral idylls of the 1930s, some postwar writers tried to deal more directly, though distantly, with the world around them. For example, the nostalgic and warm-hearted Oh Yong-su wrote lyrical escapes

---

[6] Kwon Youngmin, *Han'guk kundae munhak kwa shidae chongshin* (Seoul: Munye ch'ulp'an-sa, 1983).

about good country folk,[7] while existentialist writers like Yi Pom-sok confronted their readers with litanies of despair as they told of the people's struggles in the face of adversity or of the failure of weaker ones to escape their fate.[8]

Mature craftsmen, schooled in the 1930s and tested in war, began to tower over the literary establishment at about this time, relinquishing their position only when displaced in the 1970s by a new generation that knew nothing of the colonial experience and were only toddlers during the Korean War. Although most of these greats, who defined Korean literature in their turn, have now passed from the scene, two giants still remain today.

Kim Tong-ni (b. 1913) has written more and has had more written about him than any other living Korean author over the past 60 years. Koreans respond to him as the voice of their ethos, as a writer who seeks understanding of what it means to be Korean. Incorporating ethnic materials in a perfectly modern aesthetic, he is anything but a "folk" writer. Even in his early works, Kim gave voice to a "humanistic nationalism," which he believed could "overcome cultural barriers and seek identity with universal trends in world literature."[9] The universal language of symbols enables his work to reach out to readers beyond Korea's borders, even though it is heavily laden with local color.

Religious belief—whether shamanism, Buddhism, or Christianity—is an undercurrent in nearly all Kim's work. He often speaks of his deep concern about the nihilism of the 20th century and of our inability to answer it with a new set of principles. Kim believes it is his literary mission "to seek out divinity and identify the relationship between that divinity and humankind."[10] He has produced some 80 short stories and 20 novels and collections of stories. Kim is a recipient of the Freedom Literary Prize (1955), National Academy of Arts Award (1958), Samil Literary Award (1967), Order of the Camellia for Civil Merit (1968), Order of the Peony (1970), Seoul City Cultural Prize (1970), and the May 16 National Award (1983).[11]

---

[7] Oh Yong-su, *The Good People: Korean Stories by Oh Yong-su*, trans. Marshall R. Pihl (Hong Kong: Heinemann Asia, 1985).

[8] For example, see Yi Pom-sok, "A Stray Bullet," trans. Marshall R. Pihl, in *Flowers of Fire*, ed. Peter H. Lee (Honolulu: University of Hawaii Press, 1974), pp. 270–306.

[9] Ahn Jung-hyo, "Kim Tong-ni," in *19 Contemporary Korean Novelists* (Seoul: Korean Culture and Arts Foundation, 1985), p. 37.

[10] Ibid., p. 38.

[11] Two of the many books by Kim are available in English: *The Cross of Shaphan* (1958, rev. 1982), trans. Sol Sun-bong (Arch Cape, Oreg.: Pace International Research, 1983),

Hwang Sun-won (b. 1915), in addition to being Korea's most consistently productive writer, is also its most widely translated: during the 1980s alone, nearly 1,500 pages of "Hwang-in-translation" appeared.[12]

While representative of his generation, Hwang Sun-won also stands apart because of his distinctive style. Where another writer of his generation might express a certain complicated idea with a single extended sentence, Hwang typically uses a combination of two or more simple sentences, including fragments if necessary. His sentences are tight and carefully packed: every element has its function, each word seems in its proper place, and the relationship between words and phrases is linear and thus clear. The cumulative impact on the reader is of a continuous forward movement toward some reward that lies ahead.

For all his foreshadowing and logical development, Hwang is remarkably unforthcoming with informative detail. He does not paint landscapes or dally with flowers and insects; he is primarily concerned with the beauty of the human world and the expression of human feeling. And this he reveals with careful detail in telling contexts. As a result, the world of a Hwang Sun-won story is removed from the everyday world. The reader nearly always senses darkness and mystery just beyond the light.

Hwang Sun-won has been recognized with many prizes and awards, starting with the Freedom Literary Prize in 1954. Other recognitions include the National Academy of Arts Award (1961), Order of the Camellia for Civil Merit (1970), and Republic of Korea Literary Award (1983).

Self-Discovery and Social Awareness

A Sea Change on April 19, 1960.   Halfway through the second stage of South Korean literature since Liberation, while masters like Kim Tong-ni and Hwang Sun-won still towered over the scene, thousands of Korean students—elementary, middle, high school, and college—managed something their elders had long been unable to accomplish. Enraged by the news that police had killed a boy in Masan with a tear-gas canister fired at close range and tried to dump his body in the harbor, they poured into the streets of major cities by the thou-

---

and *The Shaman Sorceress* (1978), trans. Hyun Song Shin and Eugene Chung (London: Kegan Paul International, 1988).

[12] Two recent collections of Hwang's short fiction are now available in English: *The Book of Masks*, ed. J. Martin Holman (London: Readers International, 1989), and *Shadows of a Sound* (San Francisco: Mercury House, 1990).

sands. As the police scattered into hiding and the army watched from the sidelines, the students converged on downtown Seoul in massive street demonstrations that finally pulled down the deeply corrupt, authoritarian regime of the Liberal Party under President Syngman Rhee. This was a seminal event for modern Korean culture, society, economy, and politics, for it unleashed a new generation upon the scene, one that now leads in every walk of Korean life.

The day the revolt began, April 19, 1960, gave the name "April 19th generation," to its participants, who are also called the "Liberation generation" because many of its members were born in 1945, or the "Han'gul generation" because they received a purely Korean education.[13] Although the impact of this group on the literary scene was not to be felt for several years, the sea change that flowed from their accomplishment was already being reflected in the literary works of some slightly older writers by the early 1960s.

Though a decade older than this new generation, writer **Ch'oe In-hun** (b. 1936) was the first to break the taboo on the discussion of the war in creative literature with his novel *The Square*, published in 1961.[14] His work takes the then-popular victim's view of the war as having been caused by external forces, which contrasts with the treatments of two decades later that began to suggest the war was the inevitable result of internal historical factors.

Ch'oe In-hun's taboo-breaking novel notwithstanding, a more significant breakthrough occurred in modern Korean fiction when one of the April 19th generation, **Kim Sung-ok** (b. 1941), published his landmark short story "Seoul, 1964: Winter,"[15] marking the beginning of the third stage of South Korean literature in the age of division.

"Seoul, 1964: Winter" is a bellwether of Kim Sung-ok's generation. His youthful, modern vocabulary of high-frequency words is notable for its distinct and explicit quality and concomitant rare use of the sensory vocabulary that had been an essential attribute of creative writing since the colonial period. Kim's generational worldview is revealed in his slangy and sardonic characters, who brashly and egocentrically reject the reality of life around them, suggesting a generation that has tumbled from the heady sense of victory gained in the

---

[13] "Han'gul" is the name of the innovative Korean phonemic alphabet, which had been suppressed in the late years of the Japanese colonial period and therefore could not again be used publicly until 1945.

[14] *Kwangjang* (Seoul: Chonghyang sa, 1961). Translated by Kevin O'Rourke as *The Square* (Devon, England: Spindlewood, 1985).

[15] Kim Sung-ok, "Seoul, 1964: Winter," trans. Marshall R. Pihl in *Land of Exile: Contemporary Korean Fiction* (Armonk, N.Y.: M. E. Sharpe, 1993).

student revolution to a distrustful frustration engendered by the world of the Park Chung-hee coup d'état in 1961.

Although Kim Sung-ok faded after publishing comparatively few works, the crack he made in conventional literary perceptions was torn wide open in the 1970s as other members of his generation followed his lead. Notable among them is **Ch'oe In-ho** (b. 1945). An ironic and witty writer, Ch'oe made his debut in the 1960s and has since become a huge commercial success. He first came to public notice in the 1960s, when several of his short stories were selected in competitions sponsored by the *Han'guk Ilbo* and *Choson Ilbo* newspapers and by *Sasunggye* magazine. But he was not fully launched in his writing career until 1970 when, fresh out of the air force, he published "The Boozer," a story he had written some years earlier.

Critic Chong Hyong-gi has observed that Ch'oe In-ho looks beyond the human facade into what makes people who they are, "turning them inside out and indicting them for what they've lost."[16] This search and revelation can make for fun and games if the objects are the cartoonlike characters in "Parade of Fools," his 1987 collection of sardonic anecdotes about the adventures of a college boy and girl, but Ch'oe In-ho is serious as well as penetratingly witty as he looks inside drinkers and night crawlers in the dark mosaic of "The Boozer."

Literary Nationalism in the 1970s.   The decade of the 1970s, unique in Korean social and cultural history, was characterized by a rapid economic development that spawned such by-products as social and regional discord, together with a political self-righteousness that invited ideological confrontation. Rural poverty increased as uprooted workers concentrated in the major cities, which were dominated by a burgeoning, materialistic bourgeoisie that sought to amuse itself in the context of commercial culture. At the same time, a national self-awareness began to take shape as part of an effort to surmount the discord and recover a sense of national wholeness. In response, Korean literature began to orient itself toward the new realities and thus take part in the cognitive task that faced the nation.

South Korean literature came to embody the zeitgeist of the 1970s, grasping its significance and giving form to the national experience. This literature was so interrelated with the attributes of the period that it became known by the catchphrase "literature of the 1970s," identifying it as a distinct unit of literary history—to the consternation

---

[16] Chong Hyon-gi, "Iroborin shilchae rul ch'annun t'amsaek iyagi—Ch'oe In-ho ui 'Sulkkun' e puchyo" (A Tale of Searching for Lost Reality), in Ch'oe In-ho, *Sulkkun* (The Boozer), Seoul: Tonga toso ch'ulp'an, 1987, p. 362.

of those who conceive of literature as an autonomous and uninterrupted flow.

Cho Se-hui (b. 1942) emerged as an important figure in Korean fiction at this time. His *Small Ball Launched by a Dwarf*[17] is the most notable product of the "literature of the 1970s." It went through 31 printings in its first six years and continued to sell 20,000 copies yearly throughout the 1980s. Punning on its title, Kim Yoon-shik of Seoul National University states that the work "played the role of a big iron ball in the Korean society, as it moved from the 1970s to the 1980s, in that it posed the question, what would there be on the other side of the seemingly bright future promised by industrialization?"[18]

Cho's best-seller is a series of loosely connected stories. A fixed set of characters appears throughout the stories, revealing themselves in bits and snatches as Cho builds up the reality of their lives from the discontinuous fragments scattered throughout the work. Cho creates the cinematic shock effect of a split screen or jump cut by juxtaposing bits and pieces of his characters' contrasting realities. These characters' lives run parallel, intersect, and collide, summoning up life in the rapidly industrializing Korea of the 1970s.

The world of the stories is populated by people who represent a cross section of contemporary Korean society: entrepreneurs, intellectuals, bourgeoisie, and uprooted workers living on the margins of society. Their values range from humanistic to materialistic, their consciousness from unawakened to awakened, their morality from human caring to animal egoism, their view of mankind from human-as-being to human-as-instrument, and their notion of love from absolute to useless.

Cho Se-hui writes in a lean, clipped style more like the succinct, unadorned language of Ernest Hemingway than the undulant prose of Korean writers in the generation immediately preceding his. He chooses his words, particles, and inflections with care, saying no more and no less than is needed. Even the language of Kim Sung-ok, his contemporary, seems relatively conventional in comparison to Cho's.

The form of Cho Se-hui's fiction is particularly well suited to the content of his work, which mirrors, in a microcosm, the complexity of modern Korean society, where critics perceive the kind of fragmenting of human wholeness and wrenching alienation that "severs man

---

[17] The Korean title is *Nanjangi ka sswoaollin chagun kong* (1978).

[18] Kim Yoon-shik [Kim Yun-shik], "The Korean Novel in an Age of Industrialization," *Korea Journal*, Vol. 29, no. 6 (1989), p. 27.

from the natural rhythms and shapes of creation."[19] In the midst of this darkness, however, Cho's protagonists search for meaning and wholeness, for "a world spiritually bonded together by love, a world in which love defines the value of life."[20] As such, *Small Ball Launched by a Dwarf* exemplifies the central thrust of Korean literary nationalism of the 1970s, which sought to recapture the harmonious totality of human life that was so direly threatened.

Political and Social Awareness in the 1980s.   The many social changes spawned by rapid industrialization in the 1970s created social forces that informed the literature of the 1980s. The decade of the 1980s is distinguishable from preceding decades by its strong political and social orientation, direct expression of protest against political dictatorship and economic inequality, and indirect criticism of the new materialism, seen as enslaving the people and paralyzing their political and social awareness.

Two events hit the country particularly hard, spurring the literary responses that characterized this very different decade. The assassination of President Park Chung-hee in October 1979 blew the lid off a pent-up social scene, leading to labor disputes, strikes, and massive demonstrations. These events culminated in the May 1980 civil uprising in the city of Kwangju, which involved 200,000 people and was put down by military force at the cost of hundreds dead and thousands wounded. The trauma of the Kwangju massacre had sufficient impact to color the literature of a generation of young writers who were then in their twenties.

Early in the 1980s, the repressive dictatorship of President Chun Doo-hwan clamped controls on writers by forcing the closure of their literary magazines. But while the older writers, numbed by past events, were no longer as sensitive as they once had been, a few younger writers were able to grasp the impact of the Kwangju massacre on the general populace and the resulting changes in popular consciousness. At the same time, the interest of general readers was shifting toward writing in the social sciences as they searched to understand both the massacre and the ensuing social changes.

The forced closing of literary magazines led to the creation of a hybrid form of seasonal—rather than monthly—publication that was called a *mook*, telescoping the English words "magazine" and "book." The new hybrid did not fall under the registration laws for periodicals

---

[19] Georg Lukács, *Realism in Our Time* (New York: Harper Torchbooks, 1971), p. 12.

[20] O Se-yong, "Cho Se-hui ron: sarang ui ippop kwa sabop" (On Cho Se-hui: Legislation and Adjudication of Love), in *Han'guk hyondae chakka yon'gu* (Studies of Contemporary Korean Authors), Seoul: Minum sa, 1989, p. 367.

because it appeared irregularly and, in addition, it was able to avoid the scrutiny reserved for general magazines by presenting itself to the authorities as a special-interest publication. Recalling practices of the early colonial literary world of 60 years before, a *mook* was written and edited by a circle of like-minded people who used their publication as a platform to present their literary, social, and political views. Some 40 to 60 *mook*s had appeared by the early 1980s, and many have continued even into the 1990s.

With the advent of the *mook*, new writers appeared. Their work fell into two major groupings, commonly referred to as "literature of division" and "literature of the people"; these dealt, respectively, with problems of the division of national territory and with social issues stemming from the dictatorship of a political elite. In contrast to Ch'oe In-hun's 1961 *The Square*, which treated the Korean War as a clash of superpowers, the literature of division of the 1980s began to consider the war as the inevitable result of internal historical forces, such as the class struggle of landlord and tenant. Cho Chong-nae assayed this approach in his 1981 novella, "Land of Exile,"[21] and again, more forcefully, in his massive saga, *The T'aebaek Mountains* (1983–89).[22] The literature of the people, on the other hand, was based on the premise that industrialization had so enlarged the working class that its members were able to generate a culture of their own and thus could create their own works of literature. Although politically moderate critics question the quality of this output, radical intellectuals have given people's literature their enthusiastic support.

The new young mainstream novelists who emerged during the 1980s include Yi In-song, Yang Kwi-ja, Im Ch'or-u, and Ch'oe Su-ch'ol—all born in the 1950s. In spite of their shared experience of the 1980s and tendency to address larger societal issues (laborers, the middle class, and social reform; political violence, national division, and the Kwangju massacre), they nevertheless show considerable individual genius.

Yi In-song, well known for his 1983 short-story collection *Into an Unfamiliar Time*,[23] writes to change society. He enriches his work with careful research but also draws upon his own personal experience—which he heightens for artistic effect. His intellectual style makes limited use of conventional narration. **Yang Kwi-ja**, on the other hand, writes in a simple but polished classical style as she examines

---

[21] "Yuhyong ui ttang" in the *mook Hyondae munhak* (October 1981), trans. Marshall R. Pihl, is the title story in *Land of Exile*.

[22] *T'aebaek sanmaek* (Seoul: Hang'il sa, 1989).

[23] *Nasson shigan sok uro* (Seoul: Munhak kwa chisong sa, 1983).

the alienation of a weary middle class. A representative collection of her work is the 1985 *Deaf Bird*.[24]

The work of **Im Ch'or-u**, who was born in Kwangju, reveals spiritual scars of the 1980 massacre. The representative "A Shared Journey," from his 1985 anthology *Beloved South*,[25] exemplifies his uneasy but lyrical style, which projects a gloomy view of the world. In this story, two close friends and college classmates travel together by train from Kwangju to the southern port city of Mokp'o. One is the narrator. The other is a Kwangju activist—now a fugitive—whose experience has changed him and estranged him from his close friend. This delicate and sensitive story was one of the first to emerge in the wake of the Kwangju massacre and was written and published while President Chun Doo-hwan was still in power.

The most thematically wide-ranging of these representative young writers of the 1980s is **Ch'oe Su-ch'ol**, whose constantly shifting insights examine the failures in human relations, isolation of individuals, and psychological aspects of violence in society. He believes that a shared language with shared meaning is essential to all communication and that the lack of it can lead to discrimination, conflict, and violence. A representative collection of his work, *Pavilion in the Air*,[26] explores inner consciousness and psychology in an imaginary world of unreality. Typical of these stories is "Time Killing," told without dialogue, in which a commission salesman sits day after day in a third-run theater watching kung fu movies instead of making his rounds. The environment of the darkened theater—movie, other customers, and furnishings—is described through his consciousness with often unexpected results, sometimes amusing, sometimes bizarre.

Literature in North Korea

Literature in the Democratic People's Republic of Korea (DPRK) developed very differently from that of South Korea. When leftist literary leaders from the southern half of Korea and intellectuals who had spent the war years in exile in Yanan, China, flocked to the new regime in the North after Liberation, they discovered a situation quite unlike what they had anticipated. Major literary and intellectual leaders associated with the earlier proletarian school had disappeared from sight in the course of the struggle for political control of the

---

[24] *Kwi mogori sae* (Seoul: Minum sa, 1985).

[25] "Tonghaeng" in *Kuriun namtchok* (Seoul: Munhak kwa chisong sa, 1985). Translated by Bruce Fulton and Ju Chan Fulton as "A Shared Journey" in *Land of Exile*.

[26] *Kongjung nugak* (Seoul: Munhak kwa chisong sa, 1985).

North between Kim Il-sung's Soviet-oriented Korean Workers Party and the New People's Party, whose leaders had spent the last years before Liberation with Mao Zedong in Yanan.

It is ironic that this Yanan faction, consisting mainly of literate and well-to-do elements, had watched their Chinese literary counterparts knuckle under to Mao's thought-reform movement in China during the early 1940s only to return home and themselves fall victim to Kim Il-sung's Korean Workers Party, which was made up preponderantly of the illiterate and the indigent.[27] The leader of the Yanan faction, Kim Tu-bong, an established literary scholar, was purged during the Korean War.[28] Having eliminated not only noncommunist nationalists and domestic communists soon after Liberation but also the Yanan faction by the end of the Korean War, Kim Il-sung had a free hand to dictate cultural policy in line with his own anti-intellectual, party-first bias. Clearly impatient with possible criticism by intellectuals from within party ranks, as Mao had been in Yanan, Kim repeatedly expressed a distaste for literary workers as a professional group separate from the party and the people. Echoing Mao's 1942 "Talks on Art and Literature," Kim demanded that literature and all aspects of intellectual activity conform to party policy in his "Talk with Writers and Artists" delivered on June 30, 1951.[29]

In terms that recall the Stalin-Zhdanov cultural policy of Soviet Russia in the 1930s, Kim characterized writers and artists as "engineers of the human soul" and stressed that their works should serve the people as a "powerful weapon and as a great inspiration." He chided writers and artists for having "lost touch with life" and for "lagging behind our rapidly advancing reality." His basic theme was that the writers must serve the people and the party, acting as inspirational conveyors of information who help the readers learn from the "lofty spirit of ordinary people." He encouraged writers to study popular culture directly, warning that "the writers and artists should know that the genuine creator of great art is always the people." Kim con-

---

[27] This characterization of the membership of the two North Korean parties is made by Chong-Sik Lee, "Politics in North Korea: Pre-Korean War Stage," in *North Korea Today*, ed. Robert A. Scalapino (New York: Praeger, 1963), p. 9. The literary dissent and thought reform in China during the Yanan period is described by Merle Goldman, *Literary Dissent in Communist China* (Cambridge: Harvard University Press, 1967), pp. 18–50.

[28] Lee, "Politics in North Korea," p. 13.

[29] The political context and main points of Mao's talks are covered in Goldman, *Literary Dissent*, pp. 32–36. The official English translation of Kim's talk appears in Vol. 1 of Kim Il Sung, *Selected Works* (Pyongyang: Foreign Languages Publishing House, 1971, 5 vols.), pp. 305–12.

cluded by pronouncing an end to the creative independence of Korean writers: "An implacable struggle must be fought against any and every sectarian act and tendency that impedes the implementation of the Party's policy on literature and art and weakens the unity of the literary and art world."

In November 1960, Kim Il-sung announced the formation of a General Federation of Literature and Art, in which writers and other creative artists were to work collectively under the leadership and direct guidance of the party. He suggested that literature could be developed rapidly by making use of many "correspondents" living among the masses, who, he added, "could write rather better works than the professional writers who are confined to their office rooms. . . . The mistaken idea that professional writers alone are able to write . . . should be cast aside."[30]

By the 1970s, Kim appeared satisfied that his writers were under party control and successfully incorporated into the work of the state. In his report to the Fifth Congress, he spoke of "Achievements in the Cultural Revolution."

> Our socialist literature and art are in their heyday. Thanks to the successful implementation of the Party's policy in this area, all revisionist elements and restorationist tendencies have been removed. Our writers and artists are all busy creating revolutionary literature and art works thoroughly based on the working-class line; and workers, farmers, and broad sections of other working people are actively participating in literary and artistic activities. Our literature and art have become the literature and art of the Party, of the revolution, and of the people in the truest sense of the term and are becoming a powerful means in educating our working people along communist lines.[31]

Content and Style

North Korean fiction as it has evolved under party control is less a reflection of social reality than a statement of social ideals; it is expressed in characters, settings, and themes that, while recognizable to the reader, do not photographically reproduce real-life experience. Rather, North Korean fiction creates a negative image from which one might develop a picture of what the party perceives as shortcomings in the society requiring correction through education.

---

[30] Kim Il Sung, November 27, 1960, "Talks with Writers, Composers, and Film Workers," *Selected Works*, Vol. 2, pp. 594 ff.

[31] Kim Il Sung, November 2, 1970, "Achievements in the Cultural Revolution," *Selected Works*, Vol. 5, p. 423.

There are no villains in North Korean fiction set in the present-day DPRK. The only inveterate villains are found among landlords and Japanese in stories set before Liberation or American and Korean officials in modern tales that take place in South Korea. In stories set in the DPRK, we find no interpersonal conflicts involving true enmity but, rather, solvable misunderstandings, such as those between faithful believers and backsliders. The stance is optimistic, evincing a belief in human perfectibility. Since all people are seen essentially as potential believers susceptible to conversion or correction, there is no character development beyond the individual's recognition of party truth. Therefore, without productive interaction between characters, the only motive force rests with the author, who manipulates his puppetlike characters in obvious and predictable ways.

The typical story consists of five parts: description of physical setting, identification of major characters, introduction of problem to be solved, crisis, and resolution. The setting is always identified as a real one, usually agricultural, in the present-day DPRK. The next most popular type of setting after agricultural is industrial, but typically a rural locale. Most of the agricultural activity is related to change (that is, mechanization, improved fertilizers, more efficient methods, land reclamation, and highway and railroad construction), which means that virtually no attention is given to traditional farming and the natural cycle—nature cannot dominate the land, for nature is to be overcome by man's revolutionary struggle. The natural environment is typically beautiful to observe but harsh to encounter: mountains abound, and characters frequently struggle against the cold and snow (often a blizzard). The sun and moon are commonly used to punctuate the ending of a story, rising or falling appropriately in the last paragraph as if in affirmation of the resolution just achieved.

The major characters, identified at the outset by name and social function, are all local workers. Kim Il-sung appears frequently as a colonial-era anti-Japanese guerrilla fighter but not as a named participant in a contemporary setting, in spite of the many quotations from and other references to him. Although the speech of characters reflects the differences in their status, the authors tend to equalize the characters throughout the narration by referring to them by their first names. The family structure is downplayed and made ancillary to such mainstream, task-oriented groups as work brigades, rural cooperatives, military outfits, factory-worker groups, student circles, and cultural clubs. The effective, cooperative, and obedient functioning of these groups—many of them newly introduced to North Korean society since 1945—is a major concern. Interaction of individuals without reference to these groups does not occur, hence ruling out any but the most tangential recognition of family and romantic love. Strong emotion is not expressed unless invoked in the name of socialist ideals, and when characters die (they seldom do), it is for a heroic cause and as an inspiration to others. Women are typically portrayed as secondary figures who, though they frequently prove their mettle, are living in a world of male revolutionaries.

The problem introduced in the third part of the typical story is commonly a misunderstanding to be resolved, a backslider to be encouraged, a quota to be met, a new technique to be perfected, or a struggle against an adversary of the group (natural phenomena, Japanese, Americans). There is never any question about ultimate victory, and what doubters there are become converted in the course of the solution of the problem. The crucial meeting of forces in the fourth part gives way to a concluding resolution in which the problems are restated and a suggestion of future happiness and success is unveiled.

The didactic content, manipulative plot, and unconvincing characterization of the contemporary North Korean short story are functions of the same kind of social purpose that motivated the writers of the "new novel" early in the 20th century: the two are invested with a serious intent that is a function of the times. Both are valid and useful in terms of their social purposes: the "new novel" helped to spread literacy and inculcate progressive ideas in early modern Korea, and North Korean socialist realism has served to educate citizens of the DPRK along party lines.

We find, as a recurrent underlying theme in three periods of Korean literature—the enlightenment, the colonial era, and the age of division—an expression of the Koreans' sense of themselves as a people. Although enlightenment literature was never more than transitional, its intellectual momentum stimulated an awareness of Korean cultural identity that emerged in colonial literature and was able to champion a sense of moral victory over oppressive Japanese rule. The third period, initiated by Liberation in 1945, promised the opening of a new literary age, one dedicated to the establishment of a national literature in the truest sense—an ironic concept for a divided nation.

Instead of relegating North Korean socialist realism to a marginal category of political propaganda, we would benefit by considering its affinities with the 19th-century classical novel, which promoted virtue and reproved vice, the enlightenment's "new novel," which advocated modern social ideas, and the idealistic realism of passionate left-wing writers of the colonial era. Seen in this light, writing in the DPRK today is the expression of an impulse that runs deep in Korean literature.

5
The Many Faces of Korean Dance

Judy Van Zile*

If you wish to see dance in Korea today, you will have to make choices. Should you visit the small theater of the Korean Traditional Performing Arts Center for a sampling of older forms of music and dance from the court and the villages? Go to the outdoor arena of the Nori Madang and watch masked performers relate, through speech and movement, a traditional story about a supposedly celibate Buddhist monk and his cavortings with a young maiden? Sit in the plush red seats of the Little Angels Theater to see a traditional Korean story performed by lithe female dancers wearing *pointe* shoes and muscular male dancers in tights and tunics? Or trek off to the Munye Theater in the trendy student section of Taehangno to observe the latest creations of a young Korean dancer nursed on traditional Korean dance forms and reared on modern dance at an American institution?

The various dances performed today in Korea range from those that have a distinctively Korean identity to those that do not, with clusters centering around specific categories named by Koreans themselves. These categories may be placed on a continuum, with the two extremes called *chont'ong muyong*, "traditional dance," and *hyondae muyong*, "modern dance." A number of dances fall near the center of the continuum, into a category variously referred to as "new dance" and "creative dance."

*Grateful acknowledgment is made to the following organizations for providing funding assistance for research: Korean Culture and Arts Foundation (Seoul), Academy for Korean Studies (Seoul), Korean-American Educational Foundation (Fulbright Program), and International Cultural Society of Korea. Acknowledgment is also made to individuals who provided invaluable translation assistance at various stages in the research process—Alan Heyman, Joo Yun-hee, Kim Sung-ja, Lee Chun-hye, Lee Young-lan, Gary Rector, Ryu Ran, Um Hae-kyung, and Tim Warnberg—and to individuals who provided valuable comments on early drafts of the manuscript—Karen Jolly, Jane Moulin, Judy Rantalla, and Barbara B. Smith.

Traditional Dance

The variety of dances classified as *chont'ong muyong* differ in both the contexts and the manner in which they were originally performed. In former times, the royal courts supported some dances purely for entertainment and others for ritual purposes; today, all of these are classified as traditional dance. In the context of entertainment, dances were performed for the pleasure of local and visiting dignitaries. Elaborate palace banquets included grand spectacles that not only entertained but also demonstrated wealth and power. Extant paintings and written texts portray large numbers of dancers clad in rich, colorful costumes moving through precise geometric formations to the accompaniment of music played on diverse and elaborate instruments. During some periods the dancers portrayed are men, but more frequently they are women—*kisaeng*, or female entertainers.

The *Akhak kwebom* (Canon of Music), an important treatise on dance and music compiled in 1493, officially classifies these dances into *t'ang'ak chongjae* and *hyang'ak chongjae*—court entertainment dances originating in T'ang dynasty (618–907) China and court entertainment dances originating in Korea, respectively. This classification is a reminder of the early interactions between China and Korea, which included a visit by a group of Korean performers to China during the Unified Silla period (668–935); they returned with musical instruments, dance properties, and costumes. Later, in 1116, a complete music and dance ensemble from the Chinese court visited Korea. Although such interchanges might suggest substantive differences in the two kinds of dance, documents such as the *Akhak kwebom* and the manner in which the dances are performed today attest to a difference in the overall format but little difference in the movements themselves. In dances of Chinese origin, a formal procession by individuals holding various kinds of standards precedes and follows the dance, and the dance is interrupted for a brief song by the dancers in Chinese; in dances of Korean origin, the dancers begin with a bow to the king and a brief song in Korean praying for his happiness, and end by bowing to the king again, but there are no standard-bearers or processions. Any movement differences between the dances of Chinese origin and those originating in Korea no longer exist.

Many of the dances previously performed in the Korean court are performed today in concert settings in theaters, where they are perpetuated primarily by dancers and staff members of the Korean Traditional Performing Arts Center (Kungnip Kugagwon; referred to as KTPAC and until recently known in English as the National Classical Music Institute). KTPAC traces its roots to the end of the fourth century via a royal music institute in the palace. The institute moved several times when the government was relocated, but in 1955, with the dissolution of the last remnants of the former Korean court, it became independent and established itself in Seoul. The center's original goals were to preserve and transmit court dance, but in the late 20th century they were broadened to include the fostering of all forms of traditional music and dance as well as new creations. However, the center is best known for court music and dance. Original court dances are believed to have been quite long, and full performances are rarely given today. Every Saturday throughout most of the year, the center presents a 90-minute program of excerpts from the traditional music and dance repertoire. It is only here that one can regularly see the slow, stately movements of brightly attired women in dances that have been reconstructed from old documents describing court festivities.

Court dance repertoire is also taught at some universities. For example, Ewha Women's University provides students with the opportunity to major in ballet, modern dance, or "Korean dance," including court dance. As part of ongoing university activities, students occasionally perform selections from the court dance repertoire. Adaptations—some more extreme than others—of what are believed to be the most historically accurate versions of court dances are performed by many companies whose repertoire is touted as being "Korean."

Most of the court dances performed today involve large numbers of dancers who move elegantly through circular, square, and linear formations. They generally wear colorful costumes with long sleeves of stiff, multicolored silk—considered by some to be related to the long sleeves used in Chinese opera forms. With arms frequently extended sideward, the dancers walk, almost as if floating, while gently bending and extending their knees. They punctuate their movements with flicks of the wrist that propel their sleeves upward and outward. At KTPAC performances, accompaniment is usually provided by a live orchestra composed of traditional instruments and led by a musician playing the *pak*, an ancient instrument with six slats of wood fastened at one end with a leather thong; the slats are spread apart and then snapped shut to provide a loud clap signaling transitions between sections.

The movements of some dances are literal, as in *Kainjon mokdan* (Beautiful Persons Picking Peonies), in which the dancers, representing court women, move around a large vase containing flowers that they eventually pick and hold while dancing. Another court activity is depicted in *Pogurak* (The Ball-Playing Dance). This time the dancers try to throw small, pincushion-like balls through a hole in a simulated gate. Those who succeed are rewarded with a flower; those who fail receive a black stripe painted on the cheek.

Many dances, however, are very abstract. *Ch'unaengjon* (The Nightingale in Springtime), one of the few solo dances performed today, suggests the quality of a nightingale through its delicate movements; the gentle, sometimes wavelike motions of the arms, often extended sideward, are birdlike, but there are no movements that mime the flapping of wings or the soaring of a bird.

Two of the court dances performed today are distinctive because the dancers wear masks. *Hak ch'um* (The Crane Dance) undoubtedly had ritualistic origins. For Koreans, the crane is a symbol of longevity that figures prominently in paintings and embroidery. In the version of this dance performed today, two dancers in realistic crane costumes that extend over the head to form a kind of headdress—concealing the entire torso, arms, and head—execute pantomimic movements of flying, roaming through fields, and pecking at food. Historical sources suggest that *Ch'oyongmu* (The Dance of Ch'oyong) was also once part of rituals—specifically, those to expel evil spirits at New Year—and that it was performed outdoors. Five dancers said to represent the directions (north, south, east, west, and center) wear large masks suggestive of Ch'oyong, a son of the Dragon of the Eastern Sea. At some time *Ch'oyongmu* was brought into the court, where it was transformed into a dance done purely for entertainment and incorporated into a suite of dances that included the Crane Dance.

Besides dances for entertainment, the royal court also supported dances that continued to serve ritual purposes: *Munmyocheriak*, to honor Confucius, and *Chongmyocheriak*, to honor royal ancestors— both examples of Chinese influence. Although Confucianism entered Korea from China as early as the fourth century A.D., it did not become official orthodoxy until the Choson dynasty (1392–1910), when it replaced Buddhism as the state's main philosophical tenet. These ritual court dances are perpetuated today primarily at shrines in central Seoul by royal descendants and students of the High School of the Performing Arts. Despite the different reasons for which these dances have traditionally been done, there is little difference in their performance. Large groups of men (or boys and girls, in the case of performances by the performing arts school), in a square formation of precise rows and columns, execute simple arm movements and bows to a measured tempo, all to pay tribute to Confucius or important ancestors as a part of larger ritual celebrations. The simplicity of movement and ponderous tempo contribute to a meditative and highly ritualistic atmosphere. The performers hold symbolic implements: for dances classified as *munmu* (civil), a stick decorated with a dragon's head and pheasant feathers in one hand and a flute in the other, symbolizing peace and prosperity, and for dances classified as *mumu* (military), an ax and mallet or wood sword and spear, symbolizing war.

Masked dance dramas, *t'alch'um*, were at one time associated with the court, but they originated in conjunction with village shaman rituals and eventually became largely an entertainment form. They evolved to cleanse houses and villages, afford protection from calamities, and assure good crops. Their support from the court varied: during the Koryo dynasty (918–1392), the court maintained an Office of Masked Dance Drama, and *t'alch'um* were performed at royal banquets; during the Choson dynasty, possibly because of the new importance of Confucian values, the office was abolished. Despite former occasional affiliations with the court and frequent performances today in large cities, *t'alch'um* are still closely associated with villages. There are many regional variants, but most revolve around humorous themes that allowed the people of former times the opportunity to poke fun at things they would normally not discuss in public—liberties taken by ostensibly serious, wholesome monks, frivolous rompings of upper-class noblemen, and bawdy activities of matchmakers. As performed today, *t'alch'um* perpetuate the traditional satirical stories of the past but also occasionally incorporate references to important contemporary individuals or events. Performers serve as caricatures who strut and dance as they sing and engage in sometimes risqué dialogue that creates a lively atmosphere in which audience members shout their delight at peak moments.

Although *t'alch'um* are most frequently performed today by governmentally recognized master performers and their students, they have also become a popular activity among university students, who sometimes perform them on campuses. This interest originated with the student nationalism of the 1980s, one aspect of which was a movement to heighten Korean cultural consciousness.

Farmers' band music and dance, *nong'ak*, is another traditional dance form with strong connections to villages. Believed by some to be the oldest form of dance in Korea and to have shamanistic origins, this is a loud, extremely vigorous performing tradition originally engaged in by farmers in connection with agricultural events. Performers paraded through villages, then stopped in open areas to perform, playing wind instruments, drums, and gongs that created a piercing cacophony as they danced. In *nong'ak*, as in many other Korean dance forms, the interplay between music and dance and musicians and dancers is particularly important: musicians perform highly stylized movements, and dancers play musical instruments. Dancers play several varieties of drums, ranging from the small, handheld *sogo* to the larger, hourglass-shaped *changgo* (the latter fastened to their bodies with sashes around the waist and shoulder), and a musician playing the harsh brass *kkwaenggwari* gong skips and leaps at the head of the group as the ensemble's conductor. A highlight of *nong'ak* is the performance of an individual wearing a tightly secured hat with a small, revolving rod on top. Affixed to the rod is a long streamer. With continuous small, strong, abrupt movements the dancer rapidly tilts his head forward, to one side, backward, and then to the other side, causing the streamer to whip through the air as it traces large circular designs in space. He may also play the *sogo* and fly breathtakingly through the air in gymnastic aerial turns—all simultaneously!

Today *nong'ak*, like *t'alch'um*, is performed by governmentally recognized masters and their students, by groups of villagers who get together for entertainment and to maintain community spirit, and by students from the elementary through university levels.

The shamanism that contributed to the development of *t'alch'um* and *nong'ak* also gave rise to dance and stylized movement that remain a part of shamanic rituals. Although not always looked on favorably by the government, shamanism has never completely disappeared and is practiced today in both villages and large cities. "Clients," who enlist the services of a shaman to heal the ill, appease the spirits of the deceased, or thwart other negative forces, participate in elaborate rituals that include food and monetary offerings, singing, and dancing. The singing is generally done by the shaman, who in most regions is female and who also engages in various forms of structured movement. Stylized movements are often used when the invoked spirits descend and speak through the shaman or when the shaman approaches clients while holding out a fan to insist that monetary offerings have been insufficient. At climactic moments the shaman will insist that the client don special clothing, make arm movements similar to those of traditional dance forms, and jump up and down. As in the *t'alch'um*, regional variants of the rituals and movements used in shamanic activities abound. Shamanic dances are still performed today as rituals by practicing shamans, but they are also the basis for creative works performed by trained dancers in theaters.

Formalized movements are also found in the traditional dances of Buddhist rituals. Like Confucianism, Buddhism was introduced from China in the fourth century A.D. It became the official national religion during the Koryo dynasty. Unlike the movements of shamanic rituals, Buddhist dance is more an adjunct activity to larger rituals than an integral part of the rituals themselves. It was originally performed by monks, usually in large open courtyards at Buddhist shrines, to the accompaniment of *pompae*, ritual chant and recitation originating in India—the homeland of Buddhism. Only four Buddhist dances are performed today. *Nabi ch'um* (The Butterfly Dance) is believed by some to be symbolic of the spreading of the Buddha's will in all directions. Performing either solo or as a duet, the dancers wear white cloaks with extremely long sleeves. They move slowly, bending and extending their knees as their lifted arms sweep gently forward and backward like the wings of a butterfly in slow motion. *Para ch'um* (The Cymbal Dance) is also said to spread the word of the Buddha. This dance is most often performed by four dancers who, as in the *nong'ak*, function as musicians, in this case each manipulating a pair of large cymbals. While playing the cymbals, the dancers turn in various directions, bend and extend their knees, and rotate their arms overhead so that the cymbals contribute to the overall visual design as well as produce sound. *Popgo ch'um* (The Monk's Drum Dance) is a solo, and the dancer again functions as a musician. He performs highly stylized movements as he plays a drum mounted in a tall wooden frame. (Originally, the drum was extremely large; nowadays, it is often small to facilitate transporting it to performance locations.) In the dance *Taju* (sometimes referred to as The Dance of the Eightfold Path), an octagonal box with inscriptions on each side—representing the eightfold way of the Buddha—is placed between two dancers. Each holds a long, thin stick and gently taps the top of the box as he moves around it.

These Buddhist dances are performed today primarily by monks of the Pongwon Temple in central Seoul on traditional religious occasions as well as at other celebratory events. In 1990, for example, they were performed in the Pongwon Temple courtyard as part of the activities celebrating the raising of the roof beam for a new building and on a small stage along the banks of the Han River for thousands of Buddhist devotees and religious leaders attending the 17th general conference of the World Fellowship of Buddhists.

Derived Dance

The various dances described thus far, whether originally supported by religious institutions or the former court and whether done for entertainment or as part of ritual, are considered traditional dances, or *chont'ong muyong*, and are readily identifiable as being Korean. If we move along the continuum to dances that are derived or adapted from some of these traditional forms, we find dances that, despite changes, still retain a distinctively Korean identity. These derived forms often display similarities to their traditional forerunners in terms of movement. They are generally performed today in formal theatrical concert settings by any of a number of dance companies that describe themselves as performing "Korean dance." It is perhaps this accessibility to the general public that has caused many Koreans to refer to these dances as *minsok muyong*, "folk dance." (The term as used here should not be confused with its use in much of the Western world, where it generally connotes dances with relatively short, simple movement patterns that are repeated continuously and that are meant to be participated in rather than observed by an audience.)

Among the derived dances is a subcategory known as *salp'uri*. The origin of *salp'uri* is unclear. Some dancers attribute it to the *kisaeng*, or female entertainers, who eventually left the court and performed for a male clientele at eating and drinking establishments. Others attribute the creation of *salp'uri* as it is performed today to Han Song-jun, a man who lived at the end of the 19th and beginning of the 20th centuries. Han supposedly based this type of dance on those used in shamanism, but he developed dances intended for the concert stage rather than for rituals. *Salp'uri* primarily draws on the spirit or feeling of the shaman dances rather than the movements themselves. The dances are solos, typically performed by a female dancer carrying a medium-length or long silk scarf that she manipulates during the dance. The dances have come to be considered the epitome of stereotypically Korean dances, and they express the essence of *han*—a term translated variously as sorrow, bitterness, or unsatisfied desire. Although individual choreographies for *salp'uri* vary, its movements are slow and display an introverted, almost withdrawn character. The dancer who can perform *salp'uri* well, which means, above all, with the correct feeling, is considered to be a true master.

Other more recently created dances derived from older traditional dance forms and intended for the concert stage include a shaman dance employing a fan and bell-tree (implements used by some shamans in movements to call forth the spirits, dispel them, or collect money from clients); a drum dance derived from *nong'ak* in which the dancer plays the hourglass-shaped *changgo* drum; a series of dances derived from the Buddhist Monk's Drum Dance in which the performer plays one or more drums in standing wooden frames; and a series of knife or sword dances rooted in ancient legends and dances previously performed in either court or village settings. There are many variants of these dances, which are most often performed by companies that stage evening-long programs of a variety of dances. But the ties to the dance forms from which they derive are sufficiently strong and the frequency with which they are performed is such that they, too, are generally considered traditional dances.

Creative Dance

Moving still farther from the traditional end of the continuum of dance forms found in Korea today leads to dances with identities that sometimes display clear Korean origins and sometimes become less easily distinguishable as Korean. The boundaries between creative dance, modern dance, and Korean adaptations of ballet are not always clear, making the notion of a fluid continuum a particularly useful analytical tool. The placement of a dance in, or nearer to, one category as opposed to another can be based on the training of the choreographer, elements of costuming and movement, or the ideas that are central to that particular dance. Creative dances form a kind of bridge between the two ends of the continuum, but one that ambles a bit. The dances in this category vary considerably, and confusion in affixing labels is evident in the fact that several terms—with unclear definitions—are used to describe them. In the early 1930s and 1940s, when some of these dances were evolving, they were described as *shin muyong*, literally, "new dance." In more recent times, they have come to be referred to as *kundae muyong*, "modern" or "contemporary" dance, following the use of *kundae* to refer to developments in many of the arts during the newfound freedom following the end of the Japanese occupation (1910–45).[1] The term *ch'angjak muyong*, "creative dance," is the most descriptive of the nature of these "bridge" dances, which emphasize experimentation, in some instances based on non-Korean dance forms and in other cases on traditional or derived forms.

Three notable members of the first generation of creative dancers were Ch'oe Sung-hui, Cho T'aek-won, and Pae Ku-ja. They all studied in the late 1920s and early 1930s in Japan with Ishii Baku, a Japanese dancer who had studied, in Europe, what is known as "modern" or "contemporary" dance. Ishii was particularly influenced by the work of Isadora Duncan and the German expressionist dance of Mary Wigman. Following their studies with Ishii, Ch'oe, Cho, and Pae returned to Korea to begin experimenting with ways to combine their new occidental training with elements of traditional Korean dance and culture, creating dances originally referred to as *shin muyong* and now generally known as *kundae muyong*.

Because much of their work occurred during the years of the Japanese occupation, less is known about the details of the creations of these three pioneers than of the works of a second generation of cre-

---

[1] In Korean usage, *kundae muyong* refers generally to dances of the prewar and immediate postwar period, while *hyondae muyong* means more strictly contemporary (literally, "modern") dance.

ative dancers. More recently, Kim Mae-ja, a former chairwoman of the Ewha Women's University dance program and former head of the Korean dance area within the program, began to experiment with new ways of creating dances. Unlike the first generation of creative dancers, however, Kim was trained solely in traditional and derived forms of Korean dance. Although many of the movements she uses can be found in these more traditional types of dance, she has expanded on them, as well as elaborated on the arrangement of performers in the stage space. The costumes in her creations depart from the purely traditional Korean attire worn in older dances, and the music employed is recently composed. Though there is a Korean flavor to many of her dances, they clearly display innovation. The 1977 premiere of her dance *Pidan kil* (The Silk Road) marked the beginning of the dances referred to today by Koreans as *ch'angjak muyong*.

What binds the diverse faces of creative dance together (whether described as *shin muyong*, *kundae muyong*, or *ch'angjak muyong*) is that although they are not considered to be traditional, they *are* identified as being Korean. The two creative dance performances described below illustrate some of the combinations and permutations that lie between the traditional and contemporary ends of the dance continuum in Korea.

Mun Il-ji, a choreographer at the Korean Traditional Performing Arts Center with strong training in traditional dance forms and who earned the first doctorate with an emphasis in traditional dance from Hanyang University, premiered an evening-long work titled *Pyo* (Rice Plant) in October 1990. Based on a poem of the same name by Yi Song-bu, the dance has a purely Korean theme. In a *Korea Herald* article, Mun stated that she tried to capture the spirit of life among the Koreans of former times: "The scene of paddies standing against each other in the rice field brought up the image of ancient Koreans who lived leaning against each other in closely associated communal societies."[2] The costumes incorporate elements of traditional Korean attire. Although the movements replicate, or are based on, those found in traditional dance, they are drawn from a variety of forms. Despite the fact that the theme, movements, and costuming are clearly Korean, the mixing of elements from different styles of Korean dance and the modification of movements found in traditional dances place *Pyo* in the creative rather than traditional category.

Another performance lying somewhere in the middle of the continuum is the 1990 production of *The Myth of Mount Paekt'u*. In the style of the elaborate extravaganzas of film director Cecil B. de Mille, the

---

[2] "Traditional Dance *Pyo* to Be Staged," *Korea Herald*, October 20, 1990, p. 10.

production was described as an "epic spectacle" and compared to Beijing opera and Japanese kabuki. The script, by philosopher Kim Yong-ok, is based on the legend of the founding of the Korean nation. A she-bear and a tigress seek the help of the son of the divine creator in enabling them to become human. They are each given a bunch of mugworts and 20 bulbs of garlic to eat and then told to stay out of the sunlight for 100 days. Only the she-bear is able to complete the task and ultimately emerge as a woman. She subsequently gives birth to Tan'gun, who is said to have descended from heaven to the highest point in Korea—believed to be Mount Paekt'u, near the Manchurian border in what is now North Korea. In 2333 B.C., Tan'gun founds the Korean nation.

In *The Myth of Mount Paekt'u* a cast of almost 200 actor-dancers, accompanied by a 50-member live orchestra, combines traditional dance movements with movements that have no relationship to any traditional Korean dances. In one section the stage is almost entirely filled with performers who are seated or kneeling. A small drum is placed on the floor in front of each performer, who strikes it using stylized movements in a manner that produces a powerful and dynamically varied rhythmic interlude as well as a visually spectacular dance. The beating of drums by dancers in a way that emphasizes both sound and movement is an integral part of many traditional Korean dances. In another section, however, intended to be symbolic of the birth of the Korean people, performers crawl, writhe, and extend their arms as they work their way over a hill created on the stage. Movements in this section have no relationship to any traditional dance forms.

Kuk Su-ho, whose training is entirely in traditional dance forms and who is currently a member of the dance faculty at Chung'ang University, is responsible for the choreography and stylized movement of this mammoth theatrical undertaking. In this case the performance incorporates many traditional movements as well as purely creative ones to tell a traditional story; it combines both Korean and non-Korean components and hence can be placed somewhere in the middle of the dance continuum.

Some of the dancers in this bridge category, such as Kim Mae-ja, Mun Il-ji, and Kuk Su-ho, have been trained only in the older forms of Korean dance. Others have studied ballet or Western modern dance, either at home or abroad.

Modern Dance

Some of the dancers who choose to move beyond Korean dance forms become involved in dances that bear little resemblance to anything uniquely Korean. They pursue either ballet or modern dance in a manner that places them at the opposite end of the continuum from *chont'ong muyong*. *Hyondae muyong* refers to what is known in the United States as "modern dance" and in Europe as "contemporary dance." First introduced to Korea in 1926 by the Japanese dancer Ishii Baku, modern dance did not really take hold in Korea until the 1960s and 1970s. In recent times modern dance owes much to Yook Wan-sun, also a former chairwoman of the Ewha Women's University dance program and former head of the modern dance area. Yook went to the United States to study modern dance at the University of Illinois and eventually moved on to New York City, where she studied with Martha Graham, one of the founders of the American modern dance movement and one of the most widely known modern dance choreographers. Yook returned to Korea in the mid-1960s and earned the first doctoral degree with an emphasis in contemporary dance from Hanyang University. She introduced the Graham technique into the dance curriculum at Ewha, and the program has subsequently become the source for most of the modern dance performed today in Korea; credentials of modern choreographers and performers almost always include study at Ewha, and a large percentage of modern dance faculty members at the countless universities and high schools that offer a dance curriculum studied, at some time, at Ewha. Martha Graham and her technique, although almost passé in the United States, have become the standard for modern dance in Korea.

At the same time, however, Korean modern dance also encompasses choreographers who have tried to go beyond the Graham mold. These include individuals who have studied in university dance programs in diverse locations in the United States, a few who have studied in Europe, and several who, despite their Ewha training, have made conscious efforts to break away from the Graham style fostered at Ewha.

Regardless of the experimental nature of modern dance, it cannot exist completely independent of the cultural roots from which it springs. Unlike other kinds of Korean dance, however, it strives to make either a broad universal or an intensely personal statement, rather than a cultural one. While the traditional and derived dances performed today seem to speak consciously of the past and make the statement, "This is the Korea of former times," a modern piece such as Nam Chong-ho's *Children, What's Behind the Mountain* seems to try to make a more universal statement—in costume, movement, and idea.

Following her dance studies at Ewha University, Nam pursued training in France. She is presently a member of the dance faculty at Kyongsong University and, according to another modern dancer, is famous in Korea because her work is "different," meaning that it breaks away from the Graham style. In the first section of *Children*, for example, a group of uniformed children goes through the rigorous disciplines of a school day. An austere teacher "calls them to order" through movement, and they mechanically perform their classroom routines. But the moment the teacher leaves or turns her back, the children become playful and mischievous. The dance movements are not literal or pantomimic, nor do they incorporate the movement vocabulary found in many of the traditional dances. Rather, they are abstractions of regimentation and repetition interspersed with spontaneity and enthusiasm. Both the theme and movements of the dance seem to make a universal statement—one that could easily have come from a German, British, or American choreographer.

Another dance that makes a universal statement is *Meeting*. Choreographed by An Ae-sun as an abstract portrayal of various encounters, this work won the grand prize at the 1990 Seoul Dance Festival. Although the theme is universal, the stage set and use of movable components are clearly reminiscent of the work of American choreographer Alwin Nikolais, with set pieces that create dynamic shapes and long strands of elastic stretched across the stage. At present a member of the dance faculty at Ewha University, An received virtually all of her dance training in Korea, taking only a few classes with American dancer-choreographer Jennifer Muller during a brief performance tour to the United States in 1987. Although Nikolais's New York-based company has never performed in Korea, Shin Sun hee, An's set designer, studied in New York for 15 years.

Traditional dances and derived dances seem to be primarily concerned with making a statement—a statement that says either, "This is *Korea*," or, "I am *Korean*." Creative dance seems to strive to say, "I am Korean, but I am also very modern." Contemporary dance, in contrast, seems to be concerned with making either a more personal or a more universal statement—"This is *I*," or, "This is one facet of *world society*." This attitude is reflected in a *Korea Times* statement attributed to Han San-gun, Chu Ok-no, and Hong Kyong-hee, who in 1992 choreographed *Flying, Something That Makes Us Sad*. The dance is described as symbolically exposing social evils, and the choreographers believe that now is the time for Korean dancers to "get out of the pattern [of] sticking to traditional image[s] of beauty and emotion."[3] This attitude is also reflected in the use of dance as a vehicle for protest. In 1987, Yi Ae-ju, a dance professor at Seoul National University, used traditional dance forms as inspiration for a dance of mourning that she performed in the streets of Seoul at a public funeral service for Yi Han-yol, a university student killed by a tear-gas bomb during the June 1987 democracy demonstrations.

Ballet

A type of dance that sometimes appears at the non-Korean end of the continuum with modern dance and sometimes slips closer to the middle with creative dance is one that most people would identify as ballet. Clearly rooted in an imported dance style, ballet in Korea continues to manifest its classical European sources as well as Korean influences. Classical and new repertoire items from Russia and the West, such as *Giselle* and the *Nutcracker*, are staged by local or visiting choreographers; perhaps the only thing that makes them remotely Korean is that they are performed by dancers who are from Korea. A piece such as one in which Buddhist-inspired costumes, prayerlike gestures, and *pointe* shoes are combined reflects a mixing of Korean and non-Korean components. When asked why she classified this dance as ballet, a Korean replied that the use of *pointe* shoes and ballet movements placed it in this category, despite the acknowledged Korean theme and Korean-inspired costumes and movements.

Another mixture identified as ballet is a work titled *Shim Ch'ong*, performed by the Universal Ballet Company. Choreographed by the American Adrienne Dellas, founder of the company and its first artistic director, the ballet tells the traditional Korean story of a faithful daughter and her blind father. With its wicked sailors, mythical underwater scene, trials and tribulations of a poor country girl who eventually marries a king, and grand palace celebration, the story lends itself perfectly to the fairy-tale tradition of 19th-century ballet. Although the designs of many of the costumes are based on traditional Korean attire, the performers are easily recognizable as a poor country girl, fairy-tale underwater creatures, or members of royalty— Korean or otherwise.

The movement in this dance, on the other hand, is drawn almost entirely from the codified vocabulary of ballet. Shim Ch'ong dances her concerns and joys using the long, outwardly projected lines of ballet and *pointe* shoes, the wicked sailors perform an athletic display

---

[3] "Metropolitan Troupe Performs 'Social-Problem' Dance," *Korea Times*, November 24, 1992, p. 5.

of strength using the elevation and intricate footwork of male ballet *allegro*, and Shim Ch'ong and her lover express their feelings toward each other in a typical *pas de deux*. In only two brief sections is there a conscious attempt to incorporate Korean dance movements: five dancers attired in costumes and executing movements taken from the Pongsan style of *t'alch'um* provide entertainment in the court of the story's king, and the village blind men to whom sight has been restored perform a dance of joy using movements traditionally found in dances portraying young male aristocrats.

Members of the cast were both Korean and non-Korean; the Universal Ballet seems to try to live up to its name and include dancers from a broad spectrum of ethnic and national backgrounds. With a Korean story as its basis, an American choreographer, performers of varied ethnic backgrounds, Korean-inspired costumes, and movements drawn almost entirely from classical ballet, *Shim Ch'ong* is described as "ballet with a Korean story," and falls near to, but not at, the non-Korean end of the dance continuum.

Characteristics of Korean Dance

The placement of dances at one end or the other of the Korean/non-Korean or traditional/contemporary continuum is based on an assumption of certain features that are distinguishable as "Korean." No discussion of Korean dance would be complete without mention of *mot* and *heung*, for example. Among the more difficult of Korean words to translate, they refer to an inner spiritual quality of charm or grace and a feeling of lively animation or interest, both of which lead to an almost irrepressible joy or giddiness. This is the ultimate quality the Korean dancer strives to achieve, and specific movement characteristics either contribute to the achievement of this desired state or are the physical manifestation of its having been achieved. These movement characteristics cut across many of the classifications on the dance continuum and stand out as being distinctively Korean. What makes many of the creative, contemporary, and derived forms so intriguing is the way they incorporate these movements as well as elaborate on them. Although these terms are not used to describe court dance, many of the relevant movement characteristics are present in the court dances too.

One of these movement characteristics is an emphasis on verticality in the use of space. Throughout much of Korean dance, there is a rather persistent alternation between up and down actions, seen in several different ways. In the slower forms, such as the court and Buddhist dances, the dancers regularly alternate between bending and extending their knees. Hence, the whole body lifts and lowers. In the faster, more vigorous dances, such as the farmers' band music and dance and the masked dance dramas, the bending of the knees serves as a preparatory push that propels the body into a jump, enlarging the up-and-down action. This is also seen in shaman dancing when the spirits take over the shaman's body, resulting in vigorous jumping.

The upward-downward action is also emphasized in a smaller but very important way in the shoulders. Koreans sometimes refer to their dance as *okkae ch'um*, "dance of the shoulders." Movement is often initiated in the chest area with what almost appears to be a quick inhalation of the breath that causes the spine to extend and eventually forces the shoulders to rise. This movement is then "released" as the shoulders and spine relax, creating a visual "sigh of relief." In court dances this movement is extremely subtle, but in such genres as the farmers' band music and dance and the masked dance dramas, it can become a very obvious, exaggerated shoulder shrug.

Another distinguishing feature that pervades many forms of Korean dance is the creation of a feeling of suspension. The dancer often begins a movement that rises, in some fashion, and then appears to stop abruptly. The dancer remains briefly poised, as if deciding whether to lift even higher or to move on to something else. As the contained energy verges on explosion, the performer rises just a bit higher before releasing everything into a gentle downward movement. This moment of suspension—a delicate hovering—creates a strong, dynamic tension for the viewer and contributes to the visual sigh of relief.

Yet another distinctive feature of Korean dance is a particular way of using the foot. Koreans are quick to point out that their dance is characterized by walks in which the dancer steps first on the heel rather than the ball of the foot or the toe. What is unique in this movement is the way in which dancers seem to almost caress the floor with their feet, flexing their toes upward before placing the heel on the floor and then gently rolling the entire foot down. This action is enhanced by the tight-fitting padded "socks" with upturned toes (*poson*) that most dancers wear. Whether done slowly or quickly, the overall effect is of the dancer walking on something delicate, contributing to the feeling of *mot* and *heung*.

In many Korean dances the arms are extended to the side at shoulder height. They are turned inward so that the thumb surface of the hand points forward, and the wrist is relaxed, allowing the fingertips to point gently downward. There are many movements in which the wrist is flicked to manipulate a long sleeve or scarf, and then the sleeve or scarf and fingertips all finish pointing downward. The arm also often rotates outward and then inward, concluding with a relaxation of the wrist that returns the fingertips to their downward orientation.

All of these elements contribute to an emphasis on motion rather than isolated positions or posturing. Koreans actually describe their dance as "motion in stillness." The fluid, ongoing movements that appear to stop are, in reality, simply collecting energy that ultimately gently explodes, or runs over, into the next series of fluid actions. Korean dancers move through positions instead of arriving at them, creating curvilinear shapes as well as an ongoing quality of energy.

The skillful use of costume components or handheld implements and the playing of musical instruments are also features of many Korean dances. In court and masked dances the performers manipulate long sleeves that are part of the costumes; in derived dances they manipulate fans, scarves, and knives; and in many different kinds of dances the performers play one or more of a wide variety of drums.

A final feature prevalent in many different kinds of dances in Korea is an emphasis on triple meter. Movement phrases are choreographed in three-beat units, and underlying musical pulses are often further subdivided into units of three. This triple meter emphasis frequently ties in with the emphasis on verticality and suspension: rising action that leads to a brief suspension on the first two pulses and a slight accent at the end of the second pulse before the downward release on the third pulse.

Musicians as Dancers

The most important musical instrument used in Korean dance is the hourglass-shaped *changgo* drum. Even when the dancer is not "wearing" it and playing it while moving, as in *nong'ak*, it provides accompaniment. So significant is the *changgo* in Korean culture as a whole that amateurs often play it, and it is even an important component of casual picnics. As people relax and inhibitions are set aside, someone will start to beat out a rhythmic pattern, which invariably results in even nondancers lifting their arms and improvising a "shoulder dance."

In a number of the dances described here, the dancer functions as a musician by playing a musical instrument and dancing to the accompanying sound. This interrelationship between dance and music also goes in the other direction; in many forms of music in Korea, stylized movement plays an important role in the music-making process. For example, in the solo narrative vocal form known as *p'ansori*, the singer carries a fan, which he or she opens and closes during the performance. Particular emphasis is placed on gestures during narrative portions, with the performer using shoulder movements like the *okkae ch'um* found in dance and often holding the arms extended sideward at shoulder height. The vocalist even occasionally performs very short dance phrases as interludes.

Drummers also employ shoulder movements and frequently display the kinds of suspended movements typically found in dance. The *changgo* is struck on several different surfaces of each of the drumheads as well as on the drum's wooden frame; the striking is done with a thin bamboo stick held in the right hand, with the bare left hand, or with a mallet-type beater held in the left hand. As the various surfaces are struck, the musician often executes elaborations of the purely functional movements necessary to strike the appropriate surface.

One of the most prominent examples of the use of stylized movements by musicians today is in a form known as *samulnori*. Deriving its name from words meaning "four things," this type of music is said to trace its roots to shamanistic forms and *nong'ak*. The four things used are two drums (the *changgo* and the *puk*) and two gongs (the *kkwaenggwari* and the *ching*), but members of the ensemble also sing. The musicians most often play in a seated position, but sometimes one or more will stand and dance while playing. Even when sitting down, though, they engage in what might be called a "seated dance," with shoulders and chest lifting and lowering in relation to preparations for and follow-through of drum strokes, arms moving in almost prescribed fashion to strike the instruments, pauses filled with suspensions, and movements following from the last sounds played.

Major Contributors to Dance in Korea Today

Although dance has played an integral role in various facets of Korean society for hundreds of years and has been supported by the court and religious institutions to greater and lesser extents at different times, there has been a phenomenal dance boom since the 1980s. This boom is manifest in both the variety and quantity of dance activities. Dance offerings in higher education have increased, dance studios have been established throughout the country, dance students and performers have gone abroad both to perform and to study, and professional dance organizations have been created. During the ten years from 1980 to 1990, the number of dance performances per year increased from 40 to 400; in 1989, 20 dance theory books were published, approximately seven times the previous average of 3 books per year; and in 1990 alone, six new dance companies were formed.[4]

Four forces have contributed significantly to this growth: the Law on the Protection of Cultural Properties, promulgated in 1962; the Dance Department at Ewha Women's University, established the following year; the Korea branch of the American Dance Festival, a series of performances and intensive courses initiated in Seoul in 1990; and increasing financial support in the form of grants from government agencies and private corporations.

In passing the 1962 Law on the Protection of Cultural Properties, the Korean government set out to preserve and promote important facets of Korea's cultural heritage. Together with historic objects and sites, scenic places, natural resources, drama, music, and handicrafts, the government chose to recognize individual dances for their merit and people for their knowledge, performance expertise, and ability to perpetuate these dances. Based on recommendations from the Committee on Cultural Properties of the Cultural Property Preservation Bureau, the Ministry of Culture identifies dances and individuals considered to be truly outstanding. A report is prepared on the history of the dance and individuals who perform it, with verbal descriptions and line drawings of the choreography. The dance then becomes an Intangible Cultural Asset (*Muhyong Munhwajae*), and the most outstanding performers become National Living Treasures *(In'gan Munhwajae* or *Muhyong Munhwajae Poyuja*).[5]

There is considerable discussion about the processes for selecting Intangible Cultural Assets and National Living Treasures, particularly in relation to the possible age and authenticity of some of the dances and performers selected.[6] There can be no question, however, about the interest the system has sparked in dance. Village people try to revive traditions from the past (leading, in some cases, to what are considered to be contemporary constructions rather than revivals or reconstructions); annual "folk festivals," attended by thousands of Koreans as well as visitors from abroad, are held, in which performers compete to receive government recognition and monetary prizes; concerts, also attended by Koreans and visitors, are staged to show-

---

[4] Kim Seong-Kon, "On Native Grounds: Revolution and Renaissance in Art and Culture," in *Korea Briefing, 1990*, ed. Chong-Sik Lee (Boulder: Westview Press, 1991), p. 113; *Korea Annual 1990* (Seoul: Yonhap News Agency, 1990), p. 280; and *Korea Annual 1991* (Seoul: Yonhap News Agency, 1991), p. 296.

[5] See Judy Van Zile, "*Ch'oyongmu*: An Ancient Dance Survives," *Korea Journal*, Vol. 8, no. 2 (Summer 1987), pp. 18–19.

[6] See, for example, Keith Howard, *Bands, Songs, and Shamanistic Rituals: Folk Music in Korean Society* (Korea: Royal Asiatic Society, Korea Branch, 1989), pp. 241–61.

case performances by acknowledged masters and their students; and publications are generated to document historical and performance details of the various traditions. Hence, whether these dances are actual historical activities or recent constructions of a perhaps romanticized past, they nonetheless contribute to an important contemporary living tradition.

Since the establishment of the Law on the Protection of Cultural Properties, more than 20 dances have been designated Intangible Cultural Assets, and more than 50 individuals have been designated National Living Treasures for their dance knowledge and performing abilities. Dances that have been so recognized all come from the traditional end of the continuum and include those from the repertoire performed in the court for entertainment, those done in the villages as both entertainment and a component of ritual, those of 19th-century origin, and one done as a part of ceremonies to honor the birthday of Confucius.

Another important contributor to dance in Korea today is the dance program at Ewha Women's University. Originally begun as part of the physical education program (a genesis parallel to the beginnings of dance in higher education in the United States), in 1963 the program became an independent department (again following a pattern common in the United States). Today the curriculum offers both bachelor's and master's degrees in one of three emphases: Korean dance, ballet, and modern dance. Graduates have contributed to virtually every aspect of dance in Korea today—founding their own companies, establishing dance programs in other universities and colleges, opening studios, going abroad to further their education, and participating in festivals. Probably not until the next generation will Korea see dancers who were not, at some point, involved with the Ewha program.

While the Law on the Protection of Cultural Properties nurtures traditional dance forms and Ewha University fosters traditional forms, ballet, and modern dance, the most recent influence on modern dance in Korea has been the establishment of a Korea branch of the American Dance Festival. The festival, which is actually a United States–based administrative body that facilitates the creativity of modern dance choreographers and fosters the appreciation and awareness of dance, began in the United States in 1934. Its goals are achieved through intensive summer classes, workshops, and performing opportunities for faculty and students.[7]

The success among Americans of festival-sponsored activities in the United States eventually led to participation by foreigners and subsequently to the establishment, by the festival administrators, of branch programs abroad. In 1980 Yook Wan-sun, a modern-dance teacher formerly affiliated with Ewha University, brought 40 Korean students to the festival in the United States. The participation of Korean dance students continued, and Yook was ultimately instrumental in the establishment of the Korea branch of the festival in 1990. From July 30 to August 11 of that year, 487 students in Seoul participated in classes taught by visiting American modern-dance instructors as well as several Korean instructors. The event continues to be extremely popular and contributes substantially to the awareness in young dancers of what is being done in modern dance in other parts of the world. The long-range impact of the American Dance Festival in Seoul on the development of modern dance in Korea, however, remains to be seen.

The fourth major impact on dance in Korea today is the increased financial support for dance. Prizes awarded by the Ministry of Culture at dance competitions and outright grants by government and nongovernment agencies afford dancers the means to pay for costumes and the rental of performance space and offer individuals financial support while they are developing their skills and rehearsing. So substantial have both the number of dance activities and the nature of support for them become that 1992 was declared the Year of Dance by the government and featured performances, workshops, and symposia.

The myriad faces of dance in Korea today reflect the array of styles and interests present in Korean society as a whole. Some people wish to maintain a unique identity rooted in a past "untainted" by contact with Western cultures; others strive to keep up with people in the "outside world," which often simply means becoming more "like them"; and still others seek to establish a new, yet clearly Korean, identity. That these many faces can coexist bespeaks a culture that acknowledges diversity as well as its homogeneous roots and, by so doing, serves to nurture a strong dance presence.

---

[7] The festival originally took place in Bennington, Vermont. It relocated in 1948 to the campus of Connecticut College in New London, and in 1978 to its present home at Duke University in Durham, North Carolina.

Kim Yong-hee submits a prayer from earth to heaven in the Korean Traditional Performing Arts Center's *Rice Plant*, choreographed by Moon Il-chi. Photo by Chae Yong-mo, courtesy of Korean Traditional Performing Arts Center.

An Ae-sun's *Meeting*. Photo courtesy of An Ae-sun.

Kuk Su-ho's recently choreographed *Myth of Mount Paektu*. Photo by Jo Dae-hyung, courtesy of photographer.

A soloist performs *Chunaengjon* (The nightingale in springtime), one of the few solo dances originally performed in the royal courts.

Kim Ch'on-hung, who performed in the court during the last days of the Choson Dynasty and is responsible for reconstructing many of the court dances performed today, dances *Salp'uri*.

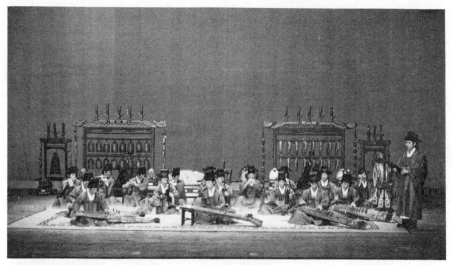

Hyangak (Native court banquet music) performed by musicians of the National Performing Arts Centre. Photo by Byongwon Lee.

Masked dance drama in which a corrupt Buddhist priest seduces a female entertainer. Photo by Byongwon Lee.

Student protest led by a *p'ungmul* group in June 1988. Photo by Tae Hwan Eom.

Komun'go, a six-stringed zither. Photo by Byongwon Lee.

P'ungmul (or *nongak*) performance in a rural village during the Lunar New Year celebration. Photo by Byongwon Lee.

6
Contemporary Korean Musical Cultures

Byongwon Lee*

This chapter presents Korean musical culture in sociohistorical perspective and describes some of its salient characteristics. It assesses the state of traditional and contemporary music in Korea and among Koreans abroad, and it places Korean music in a broader context by comparing it with relevant counterparts in China, Japan, and the West.

For nearly 2,000 years, Korea was racially and culturally homogenous. But since 1948, when the country was divided geographically and ideologically into separate republics, the cultural polarization of North and South has been increasing. The term "Korean music," therefore, must be clarified as regards separation. Here I use "Korea" and "Korean" to indicate events completed or begun prior to 1948, and "South Korean" or "North Korean" to refer to events originating after 1948.

The musical development of the two Koreas differs in many ways. Seoul, the present capital of South Korea, had been the Korean political and cultural center for nearly 500 years. Most of the musical traditions of the court and *yangban* (hereditary aristocrats) revolved around the Seoul area. The officials and musicians of Korea, South Korea in particular, chose to preserve the traditional music and the repertoires of imported music side by side. There has been no systematic reform of the traditional music or conspicuous assimilation with foreign music in South Korea, though gradual changes have occurred as the music has been transmitted from generation to generation. In contrast, the musical practice in North Korea has undergone continuous reform and modernization; many of the traditional styles, repertoires, and in-

* The author wishes to express his gratitude to Karen Drozd and Jennifer M. Oetken for their suggestions and assistance in proofreading the manuscript.

struments have been abandoned. Therefore, the music of the two countries cannot be regarded as the product of a single cultural manifestation.

The Development of Korean Music

From a historical perspective, the musical culture of Korea, particularly its classical and popular music traditions, is closely tied to that of its Northeast Asian neighbors. China was an important model for the development of high-art-music traditions in Korea, as well as being a conduit for influence from West Asia. Korea was Japan's teacher until the 9th century, in the same way that China had been Korea's teacher. Since the turn of the 20th century, however, Japan has been a dominant source for new styles of Korean popular music. Many Koreans remain fans of the sentimental Japanese *enka*-style popular song genre called *ppongtchak*, which can be heard daily on radio and television, in taxis, in coffeehouses, and in the sidewalk record stores of South Korean towns.[1]

The history of Korean music is characterized by gradual evolution rather than drastic reform of styles. Many of the long-lasting indigenous repertoires have been transmitted and preserved virtually unchanged. The imported repertoires, mostly from China, flourished side by side with indigenous music, without significant mutual influence. For this reason some of the repertoires lost in China, such as Confucian ritual music (*aak* in Korea; *yayue* in China) and popular Chinese court music, both of which were introduced into Korea before the late 14th century, are still performed in Korea along with the indigenous repertoires. Thus, despite its historical status as a crossroads of musical culture, Korean music can claim to be distinct from neighboring musical cultures because it has perpetuated its indigenous music in isolation from the music that has continuously flowed in from abroad.

In contrast, the music of both China and Japan has been characterized by conspicuous reform. Thus, establishing or tracing the original or archaic form of many traditional musics in these cultures is difficult, if not impossible. Most of the so-called traditional music and musical instruments of China are actually the products of modernization and Westernization since the turn of the century. In Japan there were

---

[1] *Ppongtchak* is a derogatory onomatopoetic term derived from the lively fox-trot dance rhythm. South Korean pop musicians in this style prefer to label it *torotto*, a corrupted and shortened Korean pronunciation of the English fox-trot, or *kungmin kayo* ("people's popular songs").

two important historical occasions of musical reform: the synthesis of various materials and the Japanization of foreign music, mainly from China and Korea, during the Heian period (794–1185), and the modernization modeled upon the Western system during the Meiji period (1868–1912).[2]

Western Influences on South Korean Music

Although the history of Western music in Korea is little more than a century long, this imported tradition is solidly ingrained in Korean society. South Korean pupils aspiring to careers in Western classical music far outnumber those in Korean traditional music. Many well-to-do Korean families plan their children's training in Western music from an early age. There are thus a number of well-known Korean musicians in the Western classical music world who have achieved an international reputation. The best-known family of musicians from South Korea is the Chung family, including the violinist Kyung-Wha, the cellist Myung-Wha, and the pianist-conductor Myung-Whun.[3] These musicians have become role models for thousands of Korean students of Western classical music.

Ever since the introduction of Western classical music to Korea in the late 19th century, the music colleges and conservatories of South Korea have referred to traditional Korean music as *kugak* ("national music"), reserving the term *umak* ("music") for Western classical music. From the time of its introduction into Korea, *umak* was accorded more respect than *kugak*, which bespeaks a certain degree of bias against Korean traditional music. Young students in particular shied away from traditional Korean music until the early 1970s, when the feeling that it was somehow inferior to Western classical music began to fade away, mainly for social reasons.

Beginning in the 1960s, efforts by well-to-do Korean families to employ prestigious teachers to give their children individual instruction in Western classical music became highly competitive. As a result, by the 1980s fees for lessons rose to an exorbitant level. Students from such families could afford private music instruction from college teachers, which gave them a greater advantage when competing for entrance into highly selective music schools. Some of the music teach-

---

[2] For details on the reform of Japanese court music, see Robert Garfias, *Music of the One Thousand Autumns: The Togaku Style of Japanese Court Music* (Berkeley: University of California Press, 1975), pp. 15–16, 27.

[3] See, for example, "Chung, Kyung-Wha," *The New Grove Dictionary of Music and Musicians* (London: Macmillan, 1980), Vol. 4, p. 383.

ers and professors were criticized for favoring their own students when evaluating applicants.

Government intervention was needed to solve the inequality of opportunity between those with money and those without. The military regime of Chun Doo-hwan enacted a law in 1980 prohibiting private off-campus music, dance, and art instruction by full-time university faculty. That law, which applied to instruction in both Korean and Western forms, is still in effect. It resulted in an immediate musical exodus from South Korea; more than 1,000 Korean students are now enrolled at a few prestigious music conservatories in Berlin, Paris, and New York. In response to this, the South Korean government in 1993 opened the National Conservatory of Arts, which features a music conservatory. (The government expects to open conservatories of dance, art, and acting in the next few years as well.) Many famous Korean artists of Western classical music, including the Chung family, have returned from abroad to serve as visiting faculty and have been successful in persuading talented students to stay and pursue training at home.

Traditional Music in South Korea

After the military coup in 1961, anti-government student riots against the authoritarian regime of Park Chung-hee and his successors occurred daily on university campuses until the late 1980s. During this time, many contemporary performing arts were subject to governmental censorship. However, because of the government's pledge to promote the traditional performing arts, these arts were exempted from censorship despite their explicit anti-establishment content. Thus, students began to opt for the easily accessible traditional performing arts as a means to avoid government censorship while expressing their feelings at rallies.

Among the traditional performing arts, *t'alch'um* (masked dance dramas) were one of the first to be performed on college campuses under the auspices of student organizations. The inherent anti-establishment content of *t'alch'um* was particularly suitable for student protests since it was traditional for *t'alch'um* performers to vary and twist the plot and libretto slightly to fit the context. One common plot in various *t'alch'um* is the ridiculing of corrupt aristocrats and a hypocritical Buddhist priest by a commoner and a monkey. Because *t'alch'um* do not require highly sophisticated dance techniques, students were able to learn the dances by themselves. In doing so, they participated not only in the production of *t'alch'um* but also in the creative experience of modifying the traditional dance drama to serve their purposes.

At the same time, *p'ungmul*, the outdoor band music and dance that in rural villages is also known as *nong'ak* ("farmers' music"), became another favorite medium at student rallies. Most of the instruments used in *p'ungmul* are drums and gongs, although an optional melodic instrument called the *t'aep'yongso* (double-reed pipe with a conical bore) may also be included. The sound of *p'ungmul* is boisterous, and its variety of rhythms is exciting, making it an ideal medium for group mobilization, encouragement, and provocation.

Beginning in the mid-1970s it became common for a *p'ungmulp'ae* (*p'ungmul* group) or a variation thereof to lead demonstrations or processions of student groups and labor unions. *P'ungmul* rhythms therefore became part of the country's emerging youth culture, and certain troupes gained followings not only in demonstrations but also for performances on stage. Of these, the most famous variation is the troupe started by Kim Tok-su in February 1978, called Samulnori. The name derived from the group's use of four main instruments (since *samul* means "four things"): a *kkwaenggwari* (small gong), a *ching* (large gong), a *changgo* (hourglass-shaped drum), and a *puk* (barrel drum). Since Kim did not register the name Samulnori as a trademark, it became a generic term for one of the most popular forms of traditional Korean music. Similar groups referring to themselves as *p'ungmulp'ae* have sprouted in universities, colleges, high schools, and labor unions all over the country.

The difference between *samulnori* and *p'ungmul* is that the former is a new arrangement of traditional materials performed on four instruments played by four players, whereas the latter is performed by a long-standing form of traditional ensemble that includes multiple players for each type of instrument. The former is associated with professional musicians and commercial concerts, whereas the latter is associated with amateurs who perform for their own entertainment and at social functions. In fact, student groups tend to distance themselves from the term *samulnori* because of its commercial and professional connotations. However, both types of ensemble share many identical musical materials. The *p'ungmulp'ae* of the present student and labor organizations, for instance, borrow material arranged by Kim Tok-su's *samulnori* group.

Through this unconventional approach to traditional music, young people began to realize that learning traditional music was not a difficult task after all. They came to understand that traditional performing arts not only provide a convenient medium for their protests, but they also have aesthetic value. This realization opened the door for students to explore more sophisticated forms of traditional music, such as *sijo* (classical lyric song), *sanjo* (long solo instrumental pieces accompanied by the *changgo*), and *p'ansori* (operatic song accompanied by the *puk*). Of these, *p'ansori* requires an especially serious commitment and intensive training in order to be appreciated and performed properly.

Most contemporary Korean intellectuals distanced themselves from *p'ansori* because of its strenuous vocal projection and extremely raspy timbre, both of which contrast with the vocal projection techniques used in Western art songs. Because of this, and because of the low social status ascribed to its music and musicians in the past, *p'ansori* was not readily accepted in South Korea. However, students began inviting *p'ansori* singers to perform on campus in the 1970s. *P'ansori* artists are known for their quick adaptation to the performance environment. Timely interjection, improvisation, and deviation from the music and libretto, traditional elements in *p'ansori* performance, have drawn enthusiastic responses from contemporary audiences.

As the interest of students in the traditional performing arts gradually increased, other age groups began to participate in this new cultural awareness. This trend was reinforced by an intensified sense of nationalism and a new search for cultural roots in South Korea. The majority of students had previously considered the traditional performing arts inferior and negligible. Ironically, though, it was the traditional performing arts that provided solidarity, a sense of identity, and a venue for social expression among disgruntled social groups in South Korea.

Professional traditional musicians no longer felt looked down upon, and they responded to their new status with wholehearted enthusiasm and seriousness. These masters now enjoy unprecedented respect and significantly improved financial security in comparison to the conditions of the pre-1970s. Since 1964 many of them have been designated as "Retainers of Intangible Cultural Assets," or "National Living Treasures," by the South Korean government, and the government provides a monthly stipend for them and their designated successor-trainees.[4]

Patronage by the merchant class has been an important factor in the dissemination and preservation of the traditional performing arts in the West, China, and Japan. In South Korea a true merchant class did not begin to emerge until after the 1961 military coup. The early members of the merchant class were preoccupied with the security

---

[4] As of 1990 the South Korean government had designated 221 Retainers of 60 different Intangible Cultural Assets.

and expansion of their businesses, leaving little capital and energy for the performing arts. During the late 1980s, the second and third generations of the "super-rich" class and the business community began to contribute some of their accumulated wealth to the performing arts; however, the extent of their commitment is as yet unclear.

In contrast, the South Korean government has played an active role in the promotion of traditional music. Under the Ministry of Culture and Information, the government established the Bureau of Cultural Property Preservation in 1962 and the Korean Culture and Arts Foundation in 1974. Through these organizations, provisions have been made for the systematic documentation, research, preservation, and dissemination of traditional music, and performance allotments have been established as well. The perpetuation of traditional music thus became a conscious national interest in South Korea, and it remains so today. In 1990 the Ministry of Culture and Information was divided into the Ministry of Culture and the Ministry of Information. Although it had been conventional before the split to appoint a journalist-politician to the post of minister of culture and information, the first minister of culture was a professor of Korean literature, clearly reflecting the growing awareness of culture in South Korea.

Earlier, in preparation for the 1988 Summer Oympics in Seoul, the South Korean government had embarked on an ambitious project calling for the construction of an enormous world-class arts complex in Seoul called Yesurui Chondang (The Great Hall of Arts). In addition to a concert hall, opera house, drama theater, experimental theater, art gallery, and calligraphy and craft exhibition hall, it included a unit for use by the Kungnip Kugagwon (Korean Traditional Performing Arts Center, formerly the National Classical Music Institute) called the Kugaktang (The Hall of National Music). Part of the project was completed in time for the 1988 Games, and the entire complex was finished in January 1993.

Musical Style

The most important feature of Korean music is its flexibility, which permits deviation, variation, and improvisation in individual performances. The extent to which musical variables are employed depends upon the performer's artistic idiosyncrasies and aesthetic preferences. They may range from merely ornamental deviation, as often occurs in court music, to full-blown improvisation, as occurs in such folk art forms as *sinawi* (improvised instrumental ensemble), *sanjo*, and *p'ansori*.[5]

Among the Northeast Asian countries, extensive improvisational musical styles are found only in Korea. The improvisation and interjection of personal idiosyncrasies in *sanjo*, *sinawi*, and *p'ansori* are all well known. Among these, *sinawi* permits the most extensive improvisation. Individual melody players spontaneously interject, intertwine, and juxtapose short tunes. The point of departure for improvisation in *sinawi* is its rhythmic patterns, whose ornamentation varies continuously with each repetition.

The melodic multipart juxtaposition in *sinawi* is highly unpredictable; the music is different each time it is played, even when the same musicians perform it. *Sinawi* typically accompanies *salp'uri* ("exorcising evil spirits"), an improvised solo dance rooted in shaman culture. It should be noted that *sanjo*, *p'ansori*, and *sinawi* all originated in Cholla, the southwesternmost province of Korea, and are related to shaman rituals of the region. Together with *samulnori*, they are the most popular types of folk music in South Korea today.

Conventionally, professional Korean performers of traditional music went through three developmental stages: learning by rote and by imitation of their own teacher, learning from other teachers while evolving a personal style, and establishing a recognizable musical style. It is socially accepted for traditional musicians to obtain instruction from more than one teacher until they establish a personal style. The result is a hybridization of the styles learned from several artists, flavored with personal innovation. For this reason, "school" or musical lineage is not clearly identifiable in Korean music.

When young musicians at the Korean Traditional Performing Arts Center perform a court music piece along with their teachers, their ornamentation, dynamic changes, and other subtle expressions often differ from those of their teachers. The teachers accept their students' deviation as reflecting the development of a personal style, and it is not subject to criticism as long as the identity of the music is not altered radically. This practice is common throughout traditional Korean music. In contrast, such a practice would be unacceptable in the performance of Japanese court music or Western symphonic music, in which exact reproduction is highly valued.

---

[5] See Byong Won Lee, "Improvisation in Korean Music," *Music Educators Journal*, Vol. 66, no. 5 (January 1980), pp. 137–45.

Sound Quality

The general sound quality of Korean music stresses rough, raspy, or buzzing timbres. Western operatic voices would therefore not suit Korean music. The extremely raspy sound of *p'ansori* and folk songs of the southwestern region is preferred by Koreans. As mentioned above, the majority of popular singers perform in the *ppongtchak* style, the sentimental style influenced by the Japanese *enka*. However, they tend to use a characteristically powerful chest voice similar to that used in *p'ansori*, rather than conforming to the typical Japanese vocal style, which employs nasal timbre, frequent narrow vibratos, and throat-controlled light projections.

The popularity and importance of the *ajaeng* (bowed zither) in Korea is one manisfestation of the preference among Koreans for rough, raspy sound. The *ajaeng* was imported from China during the Koryo dynasty (918–1392) but disappeared from China centuries ago. Its thick strings are played with a rosin-rubbed forsythia bow. The nature of the instrument and the playing method used create an extremely strong scraping sound, and the somewhat loosened strings add a rough edge. The *ajaeng* gained wide popularity and became an important part of instrumentation for both court and folk music in South Korea. It is the most popular melodic instrument for dance music.

Similar noise devices abound in other Korean musical instruments as well. The *komun'go* (6-stringed zither plucked with a slim stick) produces a scraping, scratchy sound when the strings are pushed or pulled over the convex wooden frets. This complex musical noise is compounded by the rattling noise of the movable bridges of the three drone-strings, as well as by the sound of the stick plectrum striking the soundboard. Similar sounds can be heard from the rattling bridges of the *kayagum* (12-stringed zither plucked with bare fingers). A buzzing sound is produced by the membrane-covered hole of the *taegum* (transverse flute), and the *p'iri* (double reed with a cylindrical pipe) emits a strong, reedy sound. Instruments producing a refined sound, such as the *yanggum* (dulcimer), *tanso* (high-pitched notched flute), and *tangjok* (high-pitched transverse flute), are less favored, and their use in performances is considered optional.

The manufacture of traditional Korean instruments requires little artifice and embellishment compared to that of their counterparts in China and Japan. The unpolished nature of the instruments naturally influences the sound quality. It is up to the musicians to adapt their playing technique to the idiosyncrasies of the instrument rather than perfect its tuning or improve its physical structure. Pitch gradation and raspy sound quality are two of the most important requisites for Korean musical instruments.

Sound Organization

The prevailing texture of Korean music is monophonic with occasional heterophony, in which some parts or voices perform slightly different melodies or ornaments of the main melodic line. Most of these slight variations are nonprescribed individual expressions.

Theoretically, Korean musical scales are based on five tones. However, the intervals of the scale pitches do not conform to those of Western classical music and even differ slightly among Korean musicians. The quantity of scale pitches used is not an important factor in characterizing Korean music. How individual scale pitches function musically in live performance is the most important aspect of Korean melody and musical aesthetics.

Three tones out of the five-pitch scale usually prevail in Korean music. Each of the tones may function as a central sustained tone, as a tone with a wide vibrato, or as a tone of short duration that slides a narrow interval distance down to the stable central tone.[6] Therefore, transcribing traditional Korean music onto Western staff notation without an explicit explanation of the nonequal tempered intervals and the characteristics of scale pitches is misleading. It is impossible to establish a uniform tonal theory even within one genre of Korean music, because the variants and personal renditions cannot be known until the music is actually performed.

The smallest variable in Korean music consists of the pitch gradations, which are an important characteristic of musical scale and music in live performance. Most of the musical instruments used for indigenous Korean music can make subtle microtonal pitch gradations. Thus, an instrument with fixed tuning such as the *yanggŭm* is not considered important in traditional Korean music. Other instruments with fixed tuning, such as the *p'yŏn'gyŏng* (stone chimes) and *p'yŏnjong* (bell chimes), are associated with court music of Chinese origin.

Most of the rhythms of traditional Korean music are based on triple time or triple-time groups. The most important characteristic of Korean triple time is that the third beat is either articulated or accented (see Appendix 1, p. 137). Duple time does exist in more recent traditional music, but it is very rare. In folk music duple meter is always

---

6 See Hwang Byung-ki, "Some Notes on Korean Music and Aspects of Its Aesthetics," *The World of Music*, Vol. 27, no. 2 (1985), pp. 32–46.

combined with triple meter, forming an asymmetrical rhythm. Asymmetrical rhythm abounds in regional *p'ungmul* and shaman ritual music. The length of these rhythms or rhythmic cycles may range from five beats (2+3) to as many as 36 beats (see Appendix 2, p. 138). When the rhythm is actually played on drums or gongs, the details of strokes vary considerably in each repetition to suit the melodic rhythm or express rhythmic virtuosities.

Post-1949 Musical Development in North Korea

North Korean music evolved along a different path from that of South Korea.[7] The communist-socialist ideology of North Korea set the tone for the country's musical practice. The groundwork on arts and literature was put forward by Kim Il-sung, the leader of North Korea, in his *Hyongmyongjok munhak yesullon*[8] and elaborated on by Han Chung-mo and Chong Song-mu in their collaborative work entitled *Chuch'e'ui munye riron yon'gu*.[9] These codified theories echo common Marxist-Leninist doctrines on the arts. They also contain some statements that can be traced to Mao Zedong.[10] According to these sources, North Korean policy encourages the systematic control of all aspects of music for the benefit of the people, including such practices as dictating the content of compositions, gearing performances to the masses, standardizing performance techniques, and regulating instrument manufacturing.

Music and musical instruments in North Korea have undergone drastic modernization. They no longer bear traditional traits and therefore contrast significantly with those of South Korea. Traditional ritual music and the music of the aristocracy disappeared long ago. As a result of the active modernization of Korean music, only one type of traditional instrument, the *changgo*, remains in its pre-1948 form. The rest of the instruments were modified, primarily on the model of comparable Western symphonic instruments. Modification

---

[7] The information in this section is drawn from Byong Won Lee, "Theory and Practice of the *Juche* [Self-Reliance] Ideology on Music in the Democratic People's Republic of Korea (North Korea)," unpublished paper presented at the 1988 annual meeting of the Society for Ethnomusicology, Tempe, Arizona.

[8] Kim Il-sung, *Hyongmyongjok Munhak Yesullon* (The Revolutionary Ideology of Literature and Arts), Tokyo: Miraesa, 1971, p. 186.

[9] Han Chung-mo and Chong Song-mu, *Chuch'e'ui Munye Riron Yon'gu* (Studies on the Theory of Literature and Arts of Self-Reliance), Pyongyang: Sahoe kwahak ch'ulp'ansa, 1983, p. 678.

[10] Mao Tse-tung, "Talks at the Yanan Forum on Literature and Art [in 1942]," *Selected Works of Mao Tse-tung* (Peking: Foreign Languages Press, 1965), Vol. 3, pp. 69–98.

included the enlargement of instrument size and the addition of more finger holes and buttons to the aerophones and more strings to the chordophones.

Another major musical reform in North Korea is the ongoing standardization and homogenization of styles and genres into one national style, said to be based on folk songs of the northwestern region.[11] Nevertheless, in practice the music differs from the recommended theoretical basis: the contemporary songs and music dramas of North Korea remind us of the refined tunes, but not necessarily the traditional expressions, of the northwestern folk song style. Subtle pitch gradations, microtonal shadings, and narrow and stable vibratos, which are important elements in defining the characteristic scale and mode of regional styles, have disappeared in present-day practice.

The ideal musical timbre of North Korea has also changed and become more like that of Western classical music. The traditional raspy timbre used in *p'ansori* and other regional folk songs was considered noisy and "unscientific." In order to obtain new musical timbres, the conventional musical noise-making devices of traditional instruments were either eliminated or reduced to a minimum. The *ajaeng*, for example, which is still popular in South Korea, was abandoned in North Korea because of its rough sound quality.

To a certain extent, the North Korean policy on music has succeeded in achieving its goal. The uniform folk song–like tunes, the timbre without local character, and the modernized instruments have all contributed to the dissemination of the repertoire to the wider population. Non-Koreans accustomed to the sound of Western classical music will most likely feel comfortable with the musical performances taking place in North Korea today.

Korean Musical Culture Outside Korea

Large Korean enclaves have existed for some time in China, Japan, the United States, Canada, and Uzbekistan. Each is the result of migrations at various points in the 20th century. The emigrants took their music with them at different stages of its modern development and encountered different influences in the places where they settled, so that the music associated with each community is now a significant variant of what we call "Korean" music. Ethnomusicological studies of these variants have recently been begun.

---

[11] See Han and Chong, *Chuch'e'ui munye riron yon'gu*, p. 502.

China

Among the host countries of Korean immigrants, China has the largest Korean population—approximately 2 million at present—with most being second- or third-generation Koreans.[12] Culturally and politically, Koreans in China have had more contact with North Korea than with South Korea (they had no contact with the latter until the easing of the cold war in the 1980s). In China, the host country has contributed more in the form of ideological guidelines for the production of music than it has to the musical product itself. These guidelines, put forward by Mao Zedong in 1942, characterize the relationship between music and politics—a relationship that has been ongoing since the time of Confucius.[13]

As a minority with limited opportunities for social advancement in a highly regimented society, the Koreans in China have used music, especially Western classical music, as an avenue to success and advancement. Because skill is the prime qualification in music, they have been able to use their professional talents as a path to advancement, overcoming the handicap of minority status in a country where the ethnic Han majority usually has all the advantages.

The Yanbian Arts School of the Yanbian Korean Autonomous Region in Jilin province, formerly called Manchuria, is the only institution in China that offers training in Korean music and dance. Although admission to it is still highly competitive, the Korean music program is becoming smaller every year because of the lack of Korean musical resources and the limited job opportunities. The school has an insufficient variety and quantity of North Korean instruments and repertoires to accommodate the range of its students.

Music was not a "must" for early Korean immigrants to China, whose primary motive was to escape the poverty and political suppression of the northern part of the Korean peninsula in the late 19th century. Therefore, the main Korean musical legacy in China consists of the folk songs brought by the early immigrants. Korean musicians in Yanbian felt that this was an inadequate basis for public concerts, and so they eventually began borrowing new compositions and modified instruments from the North Koreans and Chinese.

At present, Korean music in China is similar to that of North Korea. Since the end of the Cultural Revolution, though, Koreans in

---

[12] The ensuing information on Korean music in China is drawn from Byong Won Lee, "Musical Identity and Acculturation in the Yanbian Korean Autonomous Region of the People's Republic of China," *Papers of the 5th International Conference on Korean Studies* (Songnam: Academy of Korean Studies, 1988), Vol. 2, pp. 3–25.

[13] See Mao Tse-tung, "Talks."

China have gained more access to the musical materials of South Korea through unofficial channels. For example, "humanitarian family visits" and workshops held by South Korean musician-tourists for Korean musicians in the Yanbian region have provided opportunities to introduce a greater variety of traditional genres and styles, including many traditional instruments and popular songs from South Korea. Nevertheless, most of the South Korean traditional and contemporary musical repertoires were banned from public presentation in China until the establishment of diplomatic relations between China and South Korea in August 1992. Since then, Koreans in China have shown an active interest in discovering the old musical traditions that are still alive in South Korea. The introduction of traditional Korean music to the Koreans in Yanbian will likely continue as China opens up to the outside world.

Recent so-called Korean music in China is thus a synthesis of the old and new sounds of South Korea with the new sounds of North Korea. It uses modernized instruments obtained from China and North Korea in accordance with China's controlled modernization of music. Many of the ideologically embedded repertoires from North Korea have been abandoned. This music lacks a clear national character, and the perception of "Korean music" held by the Koreans in China is different from that of both South Koreans and North Koreans.

Koreans in China have retained their ethnic identity through music and have used music as an effective means for social advancement and recognition. Social developments in China will undoubtedly bring about new changes in the concept, content, and practice of Korean music there. The resulting culture will most likely differ significantly not only from the musical cultures of the Korean peninsula but also from those found among the Korean minorities in major enclaves like Los Angeles, Osaka, and Tashkent.

Japan

At present, there are approximately 700,000 first- and second-generation Koreans living in Japan. Since 1955, Korean communities in Japan have been split into two politico-ideological factions: the Chae'ilbon Taehanmin'guk Koryomindan (*Mindan*), the pro-South Korean faction, and the Chae'ilbon Chosonin Ch'ongyonhaphoe (*Choch'ongnyon*), the pro–North Korean faction. The *Choch'ongnyon* has a more tightly controlled organization and is more secretive in handling its activities. Nearly 40 years of factional division have resulted in the compartmentalization and polarization of musical practice and other aspects of Korean life in Japan.

Choch'ongnyon schools take a systematic and aggressive approach toward educating their members about North Korean music. They use North Korean textbooks for their music classes, and many of their music teachers have received training in North Korea. The Kumgangsan Kamudan (Diamond Mountain Music and Dance Troupe), based in Tokyo, is the main performing troupe of the North Korean faction. Its orchestra combines Western and modified Korean instruments from North Korea, and its repertoire consists of modern arrangements of folk songs and new compositions from North Korea. Every elementary, middle, and high school associated with the North Korean faction has a miniature version of the Kumgangsan Kamudan.

Because of the deep-rooted hostility between the *Choch'ongnyon* and South Korea, *Choch'ongnyon*-affiliated music organizations usually do not include South Korea's traditional music or contemporary songs in their repertoires. Some exceptions do exist, however. These groups make sure to include one popular South Korean protest song of the 1960s and 1970s, "Ach'im Isul" (Morning Dew), in their public concerts. Also, even staunch *Choch'ongnyon* members, ironically, prefer to sing popular songs from South Korea and Japan at *karaoke* bars; the singing of North Korean songs there is extremely rare.

The organization of the *Mindan* is loose compared to that of the *Choch'ongnyon*. There are fewer schools supervised by the *Mindan*. Its music curriculum is not as nationalistic and ideology-embedded as that of its counterpart, but rather is similar to the curriculum of South Korean schools, which is dominated by contemporary Korean and Western art songs and Western theory. There is no *Mindan*-sponsored resident performing troupe in Japan. Finally, unlike Korean musical organizations in China, which perform some of their host country's repertoire in formal concerts, the Korean factions in Japan rarely include Japan's traditional and contemporary music in their concerts.

The United States

Koreans in the United States present a different case in that most arrived from South Korea recently, beginning in the 1960s. Survival through free but tough competition, the usual lifestyle of immigrants in a capitalist socioeconomic system, contrasts with the "iron rice bowl" or guaranteed lifetime support of the socialist Chinese. The establishment of financial security and advancement in their respective occupations have been the most pressing concerns of Koreans in the United States, and adaptation and assimilation to the host country's culture and value system have thus taken precedence over concern with their cultural roots in the mother country. Also, many Korean Americans have not experienced or are oblivious to the cultural renaissance that has been taking place in South Korea since the mid-1970s.

At present, there are dozens of immigrant musicians and dancers living in major metropolitan areas. They have formed semiprofessional organizations of Korean music and dance modeled after those in South Korea. Korean music brought to North America by immigrants has not yet gone through the process of assimilation and acculturation, however. The instruments used and repertoires performed are identical to those of South Korea, revealing a continuity with the tradition as it is preserved there at the present time.

Koreans take great pride in their musical tradition. It presents a marvelous variety of rhythms, expressions, and instrumental adaptations that reflect the social and historical circumstances of their civilization. From the excitement of farmers' bands and the enthralling narratives of *p'ansori* singers to the stylized formality of court orchestras, Korea's musical past invites appreciation and study. Contemporary Korean music also offers a case study of Koreans' ability to learn from abroad and adapt foreign ideas, all the while enriching their own tradition.

The events of the 20th century have presented the world of Korean music with formidable challenges. The cultural divergence that accompanied national division in the 1940s has meant different directions for North and South Korean music as well. The social circumstances of life in South Korea have permitted a wide popularization of traditional music and an inundation of Japanese and Western popular music, while in the North the state has forced evolution along a different path, creating new and still-unique expressions. It remains to be seen whether the North and South Koreans will agree on a definition of "traditional" Korean music if and when the peninsula is reunited; yet the different adaptations in South and North Korea, as well as in Korean communities abroad, are signs of a sustained vitality in the Korean musical tradition.

Appendix 1

The basic drumming pattern of the *chungmori changdan* ("moderately rushed rhythmic pattern") in live performance.

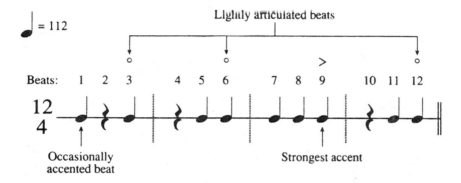

The diagram above illustrates a 12-beat folk-music rhythmic cycle. The cycle is divided into four groupings of triples, in which the loudest accent always falls on the ninth beat (or the third beat of the third triple group). The first beat is accented once in a while, but not as regularly as the ninth beat. The third, sixth, and twelfth beats are given a shuffling articulation that makes them sound slightly shorter than the rest of the beats.

Appendix 2

One cycle of the *ch'ilch'ae* rhythm from "Uddhari-poongmul," on the LP disc entitled *Samul-nori: Drums and Voices of Korea* (Nonesuch 72093-1), side 2, band 2. The diagram illustrates the transcription of the third cycle played on the *kkwaenggwari* (high-pitched gong), which begins approximately four minutes after the start of band 2.

Thirty-six beat cycle:

= 152

36:    2 1 2   2 1 2   2 1 2   1 2 1 2   2 1 2   2 2 1   2 1 2

The *ch'ilch'ae* ("seven strokes") is probably the longest rhythmic cycle in Korean music. The term *ch'ilch'ae* is derived from the seven subdivisions of the cycle, which are often punctuated by the large gong called *ching*. The subdivisions are of two types: duple plus triple (2+3), and triple plus triple (3+3).

7
The Korean American Community

Eui-Young Yu

Nearly 1 million Korean Americans live in the United States today.[1] Some are descendants of the first wave of labor immigrants, who arrived in Hawaii at the turn of the century. Others constitute the second wave, who came during and after the Korean War (1950–53) as wives of American servicemen, war orphans, and students. Most Korean Americans, however, have come to the United States since 1965, both as new immigrants and as relatives of those who came earlier.

Their reasons for coming to the United States are not hard to understand. In the 1970s and 1980s, many came to escape Korea's authoritarian political and social order. Others came in search of better lives for themselves and their children, with dreams of freedom, justice, and prosperity. Many worked 14 hours a day, seven days a week, to realize their dreams, going for years without vacations. Naturally there were problems: coming from a monocultural, monoracial environment, Korean immigrants had to learn a new language, new customs, and new ways of living in a multilingual, multicultural, and multiracial environment. As a racial/ethnic minority, they were subjected to overt and covert forms of prejudice, stereotyping, and discrimination. Slowly but steadily, however, they made progress. They settled in run-down sections of inner cities and turned them into booming commercial districts. They built Koreatowns, established churches, started businesses, bought homes, and put their children through college. Their work ethic and faith in their adopted country as a land of opportunity helped them to move ahead.

---

[1] The 1990 U.S. Census counted 798,843 Koreans in the United States as of April 1, 1990. The number of Korean immigrants who arrived here between April 1, 1990, and April 1, 1993, is estimated at about 100,000. If we add to these the natural increase (births minus deaths) during the three-year period, the present number can safely be put at between 950,000 and 1 million.

The faith of Korean Americans in the United States was shattered, however, by their experiences in the riots that occurred in Los Angeles between April 29 and May 2, 1992. The three days of violence in South Central Los Angeles following the verdict in the first Rodney King trial are now referred to in the Korean political lexicon as "Sa-I-Ku" ("4/29," or "April 29"). On that Wednesday afternoon, when the news broke that the jury had acquitted the white police officers whom the entire nation had seen on videotape brutally beating the African American motorist Rodney King, rioting erupted at the intersection of Florence and Normandie avenues and then spread quickly along the Western, Normandie, and Vermont avenue corridors as angry crowds beat up motorists, ignited fires, and looted stores. By nightfall, the violence had reached Koreatown and Hollywood.

Over these four days, the older Korean American immigrants of Los Angeles saw much of their generation's work destroyed. Approximately 2,300 Korean-owned businesses were looted, burned, or otherwise destroyed. The total damage to Korean businesses in the area was estimated at $400 million, or about half of the estimated $800 million total loss caused by the riots in Los Angeles County.[2] But even more serious was the impact of the riots on the psyche of the Korean community. Feelings of frustration, anger, betrayal, loneliness, and bewilderment still overwhelm Korean Americans. Many now question the idealism and hope that have sustained them in their new country. The future of the Korean American community is in limbo. Koreans are a resilient people, and they will certainly recover their hopes and dreams, but the wounds will take a long time to heal and will inevitably leave scars. The year 1992 will thus be remembered as a turning point for the Korean American community.

Immigration Patterns

The history of Korean Americans has been shaped by political and economic conditions in the United States and in Korea, racial dynamics in the United States, and the immigrants' own characteristics. The first Korean Americans were the 7,000 workers recruited as plantation laborers for the sugarcane fields of Hawaii between January 1903 and July 1907. They were brought in to offset the labor shortage created when the Chinese exclusion acts passed by Congress became applicable to Hawaii in 1898 and waves of anti-Japanese sentiment discour-

---

[2] *Korea Times* (Los Angeles English edition), January 6, 1993, p. 1.

aged Japanese immigration.[3] Before the 1924 immigration law revision barred the door to Koreans as well, the Korean laborers in Hawaii had managed to bring in approximately 1,100 Korean "picture brides."[4] These women were often better educated than their men, and they energized the small Korean American community. They led their families from the farms of Hawaii into the city of Honolulu, and then to California, participating in church activities and contributing to the independence movement aimed at freeing their homeland from Japanese colonial rule (1910–45).

A few Korean students also came to the United States around the turn of the century. Between 1899 and 1909, 64 students arrived, followed by a total of 541 political exiles who came by way of China or Europe without passports between 1910 and 1924, after Japan annexed Korea; 289 additional Korean students came to the United States on Japanese passports between 1921 and 1940. Many of these exiles and students found ways to stay in the United States and became leaders of the pre–World War II Korean American community.[5]

The early Korean immigrants were forced to live with open discrimination. A powerful coalition of Americans—members of labor unions, radicals on both ends of the political spectrum, and even intellectuals—opposed Asian immigration. The lives of the early Korean Americans were limited not only by immigration laws, which separated them from their families, but also by such explicitly anti-Asian laws as California's Anti-Miscegenation Law (1901), which prohibited their intermarriage with whites, and its Alien Land Law (1913), which prevented them from owning land. These conditions posed serious obstacles to their socioeconomic mobility. They were barred from decent residential neighborhoods, white schools, government employment, and even the teaching professions. Some settled on the fringes of Chinatowns or Japantowns. Many lived as migrant farm workers. Because of anti-miscegenation laws and the male-female ratio of ten to one, many of the original Korean immigrants re-

---

[3] For a detailed political and economic analysis of the early Korean immigration to Hawaii and a discussion of Chinese and Japanese immigration issues of the time, see Wayne Patterson, *The Korean Frontier in America: Immigration to Hawaii, 1896–1910* (Honolulu: University of Hawaii Press, 1988).

[4] Because most Korean immigrant laborers were unable to afford a trip home, pictures were exchanged between prospective spouses; women brought to Hawaii through such arrangements were called picture brides.

[5] See Warren Kim, *Koreans in America* (Seoul: Po Chin Chai, 1971), pp. 23–26; Won Moo Hurh and Kwang Chung Kim, *Korean Immigrants in America: A Structural Analysis of Ethnic Confinement and Adhesive Adaptation* (Rutherford, N.J.: Fairleigh Dickinson University Press, 1984), p. 49; and Bong-Youn Choy, *Koreans in America* (Chicago: Nelson-Hall, 1979), pp. 107–109.

mained single throughout their lives, resulting in a minimal growth in the Korean American population. As recently as 1950, the estimated number of Koreans in the United States was no more than 17,000, concentrated mainly in Hawaii and California.

Though their numbers were small before World War II, the early Korean Americans maintained an active community, sustained by a common dream of independence for their homeland from the Japanese. Their community centers were Christian churches, organized first in Honolulu (1903), then in Los Angeles (1904), San Francisco (1905), Oakland (1914), Reedley (1919), New York (1923), and Chicago (1924).[6] Other nonchurch organizations such as the Kungminhoe, Hungsadan, and Tongjihoe were also founded to advance community interests, and these became centers of social, educational, and patriotic activity.[7] Legendary leaders of the independence movement, such as Syngman Rhee and An Ch'ang-ho, drew support from these organizations.

At the end of World War II, however, the Korean American community began to disintegrate. An Ch'ang-ho, founder of the Hungsadan, had died in 1938. Many Korean Americans hurried home to an independent fatherland; among them was Syngman Rhee, who became South Korea's first president in 1948. Without Japan as a common enemy, the Korean American community lost much of its cohesion. By the 1950s only a few Korean churches remained, in Honolulu, San Francisco, and Los Angeles, their members aging and their children and grandchildren dispersed into the mainstream of American life.

American intervention in the Korean War triggered the second wave of Korean immigration: wives of American servicemen, war orphans, and students. Between 1951 and 1964, approximately 6,500 brides, 6,300 adopted children, and 6,000 students came to this country.[8] Whereas the prewar immigrants had been predominantly male, the Korean War–era immigrants were predominantly female, the ratio being 1 male to 3.5 females. The males were students, for the most part, and many of them stayed in the United States after completing their studies. And while the war brides and adopted children were taken into American families, the Korean students provided new life and leadership for the Korean American community.

These three groups—wives of American servicemen, adopted children, and students—have continued to be significant components of

---

[6] Bong-Youn Choy, *Koreans in America*, pp. 258–59.

[7] Ibid., pp. 141–66. See also Eui-Young Yu, "Korean Communities in America: Past, Present, and Future," *Amerasia Journal*, Vol. 10, no. 2 (1983), pp. 23–51.

[8] Won Moo Hurh and Kwang Chung Kim, *Korean Immigrants*, pp. 49–50, and Warren Kim, *Koreans in America*, p. 26.

Korean immigration to the United States. The number of Koreans who have immigrated to this country as adopted children or brides of Americans since the Korean War has now passed 100,000 in each category.[9] The 6,150 children who came to the United States from Korea in 1987 constituted 59 percent of the total adopted from abroad in that year.[10] The number has been declining since 1989 due to sentiment in Korea against foreign adoptions, but it is still significant.[11]

As a by-product of the American civil rights movement of the 1950s and 1960s, U.S. immigration laws underwent substantial change. In 1965 the quota system that had limited Asian immigration was abolished. As a result, Koreans were able to immigrate to the United States in families for the first time, and the Korean students-turned-professionals were able to apply for permanent residence and, in many cases, citizenship. These new citizens, along with the Korean wives of American servicemen, began petitioning for permission for their siblings, parents, or spouses to immigrate. Since 1970, therefore, close relatives of permanent residents or citizens have become the main category of Korean immigrants.

Korean Immigrants to the United States, 1946–1990

Year	Number
1946–50	107
1951–55	581
1956–60	6,182
1961–65	10,179
1966–70	25,618
1971–75	112,493
1976–80	159,463
1981–85	166,021
1986–90	172,851

Source: Adapted from Herbert Barringer, Robert W. Gardner, and Michael J. Levin, *Asians and Pacific Islanders in the United States* (New York: Russell Sage Foundation, 1993), pp. 24–26, Table 2.1. Statistics from the U.S. Immigration and Naturalization Service.

---

[9] Daniel Booduck Lee, "Marital Adjustment Between Korean Women and American Servicemen," in *Koreans in America: Dreams and Realities*, ed. Hyung-chan Kim and Eun Ho Lee (Seoul: Institute of Korean Studies, 1990), p. 102.

[10] *New York Times*, April 21, 1988.

[11] The Korean government plans to stop the overseas adoption program by 1996, and the number of children adopted by foreign families is declining accordingly. It was 4,191 in 1989, 2,962 in 1990, and 2,197 in 1991. See *Chung'ang Ilbo* (Seoul edition), May 5, 1992, p. 2.

Throughout most of this process, the rate of immigration has accelerated, putting Korea in the top five countries of origin of immigrants to the United States since 1975. The annual number of Korean immigrants rose from 2,139 in 1965 to 9,314 in 1970, 28,362 in 1972, and 30,803 in 1976. Between 1980 and 1990 the annual number hovered above 32,000, reaching a peak of 35,849 in 1987 and then beginning to decline.[12] In 1991 the number of Korean immigrants was 26,518, the lowest number since 1972.[13] The result over the last 20 years has been a more-than-tenfold increase in the ethnic Korean population in the United States, from 70,000 in 1970, to 355,000 in 1980, to 800,000 in 1990, according to statistics from the U.S. Census Bureau. This number nearly surpasses that of the Japanese American population.[14]

Koreans, meanwhile, have been quicker than other Asian Americans to disperse themselves across the United States. Chinese Americans are largely concentrated in California and New York, and Japanese Americans are mostly concentrated in Hawaii and California. Though Koreans continue to have their largest concentration—44 percent—in the West, the 1990 census found that 23 percent were in the Northeast, 19 percent in the South, and 14 percent in the Midwest. By state, California had the largest number of Koreans, 259,941 (33%), New York was second with 95,648 (12%), and Illinois was third with 41,506 (5%). Among cities, Los Angeles had the largest number of Koreans, 72,970, followed by New York with 69,718 and Chicago with 13,867.

The scattered residential distribution pattern is also evident in local areas. The 1990 U.S. Census counted 201,159 Koreans in Southern California—fully a quarter of the national population of Korean Americans. They are scattered in six county areas: 145,431 in Los Angeles County, 35,919 in Orange County, 6,722 in San Diego County, 6,289 in San Bernardino County, 3,877 in Riverside County, and 2,921 in Ventura County. The highest population density of Koreans is in Koreatown, an area where Korean shops and businesses are concentrated, but only one-fifth of the Koreans in Southern California live in

---

[12] Insook Han Park et al., *Korean Immigrants and U.S. Immigration Policy: A Predeparture Perspective* (Honolulu: Papers of the East-West Population Institute No. 114, 1990), p. 8.

[13] U.S. Immigration and Naturalization Service, annual reports and statistical yearbooks (various years). It is expected that the number of Korean immigrants will increase again starting in 1992, due to the changes in the 1991 immigration law, which substantially increased the occupational preference category. As of March 1992, 118,000 Koreans were waiting for immigration visas in Seoul. See *Chung'ang Ilbo* (Los Angeles edition), December 4, 1992, p. 1.

[14] The 1990 U.S. Census counted 847,562 Japanese Americans. The number of Japanese immigrants averages about 4,000 a year.

Koreatown; in fact, most residents of Koreatown are Hispanic.[15] This pattern contrasts with that of the Chinese Americans in Southern California, who are concentrated in the San Gabriel Valley between Monterey Park and Chino Hills.

The Korea that produced today's Korean American immigrants is entirely different from the one the early immigrants left at the turn of the century. Since the Korean War, Korea has maintained close economic and security relations with the United States. Today, even after the disintegration of the Soviet Union, nearly 40,000 U.S. troops are stationed in Korea. Recent Korean immigrants are already familiar with the workings of the U.S. political and economic systems.

Korea has become a highly urbanized and rapidly industrializing country. Throughout the 1970s and 1980s it recorded one of the world's highest economic growth rates. Literacy is virtually universal, and almost everyone completes at least nine years of formal education. Koreans, therefore, are one of the best educated immigrant groups coming to the United States. Many of them have a college education and urban work experience. U.S. Census statistics show that college graduation rates for Korean Americans are twice as high as the U.S. average.[16] A *Los Angeles Times* poll of 750 Koreans conducted in February and March of 1992 reveals that 49 percent of the respondents have completed at least four years of college.

People often ask why so many highly educated Koreans continue to immigrate to this country despite the sustained high economic performance of their home country. Indeed, the large-scale immigration of Koreans to the United States took place between 1970 and 1990, when Korea was experiencing rapid economic growth. The sacrifices endured by Korean immigrants in leaving suggest the degree to which they expected fulfillment in the United States, for they left behind networks of friends and relatives, a familiar culture and language, and a comfortingly monocultural environment. They also decided to come to the United States knowing that they would be saddled with the status of a cultural and ethnic minority and would confront racism, a language barrier, and social and cultural alienation from the American mainstream. And still they came. Their overriding reasons were, and continue to be, reunion with loved ones, opportunities for employment and education, and a basic yearning for freedom: many

---

[15] Eui-Young Yu, "Koreatown in Los Angeles: Emergence of a New Inner-City Ethnic Community," *Bulletin of the Population and Development Studies Center*, Vol. 14 (Seoul: Seoul National University, 1985), p. 37.

[16] U.S. Bureau of the Census, *1980 Census of Population*, PC 80-1-C1. U.S. Summary, tables 161–62.

Koreans want to be free of the strict authoritarian order, rigid male dominance, and seemingly incurable personalism, nepotism, and regionalism that are so deeply rooted in the Korean social structure. Thus, the Korean American community contains a disproportionate number of people who earlier escaped the communist dictatorship in North Korea, as well as women escaping the traditional limits placed on their lives.[17]

Their high levels of education and strong idealism motivate Korean Americans to work hard and advance. They sacrifice their leisure time, vacations, and sometimes even their health in the struggle to move up the socioeconomic ladder. They adopt self-reliant strategies and utilize their own ethnic resources in order to realize their dreams. And they have been partly successful. A 1992 *Los Angeles Times* poll found that more than one-third of the Korean families in Los Angeles County were making annual incomes of over $40,000, and 74 percent were satisfied with the way their lives were going.[18] A survey of 292 Koreans in Southern California in 1989 revealed a median annual household income of $41,730.[19] The 1990 U.S. Census showed that a full-time Asian American worker earned an annual salary of $30,027 in 1989—18 percent lower than the $36,468 for white Americans, but much higher than the $21,423 for Hispanics and $26,898 for African Americans.[20]

The Community Today

The Korean American community can be broken down into three generational categories. The first is the *il-se* (first generation), composed of those who came to the United States as adults. The second is the *il-jom-o-se* (the one-point-five, or one-and-a-half, generation,

---

[17] The author was codirector of a 1981 survey of 301 Koreans in Los Angeles and Orange counties that found that more than 20 percent were of North Korean origin, even though all had migrated to the United States from South Korea.

The ratio for Korean immigrants between ages 20 and 29 is one man per two women. U.S. Census statistics reveal that about one-third of currently married Korean women are married to non-Koreans. Eui-Young Yu, "Korean-American Women: Demographic Profiles and Family Roles," in *Korean Women in Transition at Home and Abroad*, ed. Eui-Young Yu and Earl H. Phillips (Los Angeles: Center for Korean American and Korean Studies, California State University, Los Angeles, 1987), p. 188.

[18] Karl Schoenberger, "Moving Between Two Worlds," *Los Angeles Times*, July 12, 1992, p. A24.

[19] Eui-Young Yu, *Korean Community Profile: Life and Consumer Patterns* (Los Angeles: Korea Times/Hankook Ilbo, 1990), p. 18.

[20] Shawn Hubler and Stuart Silverstein, "Schooling Doesn't Close Minority Earning Gap," *Los Angeles Times*, January 10, 1993, p. A16.

born in Korea but raised in the United States),[21] and the third is the *i-se* (the American-born second generation). The *il-se* speak Korean and tend to think and behave like Koreans. The *il-jom-o-se* and *i-se* speak English and tend to think and behave like Americans. All Korean churches and community organizations are defined on the basis of the language they use, for the Korean-speaking adults and their English-speaking children lead separate lives and socialize in different orbits.

The 1992 *Los Angeles Times* poll found that 53 percent of respondents use Korean as their primary language, and in fact Korean-language maintenance is not difficult in the Los Angeles area. At any time during the day or night, *il-se* Koreans can tune into one of many Korean TV channels and radio stations. Serialized TV dramas transmitted daily from Seoul have become favorite evening pastimes for the immigrants. Korean churches and community centers further reinforce Korean-language use, and workers in Korean businesses speak Korean to each other. Indeed, from dawn to dusk it is quite possible to use not one word of English. Moreover, the political interests of the *il-se* immigrants remain distinctly Korea-oriented, even though most of them acquire U.S. citizenship as soon as they can meet the five-year residency requirement. Korean presidential and National Assembly elections generate as much interest and excitement in Los Angeles as they do in Seoul. Politicians in Korea also tend to view the Korean American community as a part of their own constituency, half-seriously referring to Los Angeles as Nasong-gu (Los Angeles District), a constituency of So'ul-shi (Seoul City).

Unlike their elders, however, most of the second generation and a great majority of the one-and-a-half generation speak English exclusively and show little interest in Korean politics. The author's own 1991–92 survey of 203 Koreans of high school and college age in Los Angeles, Washington, D.C., and Vancouver finds that they mostly speak English, a fact that creates distance between themselves and their elders. And yet, despite the different language-use patterns and levels of assimilation, in many respects the Korean American community holds together across generational lines. The sense of belonging created by family ties, common goals, and common ethnic identity is a powerful force for social cohesion.

---

[21] For a detailed discussion of the one-and-a-half generation, see Won Moo Hurh, "The '1.5 Generation': A Paragon of Korean-American Pluralism," *Korean Culture* (Spring 1990), pp. 21–31.

Family: Generational and Gender Issues

About 80 percent of Korean American families are nuclear families made up of adult couples with young children.[22] According to the 1980 U.S. Census, the percentage of children under age 18 living with both parents was 89.4 percent for Korean Americans, 82.9 percent for white Americans, and 45.4 percent for African Americans.[23] A 1989 survey taken by the author in Los Angeles reveals that 14 percent of Korean American families have grandparents living with or near them. The grandparents care for the grandchildren while their children are at work.[24] Korean parents make enormous sacrifices to provide their children with a good education, and most Korean children understand their parents' plight and try to live up to their expectations. As a result, many Korean children excel in school.

The language and culture gap between generations, however, plagues the Korean American family. Language use is the most conspicuous difference. Communication, though not especially difficult between parents and very young children, who usually can speak simple household Korean, becomes a problem when the children enter school. School-age Korean children quickly realize that they are different from others. Many parents find that their children rebel violently against going back to school after classmates make fun of them for being Korean. After they start school, therefore, most Korean American children begin the difficult and painful process of redefining their ethnic, cultural, and individual identity.

As they grow, the children often turn against their Korean ethnicity, hating their own looks and other markers of their cultural identity. The process of rebellion, self-redefinition, and eventual self-acceptance is long and convoluted, and inevitably some children fall through the cracks into a delinquent subculture.

Because of this process of rejection and redefinition, Korean American children begin to lose their Korean-language proficiency rapidly after they start school. Without English skills, however, parents lose their primary means of communication with their children. Many immigrant families are forced to live without effective parent-child communication, a vital part of stable emotional and intellectual development.

When the children reach college age, many express regret that their Korean-language proficiency is limited and begin to attach significance

---

[22] Eui-Young Yu, *Korean Community Profile*.

[23] Herbert Barringer, Robert W. Gardner, and Michael J. Levin, *Asians and Pacific Islanders in the United States* (New York: Russell Sage Foundation, 1993), pp. 145–46.

[24] Eui-Young Yu, *Korean Community Profile*, p. 25.

to the Korean culture and heritage. Meanwhile, however, their parents have done their best to provide them with an education that has sped their assimilation into the mainstream of the Eurocentric United States. This approach has provided younger Koreans with the cultural qualities and skills needed in order to assimilate; yet it has failed to affirm their Korean heritage and identity, consciousness of which is desirable if the Korean American child is to grow into a confident adult. By the college years, young Koreans want to keep at least a part of their Korean tradition, but by then many parents have given up teaching them even the rudiments of Korean identity.

Korean American children cannot expect to learn anything about Korea in the U.S. school system because educational materials rarely mention Korea and the teachers themselves do not know much about the country. In the Korean community's church and *Han'gul* (Korean writing) schools, the children acquire a level of Korean-language proficiency that is usually limited to the Korean alphabet and a simple vocabulary. Thus, for better or for worse, the home is the primary language-learning environment, though it may not be a good place to practice Korean because parents, especially fathers, who come from a Confucian culture, are unaccustomed to engaging their children in in-depth discussions. Their conversations are usually confined to simple directives typical of the hierarchical family order prevailing in Confucian culture.

Korean American parents and children approach life in the United States in entirely different ways. The parents already have a strong positive self-identity, since their own upbringing was in Korea, where they were part of an established culture. Most adult Koreans are proud of being Korean. Thus, they have the confidence and will to overcome the handicap of being a cultural and ethnic minority, and the courage and self-esteem necessary to venture into new territory despite their deficiencies in the English language.

Younger Koreans, however, are growing up in a minority culture. Second-generation Korean Americans generally lack the feeling of mastery over their environment that their parents possess. The adults had community leaders, teachers, and other role models who were fellow Koreans. But their Korean American children have leaders, teachers, neighbors, and role models who are usually not Korean. Under the circumstances, they have difficulty developing pride and confidence in their ethnic heritage.

Second-generation Korean Americans struggle constantly to discover and define themselves. They often find that they are not accepted as American by the mainstream population. For example, American-born Koreans are constantly asked about their national origin—"Where are you from?"—despite the fact that some of their families have lived in this country for generations. Nor are younger Koreans assimilated into the Korean community. American-born Koreans often feel alienated in Koreatown, Korean churches, and Korean community organizations because of insufficient fluency in adult-level Korean language. The resulting lack of a "positive self-identity" is one of the most serious problems younger-generation Koreans face in this country, and it can lead to a sense of alienation, helplessness, and despair. They are like flowers trying to grow in the shade.

While the first generation's social networking is largely confined to fellow Koreans, second-generation Koreans move beyond the boundaries of their parents' social world. The second generation and the one-and-a-half generation tend to create two social environments for themselves, one with fellow Koreans and one with non-Koreans. Interracial marriage is an increasing phenomenon among *i-se* Korean Americans.

Another important difference between adult and younger Koreans is the degree of hierarchy and male dominance in the lifestyle and value system. Adult Koreans tend to have hierarchical, authoritarian, and patriarchal relationships. Younger Koreans do not relate to these values, and this is a primary source of conflict in the Korean American family.

An assault on traditional Korean male dominance is also carried out by the women of the community. Korean immigrant women tend to get involved in both outside work and community activities.[25] There seems to be little change in the attitudes of *il-se* men toward women: they continue to insist on patriarchal authority within the family and relegate household tasks to the women in the family regardless of whether they also work outside the home.[26] The average Korean American woman therefore performs two full-time jobs, one outside and the other inside the home. Women are also active in church committees, *Han'gul* schools, social service centers, and literary circles, as well as in journalism.[27] Their participation and influence have been strong in younger-generation Los Angeles organizations such as the Korean Youth and Community Center (KYCC), Korean American Co-

---

[25] Eui-Young Yu, "Occupation and Work Patterns of Korean Immigrants in Los Angeles," in *Koreans in Los Angeles: Prospects and Promises*, ed. Eui-Young Yu, Earl H. Phillips, and Eun Sik Yang (Los Angeles: Koryo Research Institute and the Center for Korean-American and Korean Studies, California State University, Los Angeles, 1982), pp. 49–73.

[26] Won Moo Hurh and Kwang Chung Kim, *Korean Immigrants*, pp. 122–28.

[27] Eui-Young Yu, "The Activities of Women in Southern California Korean Community Organizations," in *Korean Women in Transition*, pp. 275–97.

alition (KAC), and Women's Organization Reaching Koreans (WORK). As Korean American women have increased both their economic power and their feminist consciousness, they have begun to challenge the traditional male order. Although the Korean male ego has hardly diminished, Korean immigrant women no longer meekly obey and accept subordination. Some resort to divorce, some marry out of the Korean American community, and some stay single in order to pursue professional careers.

Korean immigrant men, on the other hand, already feel beleaguered by circumstance. They face the language barrier and discrimination outside the home and are frustrated by the underutilization of their education and occupational skills. The erosion of their traditional authority over children and spouses makes them feel even more helpless, and the accumulated anger often explodes in the context of their relationships with their wives and children. The traditional authoritarian and male-dominant values of Korea and the egalitarian ideals of U.S. society have not yet been constructively synthesized within the Korean American family.

Community Organizations

As Ilsoo Kim points out, the Korean American community is basically an associational one.[28] Koreans are united in an intricate network of clubs, business associations, churches, and news media and maintain a socially insulated but comfortable life. Communities are organized locally. There are no active national *il-se* organizations, except for two Korean business guilds: the Korean American Grocers Organization (KAGRO) and the Korean Dry Cleaning and Laundry Association.

In the Los Angeles Korean community, there are more than 150 associations, 600 Christian churches, 17 Buddhist temples, 32 newspapers, 4 television stations, and 4 radio stations.[29] In addition, there are hundreds of high school and college alumni associations. These ethnic resources provide the bases for social and business networking.

The structure and processes of *il-se* associations exhibit characteristics that are typical of Korean tradition: they tend to be leader-centered, status-oriented, hierarchical, and male-dominated, not unlike the organizations of other Asian American communities at comparable stages in their development. Members often are the edu-

---

[28] Ilsoo Kim, *New Urban Immigrants: The Korean Community in New York* (Princeton: Princeton University Press, 1981), p. 208.

[29] *1991–92 Korean Business Directory*, published by the *Korea Times*, Los Angeles.

cated elite of Korea and have leadership experience; they know how to organize the community by providing information, mobilizing resources, and helping those in need.

Unlike earlier Asian communities, clan- or region-based associations are rare. The Honam Hyang'uhoe (an association of people from the Cholla provinces) may be the only region-of-origin-based association active in Southern California. School ties play the most important part in the social and business lives of the Korean immigrants. Alumni associations are notable for the year-end parties they give. The bond formed by attending school together makes for tight networks of business contacts. The rotating credit associations called *kye*, which pool funds to finance members' business ventures, college expenses, and weddings, are often organized through high school or college alumni networks. This is not to say, however, that the *il-se* community is not honeycombed with factions. The resultant friction reduces their organizational effectiveness, as when rival factions engage in expensive lawsuits over who is to become *hoejang* (chairman).

Because *il-se* Koreans are predominantly recent immigrants, most community and church activities are geared toward their needs. Lately, however, younger-generation organizations in Los Angeles such as KYCC, KAC, and WORK have become active in bridging the gap between first- and second-generation Korean Americans and between the Korean American community and the mainstream. Younger-generation organizations have emerged as the leading social service and advocacy organizations in the Southern California Korean community. The Sixth Korean American Students Conference (KASCON), the major national organization of young Koreans, was held in Chicago in the spring of 1992 and drew more than 700 participants from all over the country.

Churches

Since the earliest days of the Korean American community, Christian churches have been the focal point of communal interaction, serving a variety of social, economic, and psychological functions.[30] Recent surveys show that about 65 percent of Korean Americans attend Protestant churches regularly, and an additional 10 percent attend Catholic churches.[31] For many Koreans, church is the principal

---

[30] Ilsoo Kim, *New Urban Immigrants*, p. 191.

[31] Based on the author's 1989 survey of 292 Koreans in Los Angeles, which revealed that Presbyterians constitute 64 percent of Korean Protestants. See Eui-Young Yu, *Korean Community Profile*, pp. 26–27. A 1992 *Los Angeles Times* poll of 750 Koreans reported that 71 percent belong to Korean churches.

place of social activity. They make friends at church gatherings, exchange information on jobs, businesses, social service benefits, and schooling, and form the close support network necessary to cope with the conditions of immigrant life. *Kye* credit associations are often organized among church members.

The church is vital to the Korean immigrant community as a place to regain the status lost after leaving Korea. The position of an elder in the church carries with it authority and prestige. Indeed, church politics often revolve around individuals vying for these positions.[32] But more important, churches provide spiritual, emotional, and psychological comfort.

As an ethnic institution, the church also reaffirms the traditional norms and values of the immigrants, thus tending to strengthen ethnic solidarity—and isolation from the mainstream. The language of the Korean church is Korean. Children learn Korean hymns and traditional songs and dances, and many Korean churches maintain *Han'gul* education programs, the so-called Saturday schools.

The Korean American community may therefore be termed a church community. Korean churches go to great lengths to recruit members, expand buildings, and even send missionaries overseas. Yet Korean churches, with few exceptions, have not reached out to meet the diverse needs of their extended community: Korean children and adolescents, as well as those Koreans isolated from their fellow Koreans (primarily, present and former wives of U.S. servicemen and adopted children in American homes). The Korean churches, like other Korean organizations, remain *il-se*-oriented, concerned mainly with the needs of the immigrant generation.

I-se children do not respond to the authoritarian air of the *il-se* ministers and elders. Their parents keep them attending Korean church into their adolescent years, but few of them continue after high school. Recently, the number of *i-se* churches and of English services in *il-se* churches has increased. But there is little prospect that the younger generation will inherit their parents' churchgoing lifestyle.

The Media

Most Korean immigrants depend on their community media as their primary source of entertainment, information, and education. According to the author's 1989 survey, 16 percent of Koreans watch

---

[32] Eui-Hang Shin and Hyung Park, "An Analysis of Causes of Schisms in Ethnic Churches: The Case of Korean-American Churches," paper presented at the first conference of the Korean American University Professors Association, held in Atlanta, Georgia, October 2–4, 1987.

primarily Korean television programs, 24 percent watch mainly English programs, and 60 percent watch Korean and English programs about equally.[33] Korean newspapers and television serials are major sources of pleasure for the majority of elderly Koreans and other adults who have no other means of recreation.

Korean newspapers and magazines and television and radio stations define issues and build consensus, thus constituting the principal mechanism that integrates the community.[34] As enforcers of community norms and priorities, they have helped accomplish major community projects, such as fund-raising for the April 29, 1992, Los Angeles riot victims, planning the annual Korean parade in Koreatown, organizing letter-writing campaigns on community issues, and arranging political rallies. They sponsor the community's artistic and literary events, compile and record the community's history, and document and preserve information about major issues, life experiences, and community happenings. Korean newspapers give Korean American writers an outlet to publish their essays, short stories, poems, novels, life histories, documentaries, research reports, and opinions.

Although the community media have grown in quantity as well as in quality, they continue to have problems. For example, small merchants are badgered for advertising. People tend to comply with these demands for fear of losing face through negative reporting about them. In addition, fierce competition among the various stations and publications has often served to divide the community. The quality of the reporting remains in need of improvement as well. In-depth investigative reports are rare. Some of the cartoons, gossip, and advertisements lack taste, style, and even basic decency.

Most of the newspapers—the *Han'guk Ilbo*, the *Chung'ang Ilbo*, and the *Choson Ilbo*—are versions of Seoul's major newspapers.[35] Camera-ready editions are transmitted from Seoul via satellite to their subsidiaries in the major cities of the United States. The American subsidiaries then add local news and deliver the papers to subscribers. The newspapers, therefore, are basically Korean papers with home-country perspectives. The English-language weekly edition of the *Korea Times* published in Los Angeles, however, maintains an independent editorial policy. Though its parent paper is published daily in

---

[33] Eui-Young Yu, *Korean Community Profile*, p. 121.

[34] Ilsoo Kim, *New Urban Immigrants*, p. 262.

[35] The *Han'guk Ilbo* (Hankook Ilbo) and the *Chung'ang Ilbo* (Joong-ang Ilbo) are the major newspapers serving Korean immigrants all over the United States. In addition, the *Choson Ilbo* (Chosun Ilbo) covers the East Coast and Midwest and the *Segye Ilbo* covers the New York area.

Seoul by the Han'guk Ilbo Company, the Los Angeles weekly's staff members are mostly American-born second generationers, and their newspaper is decidedly a product of the immigrant community, focusing on Korean American issues and representing Korean American viewpoints.

Work

Many Koreans in the United States support themselves by running small businesses. Surveys conducted in Los Angeles, Chicago, New York, and Atlanta confirm that about one-third of Korean immigrant householders own their own businesses, about one-fifth are in profes sional work, and the rest have other salaried jobs.[36] A typical pattern in the 1970s was for a newly arrived family to start a small business after a few years of work on assembly lines or with maintenance companies. Nowadays, many start businesses shortly after arrival because they already have money, thanks to the strong economy and the liberalization of foreign exchange laws in Korea. Each emigrant family is legally allowed to leave Korea with up to US$200,000.[37]

Because of the heavy reliance on ethnic networking, Koreans tend to concentrate in certain lines of business, such as dry cleaning, grocery and liquor, fast food, and photo processing. In Southern California, Koreans own 45 percent of the liquor stores, 46 percent of the small grocery markets, and 45 percent of the one-hour photo shops.[38] Dry cleaning is the business in which Koreans are most concentrated. Nationally, there are approximately 10,000 Korean-owned dry-cleaning businesses, 20 percent of the national total. In Southern California, Koreans own 2,000 of the 3,000 dry cleaning shops.[39] In downtown Los Angeles, Koreans own a majority of the clothing, electronic, and variety retail outlets.

Why do Koreans concentrate on small businesses? Profitability is one obvious reason. But a more important reason may be the feeling of autonomy that comes from having control over one's own work environment. Downward mobility and the consequent erosion of self-

---

[36] Pyong Gap Min, "Problems of Korean Immigrant Entrepreneurs," paper presented at the annual meeting of the Association for Asian Studies, San Francisco, March 26, 1988, p. 2; Eui-Young Yu, "Korean Communities," pp. 23–35; Won Moo Hurh and Kwang Chung Kim, *Korean Immigrants*, p. 226. The *Los Angeles Times* poll was reported in Karl Schoenberger, "Moving Between Two Worlds."

[37] *Chung'ang Ilbo*, March 20, 1988.

[38] *Chung'ang Ilbo*, April 30, 1992, p. II-1.

[39] Interview with Poong San Park, president of the Korean Dry Cleaning and Laundry Association for 1989–90, January 23, 1993.

esteem are a serious problem for many Korean immigrants, whose self-esteem depends largely upon their occupation.[40] A majority of Korean immigrants have college degrees and held respected jobs before moving to the United States. Language difficulties and an unfamiliarity with American culture prevent them from finding jobs commensurate with their education and work experience. They then have to choose between working in a safe but less rewarding job environment and operating their own business in a risky and difficult environment. Many immigrants opt for entrepreneurship, which brings autonomy and status.

Not all Korean businesses are located in poor multiethnic neighborhoods. Like the residential communities, Korean businesses tend to be scattered over wide areas. They are found in suburbs as well as in inner cities. And their customers are not primarily Korean. According to the author's 1989 Los Angeles survey, Koreans are a major clientele for only 22 percent of Korean businesses. Whites constitute a majority of the customers for 48 percent, while Hispanics and blacks are a major clientele for 17 percent and 10 percent of the businesses respectively.[41]

Korean businesses located in the inner city are vulnerable to oppression from both above and below in the race/class hierarchy.[42] In Los Angeles, Korean-owned liquor stores and grocery markets in the black-majority South Central area and Korean contractors in the downtown garment district are caught in this middleman minority position. Their relationships with their neighbors have not always been smooth.

Koreatown

Significance

Koreatown in Los Angeles is a geographical manifestation of the ethnic networking that has been a major survival strategy for Korean immigrants in their new country.[43] It is located about five miles west

[40] Harold L. Sheppard, "The Potential Role of Behavioral Science in the Solution of the 'Older Worker Problem,' " *American Behavioral Scientist*, Vol. 14, no. 1 (September–October 1970), pp. 71–80.

[41] Eui-Young Yu, *Korean Community Profile*, pp. 9–10.

[42] Edna Bonacich and Tae Hwan Jung, "A Portrait of Korean Small Business in Los Angeles: 1977," in *Koreans in Los Angeles*, pp. 75–98.

[43] Ivan Light, "Asian Enterprise in America: Chinese, Japanese, and Koreans in Small Business," in *Self-Help in Urban America: Patterns of Minority Business Enterprise*, ed. Scott Cummings (New York: Kenikat Press, 1980), pp. 33–57.

of City Hall and takes up several scores of blocks in five zip code areas, bordered by Pico, Crenshaw, and Beverly boulevards and Western and Hoover avenues.

Koreans began to open businesses in the area in the early 1970s, and have since turned this run-down area into a booming commercial center boasting numerous banks, hotels, shopping malls, and supermarkets. As of 1988, Koreans owned 42 percent of the commercial lots, 40 percent of the office buildings, and 41 percent of the shopping centers in Koreatown.[44] By 1992, these figures all exceeded 50 percent. The eight Korean-owned full-service banks there reported 1992 deposits of nearly $1.1 billion.[45]

Koreatown is a symbolic center for all Korean Americans, providing a sense of community, identity, and pride. Koreans from all over Southern California frequent Koreatown to shop, relax, and conduct business. When Koreans get homesick, they go to Koreatown. The *Los Angeles Times* poll taken just before the 1992 riots revealed that 79 percent of Los Angeles Koreans personally regard Koreatown as an important business, cultural, and social center. Major *il-se* and *i-se* organizations such as the Korean Federation, Korean Chamber of Commerce, KYCC, and KAC are located in Koreatown. The KYCC, with its $1.8 million annual budget and more than 50 staff members, coordinates a variety of community services such as family counseling, youth business development, relief services, and race relations improvement programs. Koreatown tearooms, cafes, nightclubs, and *karaoke* music halls (*noraebang*) are where Koreans negotiate business deals, vent stress, and make friends and enemies. Fund-raising parties for community organizations are thrown in Koreatown hotels and restaurants, and musical performances, art exhibits, poetry readings, and plays take place in the theaters and galleries of Koreatown. And Koreatown is the Korean American community's media headquarters.

Tension and Crime

In the houses and apartments abutting the business area of Koreatown dwell elderly Koreans and newly arrived immigrants who live side by side with, yet apart from, Hispanics, Central and South American refugees, other Asian immigrants, and African Americans. According to the 1990 U.S. Census, Hispanics constitute 67.9 percent of the population in Koreatown, and Asians, a majority of whom are Koreans, make up 26.5 percent. The census also reveals that 30.8 per-

---

[44] *Han'guk Ilbo*, April 9, 1988.
[45] Ibid. January 6, 1993, p. A7.

cent of Koreatown residents live below the poverty line, a percentage second only to that of South Central Los Angeles. The squalor in Koreatown has caused tension between Koreans, who own a majority of the shops, and non-Koreans, who are their customers. It has not helped that each racial group maintains a separate social world, with interactions confined largely to business transactions. The tensions that stem from the racial and socioeconomic diversity of its residents have led to an increase in violence and crime in Koreatown.[46]

Illegal drug trafficking, its dealers and clients mostly non-Koreans, runs rampant in the backstreets of Koreatown.[47] The two divisions (Rampart and Wilshire) of the Los Angeles Police Department covering Koreatown reported a total of more than 26,000 crimes in 1992, including 188 murders, 7,810 robberies, 8,154 burglaries, and 9,871 car thefts. Among the 18 divisions of the L.A.P.D., the Rampart and Wilshire divisions had the highest and second highest number of crime reports.[48] Such high instances of crime inevitably mean that hardly a day passes without the perpetration of a serious crime against Koreans (mostly by non-Koreans).

To be sure, Koreans are conspicuous and sometimes seem insensitive to the concerns of others. Heedless of non-Koreans (and their own English-speaking *i-se* generation), Korean merchants stubbornly display signs in *Han'gul*, often without paying attention to aesthetics or bothering to provide English translations. The ubiquitous *Han'gul* signs in Koreatown are reminiscent of Korea, but they also send a message to non-Koreans that they are not welcome.

Koreatown thus far has expanded naturally, pursuing profit without a master plan. There has never been any systematic attempt to establish a dialogue or a cooperative relationship between its merchants and local residents. Koreatown has now reached the stage where it needs careful planning and coordination. It cannot maintain a healthy existence as long as it remains an insulated ethnic business entity alienated socially from its non-Korean neighbors. It can survive only if it evolves into a community of people—including non-Koreans—who live and work there together.

The Sa-I-Ku (April 29) Riots and Their Effects on the Community

The Los Angeles riots of April 1992, like the Watts riots of 1965, were partly the result of accumulated anger and frustration in black

---

[46] Edna Bonacich and Tae Hwan Jung, "A Portrait of Korean Small Business in Los Angeles: 1977," in *Koreans in Los Angeles*, pp. 75–98.

[47] *Chung'ang Ilbo*, October 14, 1992.

[48] Ibid., January 12, 1993.

America. But blacks were not the only ones who attacked Korean businesses in Koreatown and South Central Los Angeles. When it appeared that the city's law enforcement system had been incapacitated, people of various ethnic backgrounds rapidly turned into mobs. Korean stores were hit hard primarily because so many of them were situated in the poor and multiethnic (Hispanic and African American) areas of the city. But the historical origins of the attacks must also be confronted.

Relationships between Korean American merchants and their African American neighbors have not been smooth since the first Korean immigrants opened their businesses in the inner city in the early 1970s. Similar conflicts have occurred and escalated over the years in New York, Chicago, Atlanta, and Philadelphia as well. Korean-black relations rapidly deteriorated after a series of organized boycotts of Korean-owned markets in New York, Chicago, and Atlanta in 1990. The March 1991 killing in South Central Los Angeles of Latasha Harlins, a 16-year-old African American, by Korean merchant Soon Ja Du worsened the already deteriorating relationship. Bitterness escalated when Soon Ja Du was released on probation. Therefore, location, history, and ethnic tension caused Korean shops to become prime targets during the Los Angeles riots.

The aftermath of the riot destruction, coupled with the lingering recession, is seriously undermining the economic base of the entire Korean American community in Southern California. More than a year after the event, many businesses remain in ruins. According to a comprehensive survey of 1,150 victims conducted by the Korean American Inter-Agency Council, only 28 percent of businesses damaged or destroyed in the riots had reopened by February 1993.[49] Many of those who lost businesses during the riots have also lost their homes because they could not make mortgage payments. Social workers predict that many more Koreans will join the ranks of the homeless.

The riots also affected the *nouveau riche* upper crust of the Korean American community. Korean doctors, lawyers, accountants, and real estate tycoons are losing fortunes because their regular clients can no longer afford their services and their commercial and residential buildings are half empty. The California Korea Exchange Bank reported for the first time since its establishment in 1974 a $4 million loss for the year 1992, with deposits and lending having declined 21 and 29 percent respectively since 1991.[50] Community leaders have been heard to wonder aloud whether Koreatown can survive the crisis.

---

[49] *Han'guk Ilbo*, March 6, 1993.
[50] *Han'guk Ilbo*, January 6, 1993, p. A6.

During the process of rebuilding, an interethnic conflict has emerged between Korean liquor store owners and local residents. During the riots, about 180 Korean-owned liquor stores were razed. In order to rebuild, the law requires that they go through a mandatory public hearing. The community of South Central Los Angeles is organizing a campaign to oppose the rebuilding of the liquor stores, claiming that there are too many of them and that they are a principal source of crime.[51] Since the riots, racial politics have prevailed in City Hall, and the needs of Koreans have been neglected. Very few of the city's rebuilding efforts have been directed to help Korean victims. Because Koreans are neglected by police, they continue to be easy prey for gunmen. During the month of February 1993 alone, four Korean American merchants were killed in Los Angeles by non-Korean gunmen during robberies. And the fear and despair are not confined to Koreatown in Los Angeles. In the same month, a young Korean American scientist was killed in a church parking lot in Philadelphia. The gunmen took his car and abandoned his baby 10 blocks away.[52] As the number of dead and wounded mounts, Korean Americans once again feel abandoned by their city governments and police.

The 1992 riots did accelerate the process of decentralization, and Korean supermarkets and shopping malls have opened up in the suburban communities of Garden Grove, Hacienda Heights, Torrance, and the San Fernando Valley. Some merchants are going out of state in order to look for a safer location. Many people contemplate moving back to Korea. But countless others will have to start all over again with street vending, housecleaning, or gardening. Many doubt that Koreatown will ever recover its previous spirit of enthusiasm and hope.

It is interesting to note, given the informal status of L.A.'s Koreatown as an extension of Seoul, that prominent Korean politicians made a point of visiting Los Angeles during and immediately after the Sa-I-Ku riots, and some even demanded that the U.S. government pay reparations to the Korean riot victims. Because the Korean Federation of Los Angeles was paralyzed at the time due to infighting, the Korean consulate assumed a leading role in crisis management for the Korean community when the riots erupted. Although its intentions

---

[51] See Richard Reyes Fruto, "Compensation Unlikely for Liquor Store Owners," *Korea Times Weekly* (Los Angeles English edition), September 28, 1992, p. 1, and Somini Sengupta, "Incentives to Close Liquor Stores Sought," *Los Angeles Times*, October 15, 1992, pp. B1, B8.

[52] Compiled from the Los Angeles editions of the *Han'guk Ilbo* and *Chung'ang Ilbo*. On February 28, 1993, about 70 Korean Americans held a candlelight vigil at City Hall calling for an end to the senseless killings.

were noble, the Korean government inadvertently created an impression in the mainstream community that the suffering of the Korean immigrants could be taken care of by the Koreans themselves and by the government in Seoul. In this respect, therefore, the victimization of Koreans during the riots may actually have segregated them further from their American environment, leaving them more isolated and far more helpless than before.

One lesson Koreans drew from the Sa-I-Ku riots was that they need to enhance their political power by becoming more involved in local politics. This has meant shifting their political orientation from Korea to the United States. In 1992, seven Korean Americans were elected as representatives to city councils and statehouses in California, Oregon, Washington, Hawaii, and Florida. And the first Korean congressman, Jay Changjoon Kim, was elected to the U.S. House of Representatives.[53]

The Sa-I-Ku riots also brought out potential strengths of the Korean American community. When Koreatown was hit, more than 30,000 Korean Americans spontaneously assembled in Ardmore Park at the center of Koreatown for a demonstration of solidarity and appeal for peace. Responding to the suggestion of a caller on a Korean radio talk show, they gathered there from all over Southern California. They represented all walks of life and all three generations of immigrants. It was the largest political rally ever held by any Asian American group.[54] Hundreds of volunteers, first-generation immigrants, and American-born second-generation accountants, lawyers, merchants, professors, ministers, and victims themselves rushed to the several emergency relief centers set up spontaneously in Koreatown to help riot victims. The Korean media became instant command centers providing vital information to help Korean business owners and residents. Korean Americans organized relief committees and raised more than $5.5 million locally to help the riot victims. The Koreatown Emergency Relief Committee (KERC) representing community groups and churches was set up at the *Han'guk Ilbo*, which raised over $3 million to help riot victims. The Emergency Measures Task Force was also established at the Korean consulate in Los Angeles in order to co-

---

[53] The seven local representatives are Mimi Kim McAndrews, state assemblywoman, Florida; Julie Sa, city councilwoman, Fullerton, California; Martha Choe, city councilwoman, Seattle; Jackie Young, state assemblywoman, Hawaii; Ho Young Chung, city councilman, Garden Grove, California; Yong Keun Im, state senator, Oregon; Ho Bum Shin, state assemblyman, Washington. U.S. congressman Kim is a Korean-born Republican representing California's 41st Congressional District, near Los Angeles.

[54] Irene Chang and Greg Krikorian, "30,000 Show Support in Koreatown March," *Los Angeles Times*, May 3, 1992, p. A3.

ordinate relief efforts by various groups. The food centers set up in Koreatown by Korean Americans were still in operation almost a year later, helping Korean and non-Korean victims. The relatively small and politically naive Korean American community can be proud of what it did to help manage the crisis created by the riots.

Conclusion

The new wave of Korean immigrants began landing at Los Angeles International Airport in the late 1960s, a time when Jewish stores and corporate chains were withdrawing from South Central Los Angeles after the 1965 Watts riots had shattered their commercial prospects in the area. Korean immigrants filled the vacuum. They bought markets and liquor stores there, unaware of the events that had led to the creation of the vacuum or that they were placing themselves between two starkly contrasting and often hostile worlds: the poverty-stricken inner city and the affluent suburbs. Korean Americans, as newcomers to the scene, did not realize the potential danger of doing business in the poverty-stricken inner cities. It has taken the Sa-I-Ku riots to teach them that they cannot afford to be viewed as outsiders. The events of spring 1992 demonstrated that Korean Americans must build healthy relationships with other minority communities, organize themselves better, combat media stereotyping, and fight racism—their own as well as that of others. In this respect the riots were a "wake-up call," and Korean Americans are heeding it.

The 1992 riots also demonstrated that the first-generation *il-se* leaders no longer speak for the community, and provided a turning point for a transfer of leadership to the younger generation. For the past 25 years, the immigrant *il-se* generation has maintained the "Korean" community in the United States. But the *i-se*, the children born here to the early cohort of immigrants, are reaching adulthood in large numbers, and they are ready to work with the first generation to build a truly Korean American community. Over the next 20 years, this community will need to muster all its resources in an attempt to secure a place for Koreans in American life. A critical aspect of this effort will be the assumption of a constructive role in the improvement of race relations.

Koreans are resilient. They will recover what they lost during the riots and rebuild Koreatown and the Korean community. The new Korean community will be an integral part of the total community, which will benefit not only Koreans but also their non-Korean neighbors.

8
Korean Perceptions of America

Kim Kyong-Dong

As a child, I used to accompany my mother when she was summoned to help with housekeeping chores at the homes of American missionaries. At the time it was customary for ladies of our community to pitch in and help their neighbors, and since our family were loyal members of the congregation at the Presbyterian church, it was an honor for my mother to be "chosen" to assist at the missionaries' homes.

The Presbyterian mission compound was located on a hilltop in one of the most beautiful areas of town, well isolated from the rest of our fairly small provincial city. Except when they had services or church-related business, the missionaries pretty much kept to themselves, rarely leaving the compound to mingle with the Korean people. Because of the social distance they maintained, there was an aura of mystique about them that kindled strong curiosity and even a sense of awe in Korean children like myself. For this reason, whenever my mother went to the compound I made her take me with her. I was much impressed by the grandeur and exotic style of the homes and the beauty of their large gardens. At the same time, I could not help feeling a chill in my heart when they treated us like servants, in spite of the friendly attitude they generally showed us.

The Pacific War forced the American missionaries to leave Korea, only to be replaced by new faces when the war was over. During the war years the Japanese filled the minds of young Koreans with caricatures of Franklin D. Roosevelt and Winston Churchill, leaders of the cruel enemy that we were being forced to fight. One day in the fall of 1945, however, liberators, not the enemy, marched into our town. This was the first time we had ever encountered so many Americans. Truckloads of tanned GIs jammed the main street of our city. Even now, almost 50 years later, my mind retains the ghastly picture of a friend of mine lying dead in the street, still bleeding horribly after having been run over by one of the enormous GMC trucks. It was an accident, of course, but the gruesome image of that moment, together with the strange smell of gasoline engines, keeps coming back to nauseate me. We were ambivalent, though, about the GIs. After all, they were also the ones who protected us from various communicable diseases by spraying us with DDT powder each day on our way to school.

The Korean War (1950–53) brought plenty of GIs, both black and white, who liked to toss us pieces of chewing gum or chocolate and sometimes could be seen fooling around with "not so decent" Korean girls. It was an American GI and then a missionary who taught me spoken English and then the Bible when I was in high school and college. In the early sixties, when I first landed in the United States as a graduate student, I declared to myself, "This must be paradise on earth!" And I told my American friends, "You people have acquired the true art of living." Later on, in the seventies, though, while teaching at an American university in the South, I learned about "latent discrimination" as well as "equal opportunity."

Back home in Korea in the late seventies, I started out being active in the American Studies Association of Korea. By the eighties, however, I was skipping meetings and nearly dropped out of the association altogether. In the political climate of the time, many Korean intellectuals had grown wary of being openly identified as pro-American. The radical student movement was denouncing "American imperialists" for scheming to colonize the Korean peninsula, and students in the social sciences and humanities were being attracted en masse to Marxist theories of political economy.

One day, one of my graduate students came to confide in me. He wanted to go to the United States for advanced study, he said, but he did not dare apply for admission to an American university because his classmates had sworn that anyone leaving the country before finishing the master's program was to be stigmatized as a traitor to the nation. Things are different now. That student is finishing a Ph.D. program at the University of Wisconsin, and with the dampening of Korean student radicalism that has followed the demise of communism in Eastern Europe, I now have many opportunities to write letters of recommendation for students who want to go to the United States for further study.

Historical Overview

The words "ambivalence" or "love-hate complex" may best describe the underlying feelings Koreans have had toward America and

Americans over the past century or so of the Korea-U.S. relationship. The direction and intensity of the emotions have fluctuated with the changing historical circumstances surrounding the two nations. The century-old relationship between Korea and the United States has been characterized by ignorance, misunderstanding, betrayal, intervention, aid, disharmony, cooperation, and competition. The Koreans have looked upon the United States with intense feelings of unabashed gratitude, love, and trust, alternating with a sense of betrayal, heartbreak, disillusionment, and even hatred. They have come to see Americans as people who smile a lot but put their own interests first. As the status of Korea vis-à-vis the United States has improved, Koreans have become better able to view Korean-American relations with objectivity and detachment.

Early Encounters and Initial Ambivalence

Although Western ideas and practices had started seeping into Korea as early as the 16th century, the seclusion policy fostered by the orthodox Neo-Confucian state of the Choson dynasty (1392–1910) was relatively successful in keeping the country sealed as a "hermit nation" well into the mid-19th century. This China-centered worldview was based on the ancient cosmological notion that heaven was round and the earth was flat. According to this theory, any nations outside the realm of China were to be regarded as "barbarians."[1]

This concept of the outside world was to erode gradually with the introduction of maps and other books containing information on the West, mainly by French Catholic missionaries who dared risk their lives to cross the border from China into Korea. Although these new ideas stimulated certain Korean intellectuals to form a more pragmatic and scientific worldview, it was not sufficiently attractive to arouse active curiosity about the West, let alone the United States. In the meantime, the ruling elite of Korea went on to oppose Catholicism for its heretical beliefs and practices and to persecute its adherents, several times going so far as to massacre a number of Korean Catholics

---

[1] Koh Byong-ik, "A Century of Korean-American Relations," in *Reflections on a Century of United States–Korea Relations*, Conference Papers, Academy of Korean Studies and The Wilson Center (Lanham, Md.: University Press of America, 1983), pp. 28–40; Lee Kwang-rin, "Early Relations: Conflicting Images," in *Reflections on a Century of United States–Korea Relations*, pp. 65–79; and Lew Young-ick, "The Shufeldt Treaty and Early Korean-American Interaction, 1882–1905," in *After One Hundred Years: Continuity and Change in Korean-American Relations*, ed. Han Sung-joo (Seoul: Asiatic Research Center, Korea University, 1982), pp. 3–27.

and their foreign missionary teachers. It was against this backdrop that the Koreans first came into contact with Americans in the 1860s.

By then, Westerners had been shipwrecked or had approached the coastline in search of trade numerous times, always without success. Americans had been among them, speaking a strange language and being regarded as harmless by the uncomprehending Koreans. The wave of renewed American interest in East Asia that followed the Civil War, however, led to bloody encounters with the Koreans that were destined to worsen the Koreans' opinions of barbarians from the West.[2] The first such incident, in 1866, involved an American schooner, the *General Sherman*, which ignored Korean warnings and sailed up the Taedong River to Pyongyang to trade goods and disseminate the gospel, only to be attacked and burned by angry Koreans when it ran aground on a sandbar near Pyongyang. The intrusion, regardless of the nationality of the ship, was regarded as an outrageous threat. Unpardonable, too, was the incident later in 1866 wherein a group of Westerners, including an American, tried to pillage a royal tomb, violating all human—but especially Confucian—norms. Then in 1871 came America's "Little War with the Heathen,"[3] when the U.S. Navy's Asiatic Squadron approached Kanghwa Island at the mouth of the Han River and was confronted by detachments of Korean riflemen. The squadron was searching for clues to the fate of the *General Sherman*, but its manner of approaching the Korean royal capital sparked a bloody skirmish that left many dead and wounded, especially on the Korean side, which could not match the superior military hardware of the U.S. Marines.

Despite these bad omens, however, there were certain reform-minded Korean intellectuals who came to hold a favorable view of the United States as compared with other "barbarians." And beginning in the 1880s, the first American legation officials and missionaries to live in Korea managed to implant a remarkably favorable image of the United States in the minds of the Korean monarch, King Kojong, and

---

[2] In addition to the works cited in note 2, this historical overview is based on the following: Lew Young-ick [Yu Yong-ik], *Han'guk kunhyondaesaron* (The Modern History of Korea), Seoul: Ilchogak, 1992; Chong Chong-uk, "Yoksajok Kwanjomeso Bon Hanmigwan'ge" (Korean-American Relations from a Historical Perspective), in *Han'gukkwa Miguk: Kwago, hyonjae, mirae* (Korea and the United States: Past, Present, and Future), ed. Koo Young-nok [Ku Yong-nok], Seoul: Pagyongsa, 1983, pp. 3–23; and Hahm Pyong-choon [Ham Pyong-ch'un], "Han'gukui Taemiinshik" (Korea's Perceptions of the United States), in *Han'gukkwa Miguk*, pp. 27–68.

[3] The phrase "Our Little War with the Heathen" appeared as a chapter title in William E. Griffis, *Corea: The Hermit Nation* (New York: Charles Scribner's Sons, 1907), p. 403.

his entourage. At the time, Korea was beginning to come under intense pressure as rival imperialist powers—notably Japan and Russia—vied for influence on the peninsula. King Kojong apparently saw in the Americans a possibility of obtaining assistance in protecting his country from imperialist encroachment, and in 1882 Korea and the United States signed a treaty establishing diplomatic relations.

American Protestant missionaries also did much to promote pro-American attitudes by their efforts to establish modern educational methods and medical facilities and training. Some had such influence at court that they became involved in Korean national affairs, suggesting American support for the Korean government that went far beyond the bounds of official U.S. policy.

Ordinary Koreans also acquired a favorable image of the United States early on through the efforts of a leading reform group called the Independence Club (Tongnip Hyophoe), led by American-educated Koreans such as Philip Jaisohn (So Chae-p'il), who was a naturalized American citizen. The Independence Club held rallies and published a newspaper in English and vernacular Korean, spreading democratic ideas and urging resistance to the contending imperialist powers. The government, too, contributed to the favorable image of the United States through the editorial policy of the palace gazette. The stereotype that was established in the minds of Korea's reform-minded officials and intellectuals can be summarized as follows:

America is a big country (with no need for territorial expansion);

America is one of the richest countries in the world (with emphasis on trade);

America gained its independence from Great Britain through a war of independence (and so acts as a champion of the weak against the strong, governed by ethics of justice and courtesy in its international relations);

America is a constitutional democratic republic, based on the principle of equality of all people;

America is a potential military power;

America is a civilized country with a highly developed educational system, scholarship, and arts;

America is a Protestant nation adhering to the principle of the separation of church and state (whereby American missionaries do not interfere with the political affairs of other nations).[4]

---

[4] Lew Young-ick, *Hanguk kunhyondaesaron* (1992), p. 155.

Of course, not all Korean perceptions and attitudes toward the United States were favorable. The more conservative Confucian elites and the more benighted masses, faced with surging imperialist encroachment, tilted away from foreign influences, and Koreans who had actually been to the United States, either as envoys or students, had more balanced views. They worried that the United States would stay aloof when Korea urgently needed its help. They were also critical of negative aspects of American society such as slavery and racial discrimination.[5]

These worries became reality in 1905, when President Theodore Roosevelt unilaterally abrogated the 1882 Korea-U.S. treaty and sided with Japan in its plans for continental expansion. The occasion was Roosevelt's mediation of the treaty ending the Russo-Japanese War, which stated that Japan had a "paramount interest" in Korea. The United States then clarified its abandonment of Korea with the Taft-Katsura Agreement, in which it agreed not to interfere with Japan's designs in Korea in exchange for Japan's promise not to interfere in the Philippines. Shortly thereafter Japan forced Korea to become a protectorate, compelling King Kojong to accept Japanese control over his country's foreign affairs—a prelude to outright colonization, which came in 1910. The United States did nothing to deter Japan from taking over in Korea, and as a result Korean attitudes toward the United States suddenly turned cool, out of disillusionment and despair.[6] The historical ambivalence of Koreans toward the United States continued throughout the 35 years of Japanese colonial rule, turning especially negative under the influence of Japanese propaganda during World War II.

Shifting Images and Attitudes Since 1945

When Japan was defeated in 1945 and American soldiers began landing on Korean soil, they were welcomed as liberators. Koreans focused on what they knew about American ideals and anticipated receiving American help in shaping Korean democracy. Many of Korea's most famous independence leaders returned from exile in the United States with American education and even advanced degrees. It

---

[5] Ibid., pp. 58–60, and Hahm, "Han'gukui Taemiinshik."

[6] It is true that the meaning of "abrogation" is disputed, with American scholars arguing that the "good offices" clause of the 1882 treaty did not necessarily imply the use of U.S. military forces to defend Korea, even if the United States had had the means or the will to do so. The point here is that the Koreans felt then and still feel that the United States could have done more than just stand by and leave Korea to be overtaken by the Japanese.

was a time when positive perceptions of the United States prevailed at all levels of Korean society.[7]

But along with the favorable sentiments there emerged a strain of nationalism that created a new postwar ambivalence about the United States. During Japan's collapse, the United States and the Soviet Union had divided Korea at the 38th parallel, occupied the two zones north and south of the line, and planned to institute a five-year "trusteeship" to govern on the Koreans' behalf—all without consulting the Koreans and on the assumption that they were unprepared to govern themselves. Koreans in both the Soviet- and American-occupied zones rose up in protest against the trusteeship idea, forcing its abandonment. For three years, from 1945 to 1948, the United States ruled South Korea while struggling to find an alternative. When talks between the United States and the Soviet Union failed to produce a plan for the reunification of Korea, the two zones hardened into separate countries, and the cold war rivals ended up sponsoring the creation of mutually hostile regimes in North and South Korea. As this process was taking shape, South Korea's American occupiers proved themselves ignorant about local matters and inept in many respects. The American mishandling of political and economic affairs in Korea, a victim of the Japanese, was especially galling when compared with the relatively enlightened and successful U.S. regime in Japan, the former aggressor.

By 1948 the United States had determined to end its occupation and turn the business of ruling over to a South Korean government—over bitter protests from Korean nationalists that such a move would mean the permanent cleavage of Korea into separate states. And once the Republic of Korea had been established in the South under the presidency of the U.S. educated Syngman Rhee, the United States withdrew its troops from the peninsula, leaving the new government impoverished and unprepared for front-line duty in the cold war. A corresponding withdrawal by the Russians from North Korea the same year had left a communist-led government in power under the Soviet-trained marshal Kim Il-sung, which was well equipped as a base for a future communist advance. Not long thereafter, the U.S. secretary of state announced that Korea and Taiwan were outside the U.S. defense line in the Far East. It has been widely claimed ever since that this statement inadvertently encouraged the North Korean

---

[7] For U.S.-Korea relations since 1945, in addition to the works cited in notes 1 and 2, see Koo Young-nok [Ku Yong-nok], "Hanmi Paengnyon: Pansongkwa Chonmang" (One Hundred Years of Korea and the United States: Retrospect and Prospect), in *Han'gukkwa Miguk*, pp. 509–33.

regime of Kim Il-sung to invade the South in June 1950, touching off the Korean War.

All these historical perceptions have contributed to the strong Korean sense of disillusionment about the United States. The result is an underlying nationalist core sentiment that adds Americans to the list of outsiders who are not to be trusted. This sentiment was expressed by a popular saying that circulated just after World War II: "Don't be fooled by the Soviets; don't trust the United States; Japan is going to rise again; so Korea beware!"

The strange American popular culture and its GI variant, which Koreans found vulgar and often shocking, poured into South Korea in the late 1940s and contributed a new dimension to the ambivalence Koreans feel toward the United States as a country of rich material life but not so decent culture. This image was reinforced by the reintroduction of huge numbers of American soldiers during the Korean War. GI behavior was offensive, ranging from a general attitude of arrogance to outright mischief—involvement with prostitutes and other criminal acts—and even to atrocities against Koreans. Though "official Korea" was reluctant to criticize the negative aspects of the American military presence, "popular Korea" often expressed its irritation out of American earshot and in print, with stories depicting "ugly Americans."

Of course the Americans were also saviors, for they not only fought with Korea against communist aggression but also provided food, clothing, and other necessities that were in critically short supply. Amid the wreckage of the war, U.S. aid virtually kept the country alive and helped it to rebuild from the ashes. The Koreans are well aware of this support and have been duly grateful to Americans for their generosity.

Moreover, in the process of industrialization since the 1960s, the United States, like Japan, has been a major source of needed capital, plant, technology, and managerial skills and also a major trading partner, essential for Korea's historic economic take-off and miraculous growth. Throughout this period, the United States has steadfastly protected South Korea from its dangerous and unpredictable foe in the North. It is no wonder that South Korea has remained a faithful U.S. ally, probably the only country in the world where the words "Yankee, Go Home!" were unheard—at least until the mid-1980s. Moreover, the United States itself has played the historic role of beacon for the Koreans. Ever since their first direct exposure to American culture, many Korean youngsters have dreamed of going to the United States, the land of opportunity, for advanced study. The United States has attracted by far the greatest number of Korean students studying abroad, and a disproportionate number of the Korean elite in the government, academe, and business are U.S.-educated.[8]

Even in Korea, though, a sentiment that might be characterized as anti-American in nature has emerged. It would be difficult to pin down the exact timing of the origin of this sentiment, but open propaganda expressing it started appearing in the early 1980s. It was based on the foundation of nationalism that surfaced during the April 1960 student upheaval that toppled the Syngman Rhee regime and was reinforced by the student protests against normalizing relations with Japan in the mid-1960s. It increased in intensity during movements opposing the increasing authoritarianism of the Park Chung-hee regime in the 1970s and was joined by anti dictatorship elements in the religious and labor communities.

As student nationalism and anti-authoritarianism were building in the 1970s, Korean intellectuals began subscribing to the ideologically charged dependency theory and Third World philosophies such as liberation theology. These ignited a form of nationalist neo-Marxism among university students. In the context of the imperialist worldview inculcated by these ideas, Korean students gradually acquired, often implicitly, a sort of anti-American ideology.[9]

Perhaps it was President Jimmy Carter's announcement and token implementation of a decision to withdraw U.S. forces from Korea that marked a turning point in contemporary attitudes toward the United States. For one thing, it immediately aroused the Korean people's hidden worry about a new American abandonment, based on the experience of the 1905 Taft-Katsura Agreement and the American renunciation of Korea's defense on the eve of the Korean War. Carter's announcement of the troop withdrawal, seemingly so careless of Ko-

---

[8] Pak Tong-so, "Miguk Kyoyugul Padun Han'gukui Elite" (The Korean Elite Educated in the United States) in *Han'gukkwa Miguk*, pp. 401–24; Kim Kyong-dong and Lee On-jook, "The U.S.-Educated among the Korean Politico-Bureaucratic Elite: An Aspect of American Socio-Cultural Influence," *American Studies*, Vol. 6, pp. 53–69; and Kim Kyong-dong and Lee On-jook, "Educational Background of the Korean Elite: The Influence of the United States and Japan," in *Dependency Issues in Korean Development: Comparative Perspectives*, ed. Kim Kyong-dong (Seoul: Seoul National University Press, 1987), pp. 434–58.

[9] Edward Taehan Chang, "Anti-Americanism and Student Movements in South Korea," in *The Korean Peninsula in the Changing World Order*, ed. Eui-Young Yu and Terry Kandal (Los Angeles: Center for Korean-American and Korean Studies, California State University, 1992), pp. 147–72; Yun Kun-shik, "Han'guke Issosoui Kubjinjui" (Radicalism in Korea), in *Han'guk chongch'i yon'gu*, Vol. 1, pp. 163–77; and Kim Kyong-dong, "Han'gukinui Chongch'iuishik" (Political Ideas and Attitudes of the Korean People), in *Ich'onnyondaerul hyanghan han'gukui sontaek* (Korea's Options for the 2000s), Seoul: Tong'a Ilbo, 1991, pp. 319–68.

rea as an important ally and trading partner, reawakened Koreans to the cold realities of international politics.

Though the Koreans' first reaction was to fear abandonment, the Carter episode brought a paradoxical phenomenon to the surface: a public debate over the whole idea of having U.S. ground forces on Korean soil. People began to assert that it was actually shameful to have foreign "occupation" forces in Korea and that their presence was blighting hope for reconciliation between North and South. This touched a nerve, given the avowed Korean yearning for reunification, and once the question was raised it contributed subtly to the gradual crystallization of something resembling anti-Americanism, not only among students but also in the general public.

But it was not until the May 1980 Kwangju incident that anti-American ideology came out into the open. An informal coalition of people opposing the Chun Doo-hwan government blamed the American military for permitting the Korean Army to massacre the unarmed citizens of Kwangju in the process of putting down anti-government demonstrations. They charged that since the Korean Army was officially part of the United Nations Command that still defends South Korea and was therefore under the control of the American general commanding the UNC, the United States had approved the redeployment of troops to commit the massacre. During the 1980s, therefore, but especially between 1985 and 1988, the student movement openly turned Marxist-Leninist (and even Kimilsungist) and engaged in what the most radical students called a revolutionary war to liberate Korea from the shackles of the imperialists, notably the United States. The series of arson attacks on United States Information Service buildings in Kwangju and Pusan and the 1985 seizure of the USIS headquarters in Seoul are to be understood in this light.[10]

Not all of the radical students' anti-American propaganda was accepted by the general populace as fact, but the students did succeed

---

[10] Kim Kyong-dong, "Han'gukinui Chongch'iuishik," and Yoo Se-hee, "The International Context of U.S.-Korean Relations: Special Focus on 'Critical Views of the United States' in Korea Since 1980," in *United States–Korea Relations*, ed. Robert A. Scalapino and Han Sung-joo (Berkeley: Institute of East Asian Studies, University of California at Berkeley, 1986), pp. 112–32. Also see Donald N. Clark, "Bitter Friendship: Understanding Anti-Americanism in South Korea," in *Korea Briefing, 1991*, ed. Donald N. Clark (Boulder: Westview Press, 1991), pp. 147–67. For the Kwangju incident and discussions of the degree of American involvement, see *The Kwangju Uprising: Shadows Over the Regime in South Korea*, ed. Donald N. Clark (Boulder: Westview Press, 1988). For the U.S. government's view of its role in the Kwangju incident, see "United States Government Statement on the Events in Kwangju, Republic of Korea, in May 1980," issued simultaneously in English and Korean by the Department of State in Washington and the U.S. Embassy in Seoul on June 19, 1989.

in reviving consciousness of the historic turnabouts in U.S. policy that had so affected Korean history, and they undoubtedly spurred a greater awareness of the need to see the United States more objectively. This shift in attitude had consequences, of which the following are two examples.

In 1988 the city of Seoul hosted the 24th Summer Olympics. This was to be an eye-opener as well as a national ego-booster for many Koreans. One country, however, was uncooperative—or so the Korean people came to believe—and that was the United States. The American media, in particular, left an unfortunate impression on ordinary Koreans during the games. In an effort, presumably, to present an objective pro-and-con picture of Korea and its people, the media exposed the soft spots of Korean society, thereby wounding Korean national pride just at the moment when Koreans felt they had restored it. In short, to the Korean people, the American media came all the way to Seoul to spoil the party.[11]

Then came Carla Hills, the U.S. trade representative, against the backdrop of several years of American trade deficit with Korea. To ordinary Koreans she represented not merely American trade interests but also American arrogance and selfishness. She was once depicted in a newspaper cartoon as a flying witch on a broomstick. Looming behind her, of course, was the giant, the United States, whose national interest must never be overridden by anyone, friend or foe, on any issue. The caricature reflected what Koreans took to be an assault on national pride and a form of betrayal.

Thus a cooling of favorable attitudes toward the United States set in, often accompanied by strong emotion. Few would characterize this as a general shift to anti-American sentiments, let alone outright anti-Americanism. In fact, the historically long-standing pro-American feelings have not completely dissipated. But what has occurred is an intensification of the old ambivalence born of a complex mix of feelings, perceptions, and experience.

Even when the radical students cried out in dead earnest, "Yankee, Go Home!", few ordinary Koreans ever took significant action against Americans on Korean soil. But the American presence in Korea has left indelible marks on Korean perceptions. Among the most striking negative images are those based on the American habit of living on

---

[11] At issue in particular was a series of two-minute spots on Korea by NBC, in which the network covered not only many positive aspects of the culture and life but also touched upon the black market, overseas adoption, excessive drinking, shantytowns, labor unrest, and the like. The important point here is that the network's "objectivity" was seen as "unfair." In addition, there were some unfortunate incidents involving individual American athletes and during the games themselves that upset the Koreans.

"compounds" well insulated from "lowly" Koreans, of toying with poor Korean girls and then abandoning them when they return home, and of hurting and even killing Koreans in violent altercations. The Korean government has done little about such felonies (largely because of legal and administrative agreements with the United States that few Koreans comprehend). This long-standing irritation has been aggravated now that the United States, a superpower, is attempting to wrest concessions from Korea in such areas as the rice market, the last bastion of Korean agriculture, and American banks with access to the financial markets of the world make windfall profits in Korea while Korean banks go through hard times.

The descriptions above constitute impressionistic sketches of the way Koreans have seen the United States and the American people over the years. These impressions are supported below with hard data.

Empirical Findings

The data presented below are mostly from attitude surveys and opinion polls conducted since the 1950s. Although Korean academics used survey techniques as early as the fifties, it was not until the eighties that they came into wide use. Most of the data summarized here, therefore, were collected in the 1980s. Caution is in order, for the surveys vary in format and questions asked, and they employ different analytical techniques.

Korean Stereotypes of Americans and the United States

One of the earliest studies dealing with Korean perceptions of the American people was conducted in 1955 by the Department of Psychology at Seoul National University. The response choices were provided by the researchers, and the respondents were asked to select from among them the words they thought were most descriptive of Americans. The college students in this study saw Americans as aggressive, practical, creative, selfish, money-oriented, and arrogant.[12]

The major characteristics of the American people mentioned by a national sample of adults in 1988 were, in order of frequency: individ-

12 Ch'a Chae-ho, "Wegugine Taehan Haksaengmit Songinui T'aedo" (The Attitudes of Students and Adults toward Foreigners), mimeographed report to the Ministry of Education, 1992, p. 26. This report contains a comprehensive review of studies concerning Korean images of foreigners, Americans being one of the most often researched groups.

ualistic, democratic, freedom-loving, selfish and calculating, scientific, rational, seeking their own national interest, looking down upon weaker nations, strong frontier spirit, open-minded, respecting individuality, order-conscious, getting along well with others, and authoritarian. In order of frequency, the features chosen by college students in the same survey were individualistic, selfish and calculating, seeking their own national interest, looking down upon weaker nations, rational, practical, materialistic, respecting individuality, strong frontier spirit, and scientific.[13] Four years later, in 1992, a survey of college students listed the following characteristics (again, in order of frequency): free-spirited, individualistic, selfish, rational, arrogant or having a superiority complex, and practical.[14]

In an earlier survey featuring questions that referred to characteristics of America's culture rather than its people, similar responses were obtained. Korean college students in 1976 mentioned frontier spirit (12.2%), pragmatism (7.8%), democracy (7.7%), autonomy (6.2%), and rationalism (5.6%) as positive ingredients of American culture, whereas epicurism or decadence (20.2%), individualism (16.1%), materialism (15.0%), family system (4.8%), and racial discrimination (2.1%) were cited as negative elements.[15] On balance, it appears that Americans continue to be seen in a positive light, with personal and cultural characteristics that Koreans admire and perhaps even envy.[16] College students, however, hold more negative stereotypes than other adults. At a symposium in the early 1980s celebrating the centennial of Korea-U.S. relations, a Korean journalist suggested a useful summary of Korean perceptions of the United States, shown in Table 1. Opinion polls reveal similar stereotypes. For example, the image of the United States as reported in a 1981 national sample included superpower (33.8%), neocolonialist (32.5%), and imperialist (26.8%),

[13] Ibid., pp. 70, 80.

[14] Ch'a Chae-ho and Ch'oe In-ch'ol, "Wegugine Taehan Taehaksaengui T'aedo, 1992" (College Students' Attitudes toward Foreigners), *Shimni kwahak* (Psychological Science), Vol. 1 (1992), p. 10.

[15] Auh Taik-sop, "Korean Perceptions of U.S.-Korean Relations," in *United States–Korea Relations*, p. 104, and Lim Hy-sop, "Acceptance of American Culture in Korea: Patterns of Cultural Contact and Korean Perception of American Culture," in *After One Hundred Years*, p. 38.

[16] At this juncture, it should be mentioned that the images of African Americans held by the Korean people are largely negative and that recent conflicts between Korean immigrants and African Americans in the United States have exacerbated negative perceptions. For more detailed information, consult Ch'a Chae-Ho and Ch'oe In'ch'ol, "Wegugine Taehan Taehaksaengui T'aedo, 1992."

TABLE 1

Positive and Negative Images of the United States

Positive Images	Negative Images
America is a big and beautiful country.	America is a country where pragmatism, materialism, and utilitarian values are dominant.
America is a land of liberty, democracy, and justice.	America as a nation of many races and diverse elements has racial unrest, and is WASP-dominated.
America is a land of opportunity.	America is a nation where morality is breaking down.
America is a wealthy nation, a leader in science and technology.	America is a country where the press is formidable.
America is a Christian nation with a Puritan work ethic.	America is a nation whose policy toward Korea has been inconsistent.

Source: Park Kwon-sang, "Korean Perceptions of America," in *Reflections on a Century of United States–Korea Relations*, pp. 134–35.

while another national survey in 1985 produced the following responses: superpower (35.0%), ally (27.0%), and democracy (17.0%).[17]

Relative Popularity of Americans and the United States

Over the years there have also been surveys asking respondents to rank foreigners according to popularity. It is interesting to note a clear pattern of change in the responses to surveys of this type. Table 2, which summarizes the results of a series of studies of college students, indicates that Americans were the best liked of 11 nationalities in the 1950s, came in second or third at least into the early 1970s, but then dropped sharply in popularity in the 1980s and remained very low in the early 1990s. (One of the 1988 surveys was of adults, and there was a noticeable discrepancy between adults and students in their ranking of Americans.)

---

[17] Yoo Se-hee, "International Context," p. 115.

TABLE 2

Ranking of Americans by Korean College Students and Adults

Year of Study	Ranking (Out of 11 nationalities)	Size of Sample
1955	1	2,000
1962	3	268
1973	2	125
1982	6	150
1985	6	302
1988	9	407
1988	4	600 (adults)
1992	8	150

Source: Ch'a Chae-ho and Ch'oe In-ch'ol, "Wegugine Taehan Taehaksaengui T'aedo, 1992," pp. 14, 17–18.

Other surveys have examined the popularity of selected countries among South Koreans. Table 3 summarizes the findings of several newspaper polls, with figures representing the percentage of respondents opting for the United States as "the country I like most." In both 1980 and 1989 the United States trailed Switzerland in second place, but it was the first choice of the Korean people even during the early and middle 1980s, with support from over one-third of the respondents.

Still another way of examining how much Koreans favor the United States is to pair it with another country. The findings summarized in Table 4 indicate that to the South Korean people, the United States is no match for North Korea, but it is a clear favorite over other countries. It is also true, however, that the percentage expressing preference for the United States seems to have diminished over time, though this may be a function of the brief span of comparison.

A comparable set of data may be mentioned here. In a national survey conducted in 1984, the percentage of respondents reporting "I like America" (69.9%) was far above that reporting "I like Japan" (22.6%) or "I like Red China" (12.5%). Moreover, further analysis indicates that the proportion of those expressing favorable attitudes toward the United States is smaller among city dwellers than among farmers, among people who are under 30 years of age than among

TABLE 3

Percent Choosing the United States as the "Country I Like Most"
(Newspaper Polls of Nationwide Samples of Adults)

Year Polls Taken	First Place Country (%)	Second Place Country (%)
1980	Switzerland (37.5)	United States (28.1)
1981	United States (60.6)	Switzerland (9.4)
1984	United States (37.3)	—
1989	Switzerland (19.3)	United States (9.3)

Sources: Choson Ilbo, March 5, 1980, pp. 22–23, for the 1980 data; *Tong'a Ilbo*, January 13, 1982, pp. 10–11, for the 1981 data; *Chung'ang Ilbo* for the 1984 data, as cited in Auh Taik-sop, "Korean Perceptions of U.S.-Korean Relations," p. 106; and *Chung'ang Ilbo*, January 1, 1990, for the 1989 data.

TABLE 4

Percent Who "Would Cheer for the U.S. Team in an Athletic Match"

Year of Survey	Against Japan	Against Russia (USSR)	Against North Korea
1986	86.5	96.5	76.6
1988	74.1	73.9	38.7
1989	83.1	78.7	27.8
1990	82.5	72.8	15.5

Sources: For the 1986 data, see Han Wan-sang, Kwon T'ae-hwan, and Hong Doo-sung, *Han'gukui chungsanch'ung* (The Middle Class in Korea), Seoul: Han'guk Ilbo, 1987; otherwise, Kwon T'ae-hwan, Han Wan-sang, and Hong Doo-sung, *Chonhwan'giui han'guksahoe: '90 kungmin uishikjosa* (Korean Society in Transition: National Attitude Survey, '90), Seoul: Population and Development Studies Center, Seoul National University, 1991.

those who are older, and among professionals than among industrial and agricultural workers.[18]

The national survey was repeated in 1989 and 1990, and the percentage of "I like America" responses came to 36.7 percent and 38.7 percent, respectively, for the two years. This was topped only by that of "I like North Korea" (43.7% and 62.5%). The United States fared better than Russia (26.3% and 35.8%) and much better than Japan

---

[18] Kim Kyong-dong, Kim Se-won, and Lee Hong-koo, "Kungminsaenghwal-gwa Taewegwan'ge Uishik" (Survey of Attitudes toward Livelihood and External Relations), *Sahoegwahakgwa chongch'aek yon'gu* (Social Science and Policy Studies), Vol. 7, no. 22 (October 1985), pp. 125–212.

(12.3% and 13.2%); yet here, too, we see a marked decline in the favorable attitude toward the United States compared to earlier years.[19]

In general, the empirical findings indicate that the United States has been a favorite nation of ordinary Korean people all along, despite a lessening of the extent of such feelings in the 1980s. The largest shifts have been among college students, whose favorable sentiments toward the United States have shown a significant decline over the years, especially in the 1980s.

One question that naturally arises when the attitudes of students are under consideration is, "Is anti-Americanism a reality, and if so, how strong is the sentiment?" Not many empirical studies have touched on this matter directly, but an interesting set of findings resulted from a 1992 survey of 782 students of Yonsei University, a relatively middle-class, conservative school founded by Christian missionaries. According to this poll, slightly more than one-quarter of respondents (26.7%) expressed anti-American attitudes, while the majority (67.8%) were ambiguous in their responses and a mere 5 percent manifested pro-American attitudes. When they were asked, "What do you think of anti-Americanism among Korean college students?" however, three-quarters of the respondents said that it was the dominant view, and only 21 percent replied that it was a minority sentiment.[20] Thus, even though a great majority of college students believe that Korean university campuses are permeated with anti-Americanism, they are not necessarily anti-American in their own orientation.

Attitudes Toward the United States as an Ally

Other findings touch upon Korean conceptions of Korea-U.S. relations. In this respect as well, the United States has been viewed in both a positive and negative light, and the negative images have tended to gain force over time.

From early on, the United States has been viewed as an ally essential to the security of Korea. As shown in Table 5, in a 1976 survey of college students, military assistance was chosen out of several re-

---

[19] Kwon T'ae-hwan, Han Wan-sang, and Hong Doo-sung, *Chonhwan'giui han'guksahoe: '89 kungmin uishikjosa* (Korean Society in Transition: National Attitude Survey, '89), Seoul: Population and Development Studies Center, Seoul National University, 1990, p. 66, for the 1989 data, and Kwon T'ae-hwan, Han Wan-sang, and Hong Doo-sung, *Chonhwan'giui han'guksahoe: '90 kungmin uishikjosa* (Korean Society in Transition: National Attitude Survey, '90), Seoul: Population and Development Studies Center, Seoul National University, 1991, p. 48, for the 1990 data.

[20] Ch'a Chae-ho, "Wegugine Taehan Haksaengmit Songinui T'aedo," pp. 24–25.

TABLE 5

Positive and Negative Aspects of Korea-U.S. Relations

Positive	Negative
U.S. military assistance during the Korean War (22.9%)	Territorial division of Korea (13.2%)
U.S. economic assistance (20.8%)	Excessive dependence of South Korea on the United States (12.8%)
Institution of a democratic system of government in South Korea (9.6%)	Weakening of traditional Korean values and culture (10.1%)
Introduction of modern science and technology (5.7%)	Materialism (9.4%)
Introduction of Western thought and ideology (3.9%)	Epicurism (6.4%)

Sources: Auh Taik-sup, "Korean Perceptions of U.S.-Korean Relations," p. 104, and Lim Hy-sop, "Acceptance of American Culture in Korea," p. 38.

sponse alternatives as the most important positive factor in Korea-U.S. relations, followed by economic aid, democratic institutions, and the introduction of modern science and technology and other Western culture.

Even in the mid-1980s, these conflicting images did not change. In a 1984 survey, America was the overwhelming choice as "a partner that plays a pivotal role in Korea's security" (84.3%), as "the country most vital to Korea's economic prosperity" (55.9%), and as "the nation that has had the greatest cultural impact on Korea" (50.7%).[21]

On the issue of U.S. troop withdrawal from Korea, a national poll taken in 1984 found that 41 percent of respondents felt U.S. forces should remain in Korea until Korea becomes militarily self-supporting, 31 percent maintained that they should stay until Korea is reunified, 24 percent replied that they must be stationed in Korea as

[21] Auh Taik-sop, "Korean Perceptions of U.S.-Korean Relations," pp. 104, 106; and Lim Hy-sop, "Acceptance of American Culture in Korea," pp. 38–39.

long as the North Korean threat of invasion persists, and only a negligible 4 percent advocated a prompt withdrawal.[22]

By 1990, though, the proportion of Koreans who believed that U.S. forces should leave had increased. According to a national survey conducted in 1990, 12 percent thought that American troops should withdraw from Korea as soon as possible, 48.2 percent advocated gradual withdrawal, 23 percent believed that the troops should stay, though their numbers could be reduced, and 15.9 percent insisted they should not leave Korea at all.[23]

Finally, one finds an interesting shift in South Korean perceptions of the U.S. posture toward Korea. In a 1984 national poll, 58 percent of respondents said they thought that the United States had benefited more from the Korea-U.S. political and diplomatic relationship than had Korea, while only 22 percent thought that Korea had been the primary beneficiary. Regarding the economic and trade relationship, too, a majority (53%) thought it was to the advantage of the United States, while 30 percent believed it was advantageous for Korea. A related finding was that Koreans in general tended to be optimistic about the possibility of a more balanced bilateral relationship in the future.[24]

In another national poll the following year, 57.7 percent of respondents thought the preceding 40 years of the Korea-U.S. relationship had been American-interest-centered, while 22.5 percent believed it had been Korean-interest-centered. The younger the respondents and the higher their standard of living, the more they were inclined to think of the political and economic relations between the two countries as "American-interest-centered."[25]

These findings compare interestingly with the response patterns of a student sample reported by the Seoul National University Student Council. The proportion of students expressing the view that the relationship has been American-interest-centered amounted to 95.0 percent, while that of those who replied it was Korean-interest-centered was a meager 2.3 percent.[26]

By 1987, however, the feeling that the United States was taking advantage of the relationship had spread to the middle and working classes. Nearly 90 percent (89.6% of middle-class and 85.6% of working-class respondents) expressed the view that the United States

---

[22] Auh Taik-sop, "Korean Perceptions of U.S.-Korean Relations," p. 106.

[23] Kwon T'ae-hwan, Han Wan-sang, and Hong Doo-sung, *Chonhwan'giui han'guksahoe: '90 Kungmin uishikjosa*, p. 49.

[24] Auh Taik-sop, "Korean Perceptions of U.S.-Korea Relations," pp. 105–106.

[25] Yoo Se-hee, "International Context," pp. 114–15.

[26] Ibid.

seeks only its own national interest even at the expense of Korea's.[27] A 1988 newspaper poll reported that 38.6 percent of those surveyed said that "America will be friendly to us only when its national interest is protected," while 31.1 percent were of the opinion that "the United States has traditionally been our ally and will be one in the future, too." Again, the younger the respondents, the more critical their views of the United States.[28]

How satisfied, then, are the South Korean people with the current Korea-U.S. relationship? In a 1981 newspaper poll, 58.1 percent said they were satisfied, 32.6 percent expressed reservations, and 9.3 percent were dissatisfied. But in a 1985 survey taken among students of Seoul National University by the Student Council, a great majority (80.9%) said that the relationship was unsatisfactory, and only 5 percent claimed to be content with it. By 1990 concern had grown in the general population, too, as 66.3 percent of a national sample of adults said that the relationship needed improvement.[29]

The Meaning of the Polling Data

The South Korean people have been grateful for the help the United States has given them in the military, economic, political, and cultural spheres. This gratitude contributed to the long-held view that the United States was a powerful country with economic, technological, and military prowess and unique religious, social, and political qualities that made it worthy of respect from the world community. Such was the mood until the early 1980s, when Koreans began to view the United States with greater objectivity.

Since that time, the image of the United States and of Korea-U.S. relations has been changing. Koreans have begun to realize that they have depended too much upon the United States, that America has been seeking to defend its own interests all along—more often than not at the expense of Korea's—and that America has corrupted "pure" Korean culture with vulgar materialism, hedonism, and individualism. Koreans have learned more about the United States and

---

[27] Han Wan-sang, Kwon T'ae-hwan, and Hong Doo-sung, *Han'gukui chungsanch'ung* (The Middle Class in Korea), Seoul: Han'guk Ilbo, 1987, p. 63.

[28] *Chung'ang Ilbo* (Seoul), June 6, 1988, as cited in Ch'a Chae-ho, "Wegugine Taehan Haksaengmit Sanginui T'aedo," pp. 27–28.

[29] For the 1981 data and the SNU student poll, *Tong'a Ilbo*, January 13, 1982, pp. 10–11, cited in Yoo Se-hee, "International Context," p. 114. For the 1990 data, Ch'oe Myong et al., *Ishipilsegirul hyanghan kungminuishik songhyang chosayon'gu* (National Survey Looking to the Twenty-First Century), Seoul: Institute of Social Sciences, Seoul National University, 1990, p. 51.

recognize, somewhat to their disappointment, that it has its share of social and moral problems.

Even though it is incorrect to characterize this shift in Korean perceptions and attitudes as a turn to anti-Americanism, one cannot help detecting increased negative feeling in the Koreans' new objectivity about the United States. This is partly the result of growing sophistication on the part of Koreans and partly of a decline in the relative economic, military, and political advantage enjoyed by the United States through most of the cold war era.

Conclusion

Any bilateral relationship is affected by a variety of factors, some of which relate to the immediate political and economic interest of each nation and others that are rooted in history, society, and culture. Such relationships are also affected by attitudes—stereotypes, perceptions, and normative judgments—on each side. These, in turn, are created and colored by interactions between the two peoples.

The relationship between Korea and the United States has been asymmetrical from the outset. In terms of tangible power, represented by modern science and technology, economic wealth, and military might, the United States has been the stronger party. With respect to intangibles, however, Korea has been proud of its traditional culture of spiritual enlightenment, regarding it as superior to Western culture. This was the Korean stance at the beginning of the relationship in the 1880s, and it has been a factor in the relationship ever since. Historical circumstances, however, yielded something unnatural: an unbalanced pattern of contact that enabled the materially more powerful side to overwhelm the other. This "tilted acculturation" has continued through the history of the Korea-U.S. relationship and had a profound but unilateral impact upon Korean society and culture.[30]

This asymmetry naturally affects the level of interest of each nation's people in the other country. And it follows that, since the American people are less interested in Korea than Koreans are in the United States, the level of knowledge about Korea among Americans is much lower than that of Koreans about the United States; as a result, the distortions on the American side are more pronounced, as is the ambivalence on the Korean side.

The Koreans, therefore, are ahead of the Americans in understanding the nature of the bilateral relationship. If the two nations wish to

---

[30] Kim Kyong-dong, *Rethinking Development: Theories and Experiences* (Seoul: Seoul National University Press, 1985).

develop a more cooperative and friendly relationship, there ought to be a much greater effort to promote mutual understanding. It may not be realistic to hope for complete symmetry between the two countries (or *any* two countries); nonetheless, whether about trade, politics, diplomacy, education, or military affairs, better information is necessary on both sides.[31]

---

[31] Kim Kyong-Dong, "Sociocultural Relations Between Korea and the United States," in *United States–Korea Relations*, pp. 1–15.

9
American Attitudes Toward Korea

Donald N. Clark

Most Americans who know Korea have encountered it as adults, and of these, the majority are members of the military who recall yearlong tours of duty on bases surrounded by walls and barbed wire. Others know Korea secondhand, through neighbors in the Korean American communities of the United States. I am one of a relative handful of Americans who have known Korea since childhood and seen it recover from the devastation of war to become one of East Asia's strongest, most viable societies.

Growing up in Seoul as the son of missionaries in the 1950s, I lived on an American compound and saw Korea at close range—albeit usually through the windows of cars or buildings. In the years just following the Korean War, Seoul was a depressed city full of terrible human suffering. On Sundays, however, my father, whose work included visiting country churches in a territory in eastern Kyonggi province, would sometimes take me in his Jeep to distant villages. A crowd would gather as we entered the village. My father, who had been born in Korea and spoke the language well, would give greetings and conduct negotiations. Invariably he would be spirited away to guest-teach the adult Sunday school class, leaving me to strike out on my own. Liberated from my father's protection and the material significance of his Jeep, I would head across the paddy dikes toward the nearest hill in search of a quiet spot in which to pass the morning. Behind me would be a host of curious village children hollering "Hello!" "Hello!" in what I took to be a mixture of friendliness and derision.[1] Eventually, all but the most determined of my pursuers

---

[1] Over time, the things shouted by pursuing children became a barometer of sorts. In the 1950s it was "Hello!" In the 1960s it was "Hello! You are a monkey!" In the 1970s, especially in some of the rougher Peace Corps assignments, the above might be accompanied by a flying rock. And in the 1980s it turned ominous with "Miguknom!" (loosely translated as "American S.O.B.!").

would fall away, and I would find myself more or less alone in the most pleasant of places: on a height overlooking a Korean farm valley on a warm May day, with nothing to do but enjoy the bucolic silence. From a distance would come the gentle mooing of an ox pulling a plow, with his master's voice gently calling "doh, doh, doh" to encourage him along. From another direction might come the rattle of a country bus, trailing a cloud of dust, or the distant striking of a tool, perhaps a hammer, or the clanging of the metal scissors used by the village candyman to cut lengths of the sweet *yot* candy so beloved by farm children. The rich aroma of manure in the fields would rise in the heat, strangely comforting in the quietness. Gusts of wind would rustle the small pine trees on the hillside, and ants would stop to inspect my shoes. Though I often dreaded "itinerating" with my father and becoming the object of "Hello"-ing, I did grow to love the serenity of spring days on hillsides in what I came to think of as my own version of Korea.

Later, as a student at Seoul Foreign High School, I made some Korean friends and began learning about "their" Korea. Our teams played their teams in basketball. I was asked to be an English-speaking "adviser" for a high school English club, and on weekends the students would take me to fascinating places to learn about Korea: not only to the palaces and museums but also to the markets where they shopped, the libraries where they did their homework, the tearooms and music halls where they killed time gossiping, and even to their homes, where there always seemed to be a feast in progress. Eating things and visiting places my mother had always warned me about, I began to appreciate Koreans as friends. It was an important lesson for an American young person brought up in an environment in which Korea could easily be mistaken for nothing more than a ruined land with poor and backward people.

Later still, on return trips to Korea as a Peace Corps volunteer, as a graduate student at a Korean university, and finally as a professor, I learned to know Korea in other ways and to feel a personal investment in U.S.-Korea relations. I have always found it regrettable that the relationship is so lopsided, with Koreans having to take such careful cognizance of the United States while Americans are so oblivious to Korea as a nation. Yet this imbalance has its logic. From the American point of view there are more important relationships: those with Canada, Mexico, the European Community, the former Soviet Union, and Israel—and that with Japan, which former U.S. ambassador Mike Mansfield once characterized as our most important bilateral relationship "bar none." Of course, it is also true that much has been changing in Korean-American relations. With a million Koreans living in the

United States, many of them U.S. citizens, many Americans now have direct knowledge of Koreans. With South Korea as America's seventh-largest trading partner, most Americans are familiar with Korean products. But these personal encounters with Korea take place here, in the United States. Korea, "over there" on the Asian mainland between China and Japan, still seems a distant and dangerous place. This aspect of Korean-American relations remains virtually unchanged.

Early American Images of Korea

In 1982 the United States and Korea marked the centennial of their first "Treaty of Peace, Amity, Commerce and Navigation." The intent of the treaty was to open Korea to Western contact, both diplomatic and commercial. Until then, Americans knew Korea as the "Hermit Kingdom," a most inhospitable place. American shipwreck victims had been tolerated for only as long as it took to deposit them at the Chinese border. American explorers and traders had been repeatedly rebuffed, and one American ship had been burned with the loss of all hands near Pyongyang in 1866. Nor had gunboat diplomacy been effective. A military engagement on Kanghwa Island in June 1871 merely had the effect of stiffening Korean resistance.[2] No foreign power was able to pierce Korea's isolation until after Japan's forcible "opening" of the country in 1876.

The 1882 U.S.-Korea treaty was part of a Korean process of reorientation, an opening to the West that was undertaken with many misgivings. Most Korean officials were wary of Westerners, and only the hardiest Americans ventured to Korea. They went for the most compelling of reasons: God and gold. Missionaries pushed the limits of Korean toleration by venturing into the hinterland to open stations, and an intrepid band of American gold entrepreneurs finagled leases on Korea's most productive mineral deposits. However, between the 1880s and the 1940s, Korea remained a little-known Asian backwater, far off the beaten track for tourists.

One reason for Korea's obscurity was its ambiguous status. Until 1895 it was claimed by China as a tributary state, somewhere between

---

[2] The *New York Herald* called the engagement "our little war with the heathen," a characterization that took on a life of its own in the literature of Korean-American relations, especially on the Korean side. Cited in Shannon McCune, "The American Image of Korea in 1882: A Bibliographical Sketch," in *U.S.-Korean Relations, 1882–1982*, ed. Tae-Hwan Kwak et al. (Seoul: Institute for Far Eastern Studies, Kyungnam University, 1982), p. 144.

vassalage and independence. Between 1895 and 1905 it was the object of contention between Russia and Japan, apparently unable to protect itself.[3] And in 1910 it became a Japanese colony and remained so until 1945, when it was "liberated" by the victorious Allies.

The century of U.S.-Korea relations therefore included approximately 40 years during which the United States had no direct relations with Korea at all. True, an American consulate-general existed in Seoul between 1905 and World War II, but it was accredited to Japan, not to Korea, and its officers recognized Japan's authority in Korea without question. During the period, U.S. immigration laws made it exceedingly difficult for Koreans—who were Japanese nationals at the time—to emigrate or study in the United States, so the flow of information about Korea was almost entirely through consular and missionary channels. The consular staff faithfully reported on conditions in Korea, contributing to what is now a bulky historical file in the National Archives. Archives of the various missionary societies that operated in Korea until World War II also contain much information about events and conditions in prewar Korea. Missionary reportage about the March First (1919) Independence Movement, for example, is extensive and insightful.[4] Much of what the missionaries wrote was for consumption by supporting churches back in the United States and was highly critical of Japanese methods in Korea. Though the effect on U.S. foreign policy was insignificant, the message does appear to have gotten through to many American Christians that Koreans wanted and deserved to be free of Japan.

The early period of American contact with Korea is also documented in a number of travel accounts and missionary books. The travel accounts, by such world-renowned explorers as Percival Lowell, A. Henry Savage-Landor, Isabella Bird Bishop, and Burton Holmes, depict a primitive land of simple, hard-working people being victimized by a medieval ruling class and a corrupt court.[5] Korea has its

---

[3] In response to the idea that the 1882 U.S.-Korea treaty somehow committed the United States to oppose Japan's creation of a protectorate in Korea in 1905, President Theodore Roosevelt remarked, "We cannot possibly interfere for the Koreans against Japan. They could not strike one blow in their own defense." Quoted in Howard K. Beale, *Theodore Roosevelt and the Rise of America to World Power* (Baltimore: The Johns Hopkins Press, 1956), p. 280.

[4] See Donald N. Clark, " 'Surely God Will Work Out Their Salvation': Protestant Missionaries in the March First Movement," *Korean Studies*, Vol. 13 (1989), pp. 42–75.

[5] Percival Lowell, *Choson, the Land of the Morning Calm* (Boston: Ticknor and Co., 1886); A. Henry Savage-Landor, *Corea, Land of the Morning Calm* (London: Heinemann, 1895); Isabella Bird Bishop, *Korea and her Neighbors* (New York: Revell, 1898); Burton Holmes, *The Burton Holmes Lectures, Vol. II: Manila, and Seoul, Capital of Korea* (Chicago: Travelogue Bureau, 1910).

charms, but it is mainly a place to be improved—that is to say, Westernized. The assumption that Korea needed improvement is a theme of all missionary writing, and although the "White Man's Burden" logic in the literature grates today, it is nonetheless an accurate representation of the American approach at the time. Books like Lillias Underwood's *Fifteen Years Among the Topknots* were dutifully read in churches across America, with discussions conducted by Sunday school teachers who had never seen Korea.[6] It is sobering to reflect on the fact that this was many Americans' only source of information on Korea for more than 50 years. And it is easy to see why, when confronted with a world crisis on the Korean peninsula in 1950, people seeking information about Korea were led into the habit of looking on it as a backward place.

When the Korean War broke out in June 1950, a Seattle reporter called a history professor at the University of Washington to ask whether Korea was an island—to which the professor answered yes, in a manner of speaking, since the Yalu and Tumen rivers originate in the same lake atop Mount Paekt'u on the Manchurian border.[7] Given the scanty information available, it seems all the more remarkable in retrospect that the American people were willing to commit such vast military and budget resources to defend one part of Korea against the other.

Images Surrounding the Korean War

Although more than 2,000 American missionaries, miners, traders, and consuls lived and worked in Korea between 1882 and 1942, when the last of the missionaries were repatriated aboard the M/V *Gripsholm,* an image of Korea did not begin to take hold in the American mind until the late 1940s, when thousands of U.S. military personnel and occupation officials were stationed in South Korea. The terms of America's encounter with Korea after 1945 were radically different from those of the earlier period. The political and military dimension

---

[6] Lillias Horton Underwood, *Fifteen Years Among the Topknots* (Boston: American Tract Society, 1904). Other examples include Horace N. Allen, *Things Korean* (New York: Revell, 1908); Annie L. A. Baird, *Daybreak in Korea* (New York: Revell, 1909); Charles Allen Clark, *First Fruits in Korea* (New York: Revell, 1921); James S. Gale, *Korean Sketches* (New York: Revell, 1898); William Elliot Griffis, *Corea: The Hermit Nation* (New York: Charles Scribner's Sons, 1907); Frederick S. Miller, *Korean Young Folks* (New York: Revell, 1936); and Horace G. Underwood, *The Call of Korea* (New York: Young People's Missionary Movement of the United States and Canada, 1908).

[7] This incident was related to the author in 1966 by Frank Williston of the University of Washington's Far Eastern and Russian Institute.

was new: the United States had suddenly gone from official disinterest to direct control of South Korea. This control, together with the fact that North Korea was inaccessible above the 38th parallel, where the main efforts had taken place in mission work and gold mining, turned the flow of information about Korea over to the U.S. government. Internal reportage resumed in the State and War departments. In the news, Korea achieved a new, composite definition: one part conquered territory, one part cold war battleground, and one part perfectible Koreans.[8]

News images have dominated the idea of "Korea" in the American mind ever since the 1940s. Foremost are images of the Korean War (1950–53). The Korean War gripped American attention, not least because it seemed to be the realization of our country's worst nightmare: a reprise of the world war that had just ended in 1945. Peace and prosperity were in danger of being snatched away by events in Korea, which threatened to ignite a worldwide conflagration. "Korea" therefore was not a happy idea, and the news from the front made it worse. The newspapers, *Life* magazine, and Movietone newsreels presented Korea as a murderous place, a bitter, frozen, brutal land. The Korean conflict could be resented on many levels: as a war that the government insisted on calling a "police action"; as the much-dreaded land war in Asia that our generals had warned us not to get into; as a "limited war" with muddled objectives that we "couldn't win" because of political constraints. When they asked about the reasons for the war, people whose men were fighting in Korea learned that their loved ones were fighting not for Korea itself but for symbols: to uphold the containment policy, to protect Japan, to encourage NATO, and to give meaning to the United Nations Charter. The welfare of the Korean people was far from the uppermost reason for fighting the Korean War.

As this first of the cold war's "brushfire" conflicts ground on, the sacking of General Douglas MacArthur became a symbol of the public's frustration with "Korea." President Harry S. Truman fired General MacArthur for insubordination after he went public with pleas for permission to "win" the war in the conventional sense. When it became clear that the war could not be won in that manner, U.S. representatives bargained for months to bring about a cease-fire that could

---

[8] As is often the case with exotic areas of the world, Americans got much of their information from *National Geographic*, which ran articles on Korea in October 1945, June 1947, March 1949, and June 1950.

be presented to the American people as an honorable "result."[9] Indeed, General Dwight Eisenhower won the presidency in 1952 largely on a promise to stop the fighting in Korea, a promise that was accompanied by the implied threat of nuclear war.

When the war ended, the word "Korea" meant the Korean War, in the same way that the word "Vietnam" more recently has been understood to mean the war as much as the country. It has taken a long time for "Korea" to gain a positive meaning. The rotation of hundreds of thousands of American military personnel through tours in Korea has tended to infuse the word "Korea" with an element of worry and danger, reinforced by letters home that tend to describe Korea from the point of view of military camps, an artificial world peopled by Koreans as employees and surrounded by a tawdry camp town known as "the vil," whose denizens include barmaids, prostitutes, pimps, and small-time merchants.[10]

Further negatives reinforced this original impression. Though "staunchly anti-communist," which was a good thing in the 1950s, Korea was a perpetual recipient of large-scale American aid. In fact, one of the most striking aspects of South Korea's postwar economic record is the extent to which it was regarded as a hopeless case in the 1950s, only to become the "miracle on the Han" in the 1980s.[11] Korea's leadership was similarly problematic. The adjectives used to describe President Syngman Rhee were "feisty" (at best) and "obstinate," "stubborn," "refractory," and "cantankerous" (at worst). Americans commented unfavorably on Rhee's opposition to the armistice, his tolerance for corruption, his aversion to the Japanese, and his desire to tax American investors. A series of U.S. ambassadors locked horns with Rhee throughout the 1950s, and it was Ambassador Walter McConaughy who eased him out of office and into exile in Hawaii during the 1960 April Revolution.

Korea, 1960–1980: An Image Coming into Focus

The April Revolution of 1960 and the ouster of President Syngman Rhee were widely reported in the American press, which described

---

[9] For a discussion of American efforts to paint the Korean War a political success, even at the cost of delaying the military armistice, see Barton J. Bernstein, "The Struggle over the Korean Armistice: Prisoners of Repatriation?" in *Child of Conflict: The Korean-American Relationship, 1943–1953,* ed. Bruce Cumings (Seattle: University of Washington Press, 1983), especially pp. 305–307.

[10] This is precisely the image that was presented in the American television show "M*A*S*H," which was so resented by Koreans.

[11] See David I. Steinberg's review of the Korean economy in Chapter 2 of this volume.

events in Korea as progress toward democratic development.[12] A year later, when the constitutional government of Prime Minister Chang Myon had proven ineffective and there was a military coup, American comment was a mixture of regret and hope that the ROK Army could organize Korea and shore up its economy. The next three decades brought constant tension in American policy between the desire to see democratic freedoms established and the need to keep South Korea secure—all while building up its economy. The Korean administration of President Park Chung-hee clearly put military security and state-directed economic growth ahead of democracy, and in doing so enjoyed the support of successive U.S. presidents from Kennedy to Carter. The situation was particularly acute in the 1970s, when Park resorted to rule-by-decree and outlawed criticism of his political style. By then, however, the Korean economy was starting to deliver, and economic performance could be touted as the justification for repressive rule. The American image of Korea, therefore, now became a somewhat contradictory composite: a collage made up of both the negative memories from the Korean War era and images of a new Korea with modern cities, automobiles, department stores, and other accoutrements of modern life.

New types of encounters with Koreans helped enhance the image of Korea as a modernizing country. First of all, by the 1960s large numbers of Korean students had enrolled in American universities and were getting acquainted with professors and host families while gaining a reputation for hard work and academic excellence. Second, during the Vietnam War many of the negatives associated with Korea were transferred in the American mind to Vietnam. Third, American buyers and investors began making deals in Korea for quality goods made cheaply by low-paid skilled workers. And fourth, American Peace Corps volunteers began working in Korea in 1966, creating an unprecedented people-to-people program that was a positive experience for most of those involved. By the end of the seventies, the image coming into focus was one of a fast-moving industrializing country rapidly earning international respect.

Journalism, however, continued to determine how Americans thought about Korea, and Korea rarely made news unless the news was bad. The North Korean capture of the USS *Pueblo* in 1968 and the *Pueblo* crew's ensuing year in captivity renewed the impression of danger in Korea, as did the North Koreans' downing of an American

---

[12] American press commentary circulated widely in South Korea at the time. A typical compendium of columns from the *New York Times*, *Christian Science Monitor*, and other leading American newspapers is Yung Bin Min, *The April Heroes: A Report on Korea's Freedom Revolution* (Seoul: Il Shin Sa, 1960).

intelligence aircraft in 1969 and a steady stream of stories about communist infiltration of the South. In the mid-1970s Korea became associated with the Moonie cult and the "Koreagate" influence-buying scandal on Capitol Hill. The assassination of Madame Park Chung-hee in 1974 and the subsequent assassination of Park himself in 1979 further darkened the picture, as did the events of 1980 culminating in the Kwangju massacre and General Chun Doo-hwan's emergence as a new Korean strongman. For the better part of the 1980s, television pictures of riot police battling South Korean students, sometimes during demonstrations against U.S. policy, upset many Americans, who wondered why their countrymen had fought and died in Korea a generation earlier.

Korea Through 1993: The Emergence of a More Positive Image

During the 1970s, the Seoul government went to work to neutralize the negatives by promoting Korea as an admirable civilization with honorable traditions dating back to the ancient world. Between 1979 and 1981, a major exhibition entitled "5,000 Years of Korean Art" toured San Francisco, Seattle, Chicago, Cleveland, Boston, New York, and Kansas City. Included were Korea's finest ceramics, jewelry, and paintings. The Korean Cultural Service began publishing an excellent quarterly entitled *Korean Culture*, distributing it free of charge to a wide variety of professional people. The Korean Ministry of Education began addressing the fact that American textbooks contained either no information about Korea or *dis*information about the country. At the urging of the Korean government, Korean donors began funding Korean studies programs at major American universities, language and fellowship programs were begun, and libraries were encouraged to expand their Korean collections. Though there were objections to the Korean government's involvement in such funding operations and worries about the political strings attached to Korean endowments, the aggregate result was a slow improvement in the level of knowledge about Korea among Americans and the emergence of a certain appreciation for Korean culture.[13]

Contributing to the development of this new consciousness of Korea in the United States was the growth of the Korean American community. Korean immigration began a dramatic increase with the 1985

---

[13] JaHyun Kim Haboush, "Perceptions and Representations of Korean Culture in the United States," a paper presented to the U.S.-Korea conference "Enhancing Korean Studies: Scholarship and Libraries," Washington, D.C., October 8–10, 1992.

revision of the U.S. immigration laws, particularly the provision that permitted immediate relatives of Korean Americans to apply for immigration. By the 1980s there were Korean Americans in every major city in America, sending their children to public schools, building churches and community centers, and operating small businesses. The corner vegetable market in New York City became a Korean business. Koreans started restaurants, dry-cleaning stores, and swap meets. In the big cities they branched out into medicine, college teaching, real estate, banking, and car dealerships. By the end of the decade, the primary mode of contact between Americans and Korea had become Koreans themselves, in cities from coast to coast. New images eclipsed the old: of diligent Korean American students, of tight-knit Korean families, and, as Korean exports flooded the American market, of Korean-made clothing, Hyundai cars, and Samsung electronics, representing good quality at low cost.

Domestic Korean politics, of course, remained a complete mystery, subject to facile analogies with political events in other countries. For example, in 1985, when opposition leader Kim Dae-jung returned to Seoul from exile in the United States, he was accompanied through Kimp'o Airport by a phalanx of American human rights activists, an obvious reference to the 1983 return of Philippine leader Benigno ("Ninoy") Aquino to Manila, when Aquino was shot on the tarmac by government agents. By the time of the June 1987 democracy movement in Korea, however, the appropriate Philippine analogy was the irresistible force of the "people power" that swept Ninoy's widow to the presidency. Through most of that month, the major American networks broadcast scenes of the Korean demonstrations, explaining events and noting the trend as the movement gathered strength. Americans watched as candidate Roh Tae-woo was forced to break with President Chun and open the political process to the popular will. Though Roh went on to win the election, mainly because the political opposition split its vote between competing contenders Kim Dae-jung and Kim Young-sam, the impression left in American minds was of a democratic sea change in Korean politics, one that connoted the maturing of a political process appropriate to a modern country. The image of rioting students was further dissipated by news coverage of the democratic elections that took place in 1992—for the National Assembly in March and the presidency in December.

Koreans regarded their successful bid to host the 1988 Summer Olympics as a major national triumph and an opportunity to showcase their postwar reconstruction. They thought of the Olympics as their chance to achieve what Japan had accomplished by hosting the 1964 games in Tokyo: a "coming-out party" that would familiarize the world with Korean culture and economic success in one stroke.[14] Many outsiders, recalling the earlier images of Korea, thought it odd that Seoul had been picked to host the Olympics and ultimately responded by disappointing the Koreans with a low occupancy rate in the new hotels that went up prior to the games. Nonetheless, the opening and closing extravaganzas did create spectacular displays of traditional and neotraditional Korean culture, with colorful costumes and elaborate music and dance numbers. South Korean athletes did their country proud in the winning of medals, and the NBC television network aired dozens of one- and two-minute spots on Korean life and civilization, which together painted a picture of a beautiful country with a unique culture, undergoing a rapid modern transformation.[15] The fact that the games were so well organized and came in under budget further impressed American onlookers.

Changing American Images of Korea: Survey Data

Anyone active in Korean-American relations can attest to the improving image of Korea in the American mind during the late 1980s. The evidence is both informal and formal. Each year I poll my American undergraduate students on images of Korea, asking the class for ten things they "know" about Korea. In the early eighties, before there were many Korean American students enrolled in the university, it was impossible for them to come up with ten items, and the first thing mentioned invariably was "M*A*S*H." Nearer the 1988 Olympics, the list was longer, including Hyundai cars, *taekwondo*, and diligent workers. By 1992 it was easy for them to come up with ten things, whether or not there were Korean American students in the class, and much of the information was relatively sophisticated. For example, awareness of the results of the March 1992 National Assem-

---

[14] For a discussion of the seriousness with which the Koreans took the hosting of the 1988 Summer Olympics, see Ian Buruma, "Playing for Keeps," *New York Review of Books*, November 10, 1988, pp. 44–50.

[15] For Koreans, however, the nature of NBC's coverage was a problem. The short spots on Korean life and culture covered negative topics such as the black market and alcoholism alongside positive topics such as education, Confucian family values, and economic success. The network claimed to be providing a balanced picture of Korea, and Koreans claimed that the effect was to diminish their efforts as hosts—the rude guest syndrome. For a brief discussion, see Donald N. Clark, "Bitter Friendship: Understanding Anti-Americanism in South Korea," *Korea Briefing, 1991*, ed. Donald N. Clark (Boulder: Westview Press, 1991), pp. 163–64.

bly elections, the names of North and South Korean leaders, the word *chaebol*, and Korean cuisine.[16]

More reliable, of course, are systematic survey data. Potomac Associates of Washington, D.C., is an organization that has tracked American attitudes toward Korea over time. In 1978 the organization took a survey that led to a rather gloomy assessment of the way negative ideas of Korea had accumulated in the public mind.[17] While 75 percent of the respondents could locate Korea on the periphery of China, fewer than one in five were aware of Korea's standing as America's (then) 14th-largest trading partner, and four out of five thought Korea was still a recipient of American economic aid. More than half pictured Korea as "crowded" and "underdeveloped," while fewer than 5 percent thought it "modern," with "high-quality roads, railroads, airlines, etc.," or "many automobiles," or its people "well educated" and "well dressed." Watts also cited "M*A*S*H" as a source of the baneful impressions, noting that, though through no deliberate effort of the program's producers, Korea in the television program tended to be shown as war-torn, backward, underdeveloped, and dirty, its people normally in "roles of subservience, often tinged with Oriental slyness." At the time of the Potomac Associates survey, the message about Korean modernization clearly had not gotten through. In a sense, the most ominous finding of that 1978 survey was that a clear majority of respondents opposed America's coming to the defense of South Korea in case of renewed North Korean attack; nor was it possible to find any subgroup of respondents, broken down by education, profession, or income, that favored the use of U.S. resources for the military defense of the Republic of Korea. One in three respondents felt that the U.S. forces in Korea should be reduced or eliminated altogether.

In 1992, William Watts presented a new assessment of American attitudes toward Korea and Koreans based on a survey of 1,018 adults who were questioned by the Gallup organization during February 1992.[18] The survey found that the respondents actually had slightly

---

[16] I documented 12 years of informal class polling in a *Korea Herald* article (April 9, 1992) entitled "Thirty-two Minutes to M*A*S*H," referring to the time it took one class in 1992 to get around to remembering the television series.

[17] William Watts, "The United States and Korea: Perception vs. Reality," in *After One Hundred Years: Continuity and Change in Korean-American Relations,* ed. Han Sung-joo, Asiatic Research Center Foreign Policy Studies, No. 3 (Seoul: Asiatic Research Center, Korea University, 1982), pp. 41–68.

[18] William Watts, "American Attitudes Toward Korea: A Special Survey," a paper presented to the U.S.-Korea conference "Enhancing Korean Studies: Scholarship and Librar-

less favorable feelings toward South Korea than had been found in a previous Gallup survey in 1979. The Korean War was still the first thing that came to mind, with Korean exports to the United States running second. Most Americans were still "woefully ignorant" about the scale and importance of Korea's economic relationship with the United States, but they were more inclined to support the U.S. military commitment, fearing instability in Northeast Asia and the emerging nuclear threat from North Korea.

The 1992 survey did demonstrate a rising level of knowledge about Korea among Americans, especially "affluent/elite" Americans. The elite category proved to be better informed and more positive about Korea than other groups. In analyzing the data, however, Watts noted that South Korea had suffered a net "negative shift" of 10 percent in favorable ratings between 1979 and 1992. To be sure, this was not as great a shift as was the case with Japan (minus 65 percent) and China (minus 39 percent). Watts speculated that trade friction with Japan and the Tiananmen massacre in China may have helped create an "Asia factor" in the survey that hurt South Korea as well. North Korea also suffered a negative shift of 7 percent.

When the questions turned to South Korea's importance to the United States, the results were somewhat less discouraging. Of the total respondents, 79 percent said that it was important for the United States to have good relations with South Korea, up from 69 percent in 1979. The "positive shift" was even higher among "affluent/elite" respondents, 89 percent of whom said it was important for the United States "to get along well" with South Korea.

The 1992 survey went on to poll respondents on their sources of information about Korea. Print media and broadcast media were virtually tied for first place; however, between 1979 and 1992 "personal contact" with Koreans nearly quadrupled as a source (from 3 to 11 percent) and "purchase and use of South Korean products" increased from 5 to 23 percent. An inference to be drawn from these data is that Americans are becoming more conscious of Korea as a result of firsthand experience.

Other findings in the survey include the fact that Americans think that U.S.-Korea relations are "only fair" or "good" as opposed to "excellent" and that relations are likely to stay the same or improve slightly in the future. Most of the respondents still were unaware of Korea's position on the list of U.S. trading partners, and two-thirds thought the United States had a trade deficit with South Korea when

ies." Also see William Watts, "America's Changing Perceptions of Korea," paper presented to the Carnegie Council on Ethics and International Affairs, New York, February 24, 1993.

the trade, in fact, was roughly in balance in 1991. Many had reservations about changing the U.S. military presence in South Korea, indicating little change from the 1979 Gallup survey. Around half thought it "likely" that the two Koreas would be reunited "in the next few years." Three out of four called North Korea's reported nuclear weapons program a "major threat" or "somewhat of a threat."

Most people understood that South Korea was far ahead of North Korea in terms of democratic practice, and "affluent/elite" citizens seemed clearly aware (80 percent) that the recent trend in South Korea had been toward promoting democracy, apparently a reference to the period since Roh Tae-woo's June 29 Declaration in 1987. Eighty-five percent of the respondents, however, were unaware that Roh Tae-woo was president of South Korea, and the figure was not much better for "affluent/elite" respondents—only 30 percent.[19] Of the 15 percent of total respondents who could identify him, seven out of every ten thought that Roh had been "very effective" or "somewhat effective" in promoting democracy in South Korea.

Perhaps one of the most disturbing findings in the survey is Watts's "Asia Factor," a sign that Korea remained ill-defined in the American mind. For example, the U.S. trade deficit with Japan suggests a corresponding trade deficit with Korea, despite the herculean efforts of both governments to prevent Korea's becoming (and being seen as) a "second Japan." The persistent perception of South Korea as a less-than-democratic place is fostered by images from the news, of course, but it also tends to merge with mental pictures of anti-government demonstrations in China, Taiwan, and perhaps even as far away as Thailand and Tibet. More intractable, no doubt, is the stereotype of authoritarian Asian governments going back for decades, which blunts the impression being made by recent reports of "democratization" in South Korea. Also striking is the contradictory tendency among the survey respondents (as was also the case in my own annual college poll) to picture Korea as a frozen place with jungles, an obvious conflation of images and story fragments from the Korean and Vietnam wars. It is likely that the confusion between Korea and Vietnam will continue in the minds of Americans as long as the U.S. military is involved in Korea. On the other hand, North Korea is an almost total blank for Americans. The conclusion to be drawn from the conflicting images of Korea is that Americans in general still do

---

[19] Watts notes that this is typical of Americans, in that in an April 1991 poll, only 13 percent of respondents could name Prime Minister Brian Mulroney of Canada and only 3 percent could name President Cárlos Salinas de Gortari of Mexico. Watts, "American Attitudes Toward Korea: A Special Survey," p. 17.

not know—or feel they need to know—much about Korea, even though special interests such as the military and parts of the business community know a great deal about their own particular area of activity there.

What About the Future?

If the present trends continue, the American economic community will lead the way in knowledge of South Korea. With serious money on the line, investors, traders, and business executives in joint ventures will be putting forth serious efforts to get to know the Korean people better. Their success will require reliable information and cultural empathy on both sides. Their encounters with Koreans are different from those of the 37,000 American military personnel who, by the terms of their encounter with the local environment, are generally confined to viewing Korea through the fences around their bases. This bodes well for better understanding in the future.

Tourism, too, may play a larger role in shaping the American image of Korea in the future. Though efforts to promote visits to Korea in the past have been only marginally successful, even during the 1988 Summer Olympics, the changing patterns of air travel in East Asia are likely to work to Korea's benefit. A direct air route between Seoul and Beijing will make Korea, with its historic sites and shopping opportunities, a convenient stopover point. The construction of a new airport on Yongjong Island is likely to attract visitors as airlines redirect trans-Pacific flights via Korea to take pressure off Japan's congested airways. These developments in air travel, together with the discovery of world-class facilities in Korea by more and more travel agents and their clients, will enhance personal contact with Korea by Americans in the future.

The aggregate effect of these developments, together with the maturing of the "1.5 generation"—the generation of Korean Americans who immigrated as young children with their parents in the 1970s and 1980s—will make Americans view Korea much more as a neighbor than a client. The surveys point to a more harmonious future, and we can only hope that they are proved right.

Ultimately, however, the problem of American ignorance about Korea is part of the larger problem of inadequate international education in our country. The U.S. republic still has its roots in Europe, and that is not likely to change; but the acquisition of superpower status brings with it a duty to know much more about the world as a whole. Were it not for the history of geopolitical trouble on the peninsula, our investment in Korean security, our current scale of bilateral trade, and the human potential of Korea's 70 million people, our ignorance of Korea would be no more remarkable than our ignorance of India, Egypt, Hungary, or Colombia. But to settle for stereotypes about any of these places is to endanger ourselves as well as the rest of the world. We must insist that our schools and colleges, and ultimately our government and people, do better.

Chronology

Donald N. Clark

Traditional Korea: The Choson Dynasty, 1392–1910

1392–1910 Korea is ruled by a succession of 27 kings of the Yi clan of Chonju. They call the kingdom Choson, usually translated as "Land of the Morning Calm."

1446 King Sejong (r. 1418–50) announces the invention of the Korean phonemic alphabet known today as *Han'gul*, making it possible to write the Korean language instead of the classical Chinese written language normally used by educated Koreans.

1592–1598 The Japanese warlord Hideyoshi, having unified Japan, deploys armies through Korea to attack China. The invasion is halted by a combined Sino-Korean resistance, and war rages on the Korean peninsula. As a stalemate develops, the Korean admiral Yi Sun-sin develops a metal-clad warship known as the Turtle Ship, to harry Japanese supply lines. Eventually, after Hideyoshi's death, the Japanese give up their venture, leaving Korea in disarray.

1700s *Sirhak*, the Korean school of "practical learning," takes shape, involving the "investigation of things" and proposals for social and institutional reform. *Sirhak* scholars struggle to define their own civilization and in the process encounter many new ideas from the outside, including Catholicism.

Korea also produces important new works of art and literature reflecting the interests of the *sirhak* school, such as the genre painting of Kim Hong-do and Shin Yun-bok. New-style novels are also written by court women in native Korean *Han'gul* script.

1784   *Sirhak* scholar Yi Sung-hun returns from Peking after having been baptized a Catholic by Western missionaries; this is the traditional beginning of Christianity in Korea. Because of the pope's condemnation of Confucian ancestral rituals as idolatry, King Chongjo outlaws Christianity in 1785, and Korean Catholics go underground.

1866   The Korean court launches a bloody purge of Korea's Catholics and their officially unwelcome French missionary priests. An intruding American ship, the *General Sherman*, is also destroyed in the Taedong River near Pyongyang, with the loss of all hands.

A French naval squadron inquiring after the fate of the martyred French missionaries is attacked and driven off at Kanghwa Island, in the Han River estuary below Seoul.

1871   The U.S. Navy sends a squadron to inquire about the fate of the *General Sherman* and to explore opening official relations. A skirmish ensues on Kanghwa Island in which the U.S. Marines inflict heavy damage but eventually withdraw.

1876   Japan sends a naval force to Kanghwa Island and forces Korean representatives to sign a treaty establishing diplomatic relations. The Kanghwa Treaty with Japan is Korea's first venture into the wider international community. It is also Japan's first bid to pry Korea out of the Chinese tributary orbit.

1882   At China's urging, Korea begins signing a series of treaties with Western powers beginning with the United States. U.S. minister Lucius Foote is the first Western diplomat and the first American to take up residence in Seoul, in 1883. Britain, Russia, France, and Italy likewise establish permanent legations in Seoul.

Korea sends its first delegation abroad, to Japan, to learn about the process of modernization there. Its members return home to begin a small "progressive" movement in Korea. Influenced by Japanese models, they appear to be pro-Japanese and hence are anathema to Korean conservatives and their Chinese advisers. Suppression follows.

1884–85   The first Protestant missionaries land in Korea, eventually to found such significant institutions as Yonsei and Ewha universities as well as a sizeable church community.

1894–96   The Tonghak peasant rebellion in southwest Korea leads to intervention by China and Japan and the Sino-Japanese War. The war eliminates overt Chinese influence in Korean affairs and gives ascendancy to Japan, which establishes a Korean reform party to carry out what are known as the Kabo Reforms. Japanese agents also assassinate Korea's Queen Min, frightening King Kojong into refuge in the Russian Legation. The pro-Japanese reform party is purged, and Russia gains the ascendancy.

Western-educated Korean intellectuals found the Independence Club in an attempt to muster the spiritual resources of the Korean people against foreign dictation. They publish broadsides in *Han'gul* decrying corruption in the Korean system, to little avail.

U.S. minister Horace N. Allen persuades King Kojong to grant a lucrative gold-mining concession to American investors at Unsan, in the mountains north of Pyongyang. The tax-exempt concession liberally repays its owners and stockholders for 40 years before being forced out of business by the Japanese colonial regime in Korea.

1897   Liberated from his position as a virtual vassal of China and determined to withstand Japanese encroachment, King Kojong declares himself an emperor on a par with the Kuang-hsu and Meiji emperors in China and Japan.

1903   American labor contractors recruit the first of 7,000 Korean workers for the sugar plantations of Hawaii, sowing the seeds of the Korean American community which, after successive waves of immigration, now numbers nearly 1 million.

1904–05   Japan and Russia go to war over hegemony in the Far East. Much of the fighting takes place in and around Korea. President Theodore Roosevelt mediates the settlement of the conflict at his summer home in Portsmouth, New Hampshire. With tacit American approval, the Portsmouth Treaty recognizes Japan's "paramount interest" in Korea. The United States and Japan follow up with the Taft-Katsura Agreement, in which the United States promises not to interfere with Japan's actions in Korea and Japan promises not to interfere in the Philippines.

In November the Japanese government forces Korea to accept a "protectorate," by which Japan takes control of Korea's defense and foreign relations, and appoints the great Meiji statesman Ito Hirobumi as resident-general, that is, the chief adviser and director of Korea's external affairs.

1909   The Korean An Chung-gun assassinates Ito Hirobumi. Ito is replaced by Japanese Army General Terauchi Masatake.

The Period of Japanese Colonial Rule, 1910–1945

1910   General Terauchi forces Korean prime minister Yi Wan-yong to sign a treaty annexing Korea to Japan. Japan takes complete control, offering cash settlements to influential Koreans and threatening stern punishment for dissenters. Japanese Army troops and gendarmes enforce popular compliance with Japanese edicts, which include shutting down Korean newspapers and political organizations and imposing strict controls on education.

1919 On March 1, Koreans stage nationwide demonstrations demanding independence from Japan. Colonial authorities, caught by surprise, respond with brutal suppression. The movement wanes but outbreaks continue through most of 1920.

In September, Japan assigns Admiral Saito Makoto to be governor-general in Korea. Saito's policy is to coopt the Koreans through concessions designed to make Japanese rule palatable to the majority. The new Japanese mood of toleration enables hundreds of Korean organizations to sprout, generating a cultural resurgence aimed at preserving Korean identity for future independence. Saito's decade as governor-general is known as the period of Japan's "cultural policy" in Korea.

Among the activities permitted by the "cultural policy" is the publication of newspapers such as the *Tong'a Ilbo* and *Choson Ilbo* and magazines such as *Ch'angjo* ("Creation"), founded by writer Kim Tong-in and others.

1921 The Korean communist movement begins, having incubated in Korean communities in China and the Soviet Union, and seeks to confront Japan directly for Korean independence.

1924 The U.S. Congress passes an immigration act establishing quotas for the number of immigrants from various countries. In keeping with existing laws discriminating against Asian immigration, however, East Asians, including Koreans, are declared ineligible for any quota.

1927 Korean communists join with moderate nationalists to found the Shin'ganhoe (New Korea Society). Ironically, the Japanese tolerate it because it makes nationalist activity easier to watch. Communists support it because it protects them from outright suppression. By 1930 the New Korea Society has grown to nearly 77,000 members, and the work of its left wing disturbs the moderates and brings increasing Japanese repression. In 1931 a leftist majority votes to dissolve the society.

1929   Insults against a Korean schoolgirl by Japanese classmates touch off anti-Japanese student riots in Kwangju and a wave of protests across the peninsula.

1934–35   The colonial regime embarks on an active assimilation policy by which it requires Koreans to use the Japanese language exclusively in education and business and forces Koreans to engage in Shinto rituals honoring imperial ancestors and Japanese war heroes.

1937–38   Japan embarks on full-scale war in China. In Korea, the colonial regime forces Korean clubs, societies, and associations of all kinds to submit to Japanese control or disband. Foreign businesses are pressured into selling out to Japanese concerns. Christian missionaries are required to endorse Shinto worship by local Christians or cease their work.

1939   The Japanese begin forcing Koreans to use Japanese, rather than their Korean, names.

1940   The Japanese shut down nongovernment publications, reduce the number of newspapers to one, organize the population into neighborhood mutual responsibility teams to facilitate war mobilization, and increase the drafting of Koreans for labor service. Some of the draftees are "comfort women" (*wi'anbu*) sent to the front as sex slaves for the troops.

1940–41   Virtually all Westerners are evacuated from Korea. In December 1941, Japan goes to war with the West and Korea is put on a total war footing. All Koreans are expected to exert themselves for the cause, contributing labor and possessions.

1943   In China and the United States, overseas Koreans try to muster support for the cause of Korean independence. In Cairo in December, U.S. president Franklin D. Roosevelt, British prime minister Winston Churchill, and Chinese leader Chiang Kai-shek agree that Korea will be given independence "in due course" when Japan is defeated in the war. An international trusteeship is contemplated for Korea.

The Period of Allied Occupation, 1945–1948

1945   Korea is liberated by the victorious Allies as Japan is defeated. The United States and the Soviet Union agree to divide Korea into northern and southern occupation zones, with the United States occupying the southern zone, including Seoul, as far north as the 38th parallel.

Koreans oppose the idea of trusteeship with such force that the Allies abandon the idea. The United States and the Soviet Union, however, remain in charge of their respective zones until 1948.

1946   Within South Korea, a struggle between left and right in Korean politics leads to a U.S.-backed campaign of repression of the left. In North Korea, Soviet-backed Korean leftists emerge, with Kim Il-sung as their leader.

1947–48   The United States turns the Korean independence issue over to the United Nations. U.N.-sanctioned elections take place in the South, after North Korea refuses entry to a U.N. inspection team. The newly elected government in the South creates the Republic of Korea (ROK) and elects the U.S.-educated Syngman Rhee president. The Western world recognizes the ROK as the legitimate government of the Korean people. The emerging socialist bloc recognizes the alternative socialist regime in the North, where the Democratic People's Republic of Korea (DPRK) is established under the leadership of Kim Il-sung.

Within South Korea there are outbreaks of violence as leftist rebels try to thwart the separation of the

peninsula into separate republics and resist the
Rhee government. Though there has been scattered
violence since 1945, an especially bloody rebellion
occurs on Cheju Island in April 1948, with a month-
long campaign to suppress it sparking a related rebellion at the southwestern port city of Yosu. The
Seoul government and remaining Americans blame
communist agitators for the trouble.

The South Korean National Assembly passes a National Security Law, the first in a series of anti-
sedition laws amenable to abuse for partisan political purposes. Sweeping purges round up op-
ponents of the regime along with national security
risks.

The Korean War and Its Aftermath, 1949–1960

1949   American occupation forces complete their withdrawal from South Korea, leaving a 500-man military advisory group to help the fledgling ROK
Army.

In October, the Chinese Communists extend their
control over the entire Chinese mainland. The Nationalist Chinese take refuge on the island of Taiwan.

1950   U.S. secretary of state Dean Acheson gives a speech
at the National Press Club in which he draws an
American defense line in the Western Pacific to
warn that the United States will defend Japan and
the Philippines, but that the defense of Taiwan and
South Korea is a responsibility of the international
community through the United Nations.

On June 25, the endemic skirmishing along the 38th
parallel in Korea erupts into full-scale war as North
Korean units invade toward Seoul. The South Korean capital falls within three days. The United Nations decides to create an international peacekeeping force under U.S. command to confront the
North Koreans and force them to withdraw north
of the 38th parallel. The U.N. effort fails at first,

then holds a line along the Naktong River in south-east Korea—the so-called Pusan Perimeter.

In September, General Douglas MacArthur commands a surprise amphibious landing of U.S. forces at the port of Inch'on, 22 miles west of Seoul. The landing through treacherous coastal waters succeeds, and within two weeks Seoul is recaptured and much of the invading North Korean army is caught in the South.

With much of the North Korean army out of action, the United Nations gives General MacArthur permission to launch a counterinvasion of North Korea, ostensibly to extend the ROK's sovereignty over the entire peninsula.

Communist China, concerned about the destruction of the neighboring communist regime in North Korea and worried that MacArthur will carry the war into Chinese territory, diverts forces from the Taiwan Strait, recruits "volunteers," and infiltrates the mountains of central North Korea. In November, Chinese troops attack from the mountains along the advancing columns of U.N. troops, forcing a disorderly retreat. U.N. forces are compelled to abandon North Korea, and by late winter the combined communist force is in the South again. Seoul falls a second time, and then is retaken by the United Nations. Much of the western half of the city has been destroyed, and nine tenths of the city's population has fled southward.

1951 General MacArthur goes public with criticism of the way the United States and United Nations are prosecuting the war. President Harry S. Truman dismisses him for insubordination and replaces him with General Matthew Ridgway.

Officers from the U.N. Command (including South Korea) and the communist side, representing North Korea and the Chinese People's Volunteers, sit down at the border to hammer out a cease-fire. The talks, which are situated in the village of Panmunjom, drag on for more than two years.

The fighting continues, more or less along the 38th parallel, with the two sides running up huge casualties while trading the same hills back and forth. In North Korea, the U.S. Air Force bombs every target of conceivable significance, reducing the cities to rubble. The North Korean government is literally driven underground. With North Korean industry in ruins, the bombing turns to the destruction of agriculture, targeting river levees and dams and causing terrible floods.

1952   Banking on his popular reputation, especially among rural voters, Syngman Rhee has the National Assembly amend the constitution to provide for direct popular election of the president. Rhee is then reelected president.

The U.S. Congress amends the immigration laws to create modest quotas for East Asians, including Koreans, to apply for U.S. citizenship. More significant, however, is the number of Koreans entering the United States as students and as war brides.

1953   On July 27, 1953, the two sides sign an armistice agreement. The battle line, below the 38th parallel in the west, above it in the east, becomes the new north-south border. Along it a two-kilometer wide demilitarized zone (DMZ) is created to separate the warring armies, with Panmunjom remaining as the point of contact for future negotiations.

Casualty figures for the Korean War are 1.3 million South Koreans, 1.5 million North Koreans, and 900,000 Chinese killed, wounded, or missing. The United States suffers 33,629 dead, the British Commonwealth 1,263, and other U.N. participants a total of 1,931.

The Rhee government, having opposed the armistice because it left Korea divided, collects on a U.S. promise to secure South Korea's safety. The United States and the ROK sign a mutual defense treaty permitting U.S. troops to remain in South Korea indefinitely. The wartime arrangement subjecting

ROK forces to the United Nations Commander effectively continues American operational control over Rhee's army which is almost entirely dependent on U.S. military aid and training.

1954   U.S.-backed efforts to open a dialogue between the Rhee regime and Japan fail as recriminations over past abuses fill the air.

1955   The Rhee government succeeds in getting a constitutional amendment removing the two-term limit for presidential tenure so Rhee can succeed himself in 1956.

The U.S. Congress votes to allow intercountry adoption of Korean children. In the beginning this is intended to provide for the offspring of American servicemen, but it also allows adoption of war orphans. The adoption program eventually places tens of thousands of Korean and Korean American children with families across the United States. Many are not, strictly speaking, war orphans, but abandoned children. Successive immigration law revisions continue the provision to permit their adoption in the United States.

1956   Syngman Rhee is reelected by direct popular vote after his opponent dies of natural causes during the presidential campaign. Opposition vice-presidential candidate Chang Myon wins, however—a sign that Rhee's party is in serious trouble.

1960   In the 1960 election, opposition candidate Cho Pyong-ok dies a few months before the voting. Rhee's party employs massive voting fraud to ensure that his chosen successor is elected vice president. The fraud touches off demonstrations demanding a new election. Police disperse the demonstrators with tear gas. When a student is killed by a tear-gas shell, bigger demonstrations erupt in Seoul. Police fire again, many are killed, and the country erupts in revolution. Within a week Rhee resigns, and the government is turned over to interim president Ho Chong. The event is known by its date as the April 19 Student Revolution, *"Sa-Il-Ku"* for short in Korean.

A constitutional change creates the Second Republic, under Prime Minister Chang Myon of the opposition. The presidency is reduced to symbolic importance only.

The Era of Military Hegemony in South Korea, 1961–1987

1961   Nine months of relatively democratic rule create sufficient indirection and confusion to disillusion people with the Chang government. On May 16, units of the ROK Army under Major General Park Chung-hee stage a coup d'état. Prime Minister Chang is forced to resign, and Park's military junta takes over with promises of order and honest government.

Kim Jong-pil, a relative and fellow-officer of Park Chung-hee, establishes the Korean Central Intelligence Agency (KCIA), with mandates to protect the state from foreign and domestic enemies. Over time, the KCIA functions as an internal security police used for blatantly political purposes by the Park regime. In the 1980s it is replaced by the Agency for National Security Planning, which continues in the same mode under the military strongman Chun Doo-hwan.

The junta also establishes an Economic Planning Board, staffed with professional economists, which emerges as the driver of a new export-led economic growth strategy. The tax system is also reorganized to stimulate investment and production consistent with government strategies.

1963   With its goals still unmet, the Park junta bows to demands for constitutional government by resigning from the military and running for office as civilians under a revised constitution creating the Third Republic. The military leaders create the Democratic Republican Party (DRP) to furnish support in the

National Assembly, and DRP candidates win a majority of Assembly seats.

1965   Having embarked on an ambitious economic development plan, the Park government seeks capital from Japan. It concludes a "normalization" treaty establishing diplomatic relations between Seoul and Tokyo, providing for Japanese economic assistance, and opening the way for Japanese joint ventures with fledgling South Korean companies. Many Koreans oppose normalization with Japan, and the government has to overcome considerable public turmoil in order to achieve it.

The U.S. Congress liberalizes American immigration laws, easing quotas and creating new categories of foreigners eligible for immigration status. Many Koreans in the United States are able to apply for permanent residence. Others are allowed to apply for citizenship because of their occupations or relationship to immigrants who already have citizenship. U.S. citizens of Korean ancestry are able to send for immediate relatives, who then are granted permanent residence and, eventually, citizenship. The Korean American community grows accordingly.

1966   The United States persuades the Park government to commit troops to support South Vietnam, by paying all the costs of deployment, procuring supplies in South Korea, and offering construction contracts to South Korean companies. Koreans regard the sending of troops as a payback for American support during the Korean War, and the ROK economy reaps valuable dollar currency in the bargain. Korea thus benefits from the Vietnam War as Japan benefitted from the Korean War.

1967   President Park Chung-hee is reelected with 51.5 percent of the vote. Under the constitution of the Third Republic he cannot succeed himself. The DRP begins the process of amending the constitution to permit him to run for another term in 1971.

1968   With ROK troops committed in Vietnam, North Korea steps up pressure on the South. In January a North Korean hit squad is caught virtually on Park Chung-hee's doorstep, alarming Seoul residents. Later in the month the American intelligence-gathering ship U.S.S. *Pueblo* is captured by the North Koreans off Wonsan along with its crew. The 82 surviving crewmen are held for almost a year, finally being released at Panmunjom in December. The American failure to strike back at North Korea surprises many in the South. Meanwhile, a heightened rate of infiltration sets off a nationwide anti-spy campaign that is said to justify rigid anti-subversion measures and curbs on speech and other human rights.

1969   The National Assembly passes the constitutional amendment permitting President Park to run for a third term.

1971   President Park is reelected by a narrow margin, nearly losing to Kim Dae-jung of South Cholla province, who wins 45 percent of the popular vote.

In December, Park declares a state of national emergency, citing domestic and international instability—elements such as the deteriorating situation in Vietnam, the Guam Doctrine and President Nixon's decision to withdraw 20,000 troops from South Korea, the sudden warming of relations between the United States and China, and changes in the world economic system.

1972   The Park government launches the Third Five Year Plan (1972–77), targeting heavy industries such as steel, shipbuilding, and automobiles.

In July, South Koreans are stunned by an announcement that South Korean officials have met in Pyongyang with North Korean president Kim Il-sung. Amid hopes for speedy unification, a dialogue begins with North Korean representatives, but it bogs down and makes no headway. The two sides blame each other for the failure of the talks.

In October, Park proclaims martial law and a series of "revitalizing reforms," (*Yushin*) that include suspension of the National Assembly, dissolution of all political parties, restrictions on civil liberties, and presidential rule-by-decree. After a campaign in which criticism of the proposal is prohibited, voters ratify the change in a constitutional amendment creating the Fourth Republic.

1973 Former Park opponent Kim Dae-jung is abducted from a Tokyo hotel by agents of the KCIA and spirited to Korea, where he is put under house arrest on charges of speaking sedition during appearances overseas. Kim accuses the KCIA of torture, alleging that his kidnappers tried to throw him overboard on the trip from Japan during an interrogation.

1974 In an attempt on the life of President Park Chung-hee, a Japan-based Korean assassin kills Mme. Park instead.

1975 The fall of South Vietnam deals a blow to American prestige in South Korea. Many Koreans express doubts that the United States would stand by South Korea if the North were to renew its attack. The Park government takes advantage of public fear to reinforce its suppression of political dissent, citing the paramount need to foster national unity and self-sufficiency.

In May, President Park announces Emergency Decree No. 9, which criminalizes criticism of the president, the constitution, and the decree itself.

1976 On March 1, Korean Independence Day, the South Korean opposition stages the reading of a manifesto for democracy at the Myong-dong Cathedral, enlisting the support of the Catholic hierarchy for human rights and democratic reform. Kim Dae-jung is among those arrested at the church for violating Emergency Decree No. 9, and he spends the next four years in detention.

At the truce village of Panmunjom in the DMZ,
North Koreans attack an American tree-trimming
crew and kill two American officers. Though there
have been confrontations between Americans and
North Koreans at P'anmunjom before, this is the
most serious incident ever to occur there. President
Gerald Ford issues warnings and sends B-52 bombers flying along the southern boundary of the DMZ
to display American retaliatory power.

1976–77   During the U.S. presidential campaign, candidate
Jimmy Carter announces his intention to withdraw
U.S. forces from the Korean peninsula. After his
election he reconsiders and drops the plan.

In Washington, Congressional hearings follow the
discovery of a widespread South Korean program
of influence-buying in the U.S. government. Several
American legislators are implicated in the affair,
which involves Park Tong-son, a shadowy "agent
of influence," the American branch of Sun Myung
Moon's Unification Church, and staff members of
House Speaker Carl Albert. The scandal is dubbed
"Koreagate" and embarrasses both sides.

1978   Tension mounts between the Park government and
the opposition. Despite government controls, workers strike for higher wages. University students
take to the streets in democracy demonstrations,
and the government loses seats in the National Assembly election.

Kim Dae-jung, in poor health in a prison hospital,
is allowed to go home to continue his sentence under house arrest.

1979   Amid nationwide worker unrest and growing danger of social upheaval, Park Chung-hee is assassinated on October 26 by Kim Jae-kyu, director of the
KCIA. Kim is arrested; the government declares
martial law; a respected civilian leader, Ch'oe
Kyu-ha, is made acting president; and the Army
Security Command under Major General Chun

Doo-hwan launches an investigation of the assassination, avowedly in search of a conspiracy.

On December 7, the South Korean electoral college formally elects Ch'oe Kyu-ha president of the ROK.

On December 8, President Ch'oe rescinds Park's Emergency Decree No. 9, which forbade criticism and dissent. There is an amnesty and Kim Dae-jung is freed from house arrest.

On December 12, Chun Doo-hwan stages a virtual coup d'état by arresting Army Chief of Staff Chong Sung-hwa, who is the martial law commander. Firefights develop between Chun's forces and those loyal to General Chong and President Ch'oe. Chun calls in the ROK Army's Ninth Division, commanded by his military academy classmate General Roh Tae-woo, takes Army headquarters and the Defense Ministry, and arrests the chief of staff.

1980   There is a brief "Seoul Spring," in which political figures amnestied by President Ch'oe speak their minds in the media and engage in public discussions with students and other politically active groups.

Park's assassin is tried, convicted, and executed. A court martial sentences General Chong to ten years in prison for mishandling the assassination investigation.

In May, there are demonstrations by students and workers demanding more freedom and higher wages. Some of the strikes are violent, and the student demonstrators criticize Chun Doo-hwan personally. Educators and officials try to cool the situation, and the demonstrations cease briefly in mid-May; then Chun declares an extension of martial law and a ban on all political activity including meetings of the National Assembly. Hundreds of opposition politicians including Kim Dae-jung are arrested, along with many students.

Kim Dae-jung's home province erupts in protest against his arrest. In the provincial capital of

Kwangju, demonstrations are brutally suppressed by ROK Army paratroopers and several dozen people are killed. Rioting ensues, and the citizens of Kwangju expel the paratroopers and effectively wrest the city from government control. Protesters raid government installations, radio stations, and arsenals. The United States expresses concern but supports law and order. Meanwhile, Chun gets U.N. Command permission to move the ROK Twentieth Army Division, which is trained for riot control, to Kwangju to quell the uprising. The ROK Army then invades the city and takes it, with a heavy loss of life. Estimates of the number killed still range between 200 and 2,000. The Chun forces blame the uprising on communist agitators.

In August, President Ch'oe resigns the presidency. The electoral college then chooses Chun Doo-hwan as president. The people vote on a constitutional amendment creating the Fifth Republic, and General Chun is confirmed as president. He vows to obey the new constitution, which provides for a single seven-year presidential term.

Meanwhile, opposition leader Kim Dae-jung is convicted of anti-state activities and sentenced to death, but the United States bargains for a commutation of his sentence and persuades Chun to stay his sentence, allowing him to leave for "exile" in the United States.

1981   President Ronald Reagan's first official visitor at the end of January is South Korean president Chun Doo-hwan.

1983   In September, a Korean Air Lines 747 with 269 persons aboard strays through Soviet air space during a nighttime flight between Anchorage and Seoul and is shot down by a Soviet fighter. All aboard are killed. The Reagan and Chun administrations call it a deliberate act of murder by the USSR, while the Soviets claim that they confused the Korean 747 with a U.S. intelligence plane operating nearby. Conspiracy theorists suggest that the U.S. was using the Korean 747 to spy on Soviet air defenses. The International Civil Aviation Organization eventually cites Soviet negligence and pilot error as two of the prime causes of the incident.

In October during an official visit to Rangoon, 17 members of Chun Doo-hwan's entourage are killed in a bomb blast set by North Korean agents at the mausoleum of Burmese patriot Aung San. Chun Doo-hwan himself barely escapes injury.

In November, President Reagan visits South Korea and reaffirms U.S. support for the South Korean government.

1985 Kim Dae-jung returns to Korea after the Chun government eases some political controls. In the National Assembly election the opposition surprises the government by its strong showing.

In the most visible of their attacks on U.S. government installations during the 1980s, university students occupy the U.S. Information Service's headquarters in downtown Seoul and hang banners from the windows demanding a meeting with U.S. ambassador Richard Walker to discuss American complicity in the bloody suppression of the Kwangju uprising in 1980. They fail, and are arrested after several days.

1987 On June 10, the ruling Democratic Justice Party (DJP) holds its national convention, endorsing President Chun Doo-hwan's choice of former general Roh Tae-woo as the party's candidate to succeed him in the forthcoming presidential election.

Under the constitution, the president is to be chosen by an electoral college packed with DJP supporters. Demonstrations erupt in the streets protesting the procedure and demanding direct popular vote for president. The demonstrations build as office workers and middle-class citizens join the students in braving tear gas to fight riot police. After weeks of riots, candidate Roh Tae-woo surprises the country by announcing that he favors the principle of popular election and that the DJP will support an immediate constitutional amendment to make it happen. Roh's announcement, part of an eight-point "democratization package," is known as the June 29th Declaration.

Voters ratify the new "democratized" constitution in October, and the presidential campaign begins.

In December, in the first popular election of a president in 26 years, 90 percent of South Korea's voters cast ballots, electing Roh Tae-woo president by a plurality of less than 37 percent. The "three Kims"—Kim Dae-jung, Kim Young-sam, and Kim Jong-pil—splinter the majority vote for the opposition, handing the election to Roh.

A Korean airliner is destroyed by a bomb set by North Korean agents and crashes into the Andaman Sea near Burma, with the loss of all aboard. A North Korean woman is arrested in Bahrain and returned to Seoul for trial, where she reveals details of a wide-ranging program of terrorism supervised by North Korean heir-apparent Kim Jong-il. Eventually the woman displays contrition and is pardoned, released, and allowed to marry and live a normal life.

1988   In April, the ruling Democratic Justice Party suffers a severe setback in the National Assembly elections, failing to secure a majority. An unexpectedly strong showing by the "three Kims" revives their political fortunes.

In March, South Korea opens its cigarette market to American imports. Korean farmers object, and protesters accuse the Chun government of buckling to American pressure to save the failing U.S. tobacco industry by exporting narcotics that Americans themselves consider dangerous to their health.

In July, President Roh Tae-woo gives a speech creating openings to North Korea and promising support for initiatives that build bridges and shared interests with the North.

In September and October, Seoul hosts the 24th Summer Olympics after seven years of intense preparations. For the first time since 1976, teams representing both sides of the cold war participate together. The Olympics give South Korea a way to open dialogues with the Soviet Union, China, and other socialist countries, boosting President Roh Tae-woo's *Nordpolitik* diplomacy. With strict security measures surrounding the games, the North Koreans remain aloof and make no move to disrupt them, as had been feared.

In a series of post-Olympics National Assembly hearings, legislators investigate corrupt and dictatorial practices under the Fifth Republic presidency of Chun Doo-hwan. President Roh, himself vulnerable to charges of complicity in Chun's bloody takeover of the government in 1979–80, is caught in the middle. After a televised apology, Chun Doo-hwan departs Seoul for a two-year "exile" at a Buddhist temple in the mountains of Kangwon province.

In Beijing, American and North Korean diplomats quietly open a series of relatively low-level diplomatic discussions with a view to resolving their differences. The discussions continue to the present.

1989   In January, Hyundai *chaebol* chairman Chung Ju-yung cultivates contacts in North Korea, obtaining permission for a joint venture to develop the Kumgangsan (Diamond Mountains) resort area. Approval for a joint venture is a breakthrough even though it never actually develops.

In the spring, students from various universities organize federations that demand access to counterparts in North Korea as a way of pressing progress in national unification. The government steadfastly blocks the students' efforts to march north and subjects their activities to heavy surveillance.

Between December 1988 and March 1989, Hyundai workers stage strikes at the Ulsan industrial park. On March 30, 10,000 riot police invade the complex to disperse the workers.

In June, opposition leader Kim Young-sam visits Moscow and while there, confers with Ho Dam, the visiting chairman of North Korea's Committee for Peaceful Reunification of the Fatherland. Ho invites Kim to visit Pyongyang, and Kim refuses.

On June 27, opposition assemblyman So Kyong-won is arrested for his secret 1988 visit to Pyongyang in violation of the National Security Law. An investigation uncovers a connection with Kim Dae-jung, who knew of So's visit, and in August 1989, Kim is indicted for violation of the National Security Law.

In its own answer to the 1988 Summer Olympics in Seoul, Pyongyang hosts the 13th International Youth Festival in July. A South Korean student representing the anti-government Chondaehyop federation flouts travel restrictions and appears at the festival in North Korea. In August, upon returning home, she is arrested and spends more than three years in prison for violating the National Security Law.

In November, North Korean president Kim Il-sung pays an unofficial visit to Beijing, where he is assured that China has no intention of recognizing South Korea.

In December, government and opposition leaders agree that the ongoing recriminations about misdeeds under Chun Doo-hwan's Fifth Republic should stop. Chun is brought back from exile to testify before a National Assembly hearing. It is also agreed that former general Chong Ho-yong, the military academy classmate of Chun and Roh who led the initial paratroopers' assault on Kwangju in 1980, be required to give up his Assembly seat.

1990   In January, opposition leader Kim Young-sam surprises the nation by merging his political party with the ruling DJP to form the Democratic Liberal Party (DLP), loosely modeled on Japan's ruling Liberal Democratic Party and composed of factions whose presumed intention is to take turns leading the nation. Kim Young-sam, whose own party had been faltering before the merger, is widely criticized for opportunism.

Pundits speculate that the DLP expects to evolve according to the pattern of the Liberal Democratic Party in Japan, where the party rules but factions within it constantly negotiate and take turns at furnishing the prime minister. As the year passes, however, it becomes clear that Kim Young-sam opposes this "cabinet" form of party government and prefers to take his chances competing for the party's nomination in the 1992 presidential election. By the end of the year, President Roh and Kim Young-sam reach agreement that the party will support the status quo and that there will be no constitutional change.

Over the winter of 1989–90, Japanese sources publish reports of aerial photographs that show the North Koreans building something big at their existing nuclear power plant at Yongbyon, north of Pyongyang. There is speculation that it is a processing facility to make weapons-grade plutonium. North Korea, which signed the Nuclear Nonproliferation Treaty (NPT) in 1985, has not yet signed the safeguards agreement that gives International Atomic Energy Agency (IAEA) inspectors access to its facilities to verify compliance with the NPT. North Korea rejects calls from the international community to open the Yongbyon facility to IAEA inspection.

In January, North Korea breaks off contact with South Korea in protest against the annual U.S.-ROK Team Spirit maneuvers, which it deems provocative. Contact resumes after the exercises.

In March, Chinese leader Jiang Zemin pays a return visit to Pyongyang.

In April, commercial air service begins between South Korea and the Soviet Union.

In May, North Korea cancels its Diamond Mountains joint venture with Hyundai tycoon Chung Ju-yung.

In May, the North Korean Supreme People's Assembly elects Kim Jong-il to a top position in the DPRK military hierarchy, moving him one step closer to succeeding his father, Kim Il-sung.

In June, President Roh Tae-woo flies to San Francisco to rendezvous with Soviet leader Mikhail Gorbachev, who is on a trip to the United States. Their meeting is brief but historic, indicating a major shift in Soviet attitudes toward the Korean peninsula. For Roh, the encounter is a triumph for his *Nordpolitik*, by which he seeks to isolate North Korea by cultivating the nations of the socialist bloc.

In September, the prime ministers of North and South Korea meet for the first time, in Seoul. Their conference is the first high-level government-to-government encounter since before the Korean War.

In September, South Korea and the Soviet Union exchange recognition and ambassadors. The North Koreans protest bitterly.

North and South Korean prime ministers meet for a second time in Pyongyang, and then a third time in Seoul, in December.

In December, President Roh Tae-woo visits Moscow for talks with Soviet leader Gorbachev.

1991   International intelligence experts conclude that North Korea has been building a plutonium reprocessing facility and a small high-explosives test facility at its nuclear site in Yongbyon. The North Koreans deny that they are making nuclear weapons, claiming that they are building a "radiochemical laboratory."

In his New Year's message to the people of the DPRK, North Korean president Kim Il-sung accuses the South of plotting a German-style takeover and says he can develop nuclear weapons to stop it.

During the Persian Gulf War, Seoul contributes aid totaling one-half billion dollars and a 134-person medical team to the U.S.-led Allied effort against Iraq.

In February, North Korea cancels the fourth round of North-South prime ministers' talks because of the U.S.-ROK Team Spirit military maneuvers scheduled for March. The maneuvers take place, albeit on a smaller scale than usual because of the diversion of resources to the Persian Gulf War.

In March, as part of a democratization effort, South Korea holds elections for local self-governing councils. The ruling DLP wins 70 percent of the seats.

In April, South Korea, which like North Korea has only had observer status in the United Nations since the Korean War, decides to join the United Nations, confident at last that the Soviet Union and China will not veto its membership. North Korea opposes separate membership for South Korea, saying that it is a step toward permanent division of the nation.

In April, Soviet president Mikhail Gorbachev visits Cheju Island in Korea and confers with President Roh Tae-woo.

In May, Chinese premier Li Peng visits Pyongyang, where he tells the North Koreans that unification is a matter to be solved by the Koreans themselves. At the end of the month North Korea announces that it is dropping its long-standing opposition to U.N. membership for the two Koreas and will apply for membership along with the South.

In June, North Korea notifies the IAEA that it will sign the nuclear safeguards agreement giving inspectors access to its nuclear facilities, but that it will not actually permit inspections until the United States takes its nuclear weapons out of South Korea and opens its bases in South Korea to international inspection as well.

In a second round of local elections on June 20, 60 percent of the contests for local councils go to the ruling DLP.

In August, the failed coup attempt against Mikhail Gorbachev in the Soviet Union shakes the North Korean regime, and the North-South talks are put on hold.

On September 17, North and South Korea are admitted separately to the United Nations. The occasion enables the two prime ministers to confer in New York.

On September 28, President George Bush announces sweeping cuts in the numbers of tactical nuclear weapons positioned abroad, and the United States indicates that it is withdrawing nuclear weapons from South Korea. North Korea repeats its demand that the United States open suspected nuclear installations in the South to international inspection.

In October, Kim Il-sung spends ten days traveling in China, conferring with Chinese leaders. He returns praising China's economic advances.

On October 22–23 in Pyongyang, the prime ministers of North and South Korea agree to work out a nonaggression treaty.

On December 13 at their fifth meeting, the prime ministers of North and South Korea sign a historic Agreement on Reconciliation, Nonaggression, and Exchanges and Cooperation Between the South and the North, vowing to respect each other's social systems, resolve conflicts through dialogue, reestablish direct communications and transportation links, and exchange information. At the end of the month officials from both sides initial a six-point "denuclearization" declaration renouncing the production or possession of nuclear weapons. North Korea once more promises to sign the IAEA safeguards agreement.

North Korean heir-apparent Kim Jong-il is given supreme command of the North Korean military on December 24.

1992   In January, President Roh Tae-woo announces postponement of the next round of local elections, over opposition objections.

Following North Korea's agreement to sign the IAEA nuclear safeguards agreement, the United States and South Korea agree not to hold their annual Team Spirit maneuvers in 1992.

North Korea signs the IAEA nuclear safeguards agreement on January 30 and ratifies it on April 9.

On February 19, the two Koreas exchange documents formalizing their December 1991 "denuclearization" agreement at the sixth round of North-South ministerial talks in Pyongyang.

On March 24, Koreans hold National Assembly elections. The government party loses its two-thirds majority and has to create alliances by which it ends up with 159 of the 299 seats in the Assembly. Major opposition groups winning seats are Kim Dae-jung's Democratic Party, with 96 seats, and Hyundai chairman Chung Ju-yung's United People's Party, with 32. The UPP's Assembly success makes it a contender in the pending presidential election.

In April, President Kim Il-sung celebrates his 80th birthday in Pyongyang with two weeks of festivities.

After the first Rodney King trial verdict in Los Angeles on April 29, riots occur in South Central Los Angeles and spread to Koreatown. As rioters loot and burn area shops, thousands of Korean Americans lose their businesses. The violence continues for three days, devastating the economic base of the Korean immigrant community in Los Angeles.

In May and June, the IAEA sends inspection teams to North Korea to assess the nuclear facilities at Yongbyon. The North Koreans furnish lists of nuclear assets and appear to be cooperative. Suspicions linger, however, that they are not revealing everything to agency inspectors.

Throughout the summer in South Korea there is spirited infighting within the ruling Democratic Liberal Party. The party nominates former opposition leader Kim Young-sam as its presidential candidate, prompting secession by a number of important party leaders, who then prove unable to mount viable candidacies for themselves.

To rise above the fray, President Roh Tae-woo resigns the DLP in September and declares the government "neutral" in the forthcoming presidential campaign.

To emphasize the government's detachment from the partisan campaign, President Roh dismisses his cabinet in October and replaces it with a slate of "neutral" ministers—meaning officials without political party affiliations.

In October, the government cracks a ring of North Korean agents who allegedly intend to organize a branch of the [North] Korean Workers' Party in the South.

On December 18, 81.9 percent of the Korean electorate turns out to vote for president. DLP candidate Kim Young-sam is elected by a plurality of 42 percent and becomes the first nonmilitary president of South Korea in more 30 years, in the first presidential succession to take place without a constitutional change.

1993   In February, North Korea refuses a challenge inspection by the International Atomic Energy Agency. At issue are two storage sites for nuclear waste that the North Koreans say are military installations and not subject to IAEA inspection.

On February 25, Kim Young-sam is formally inaugurated president. He launches a campaign against political corruption, requiring DLP assemblymen to publish their assets and dismissing officials who have been skimming public funds. The investigations cause embarrassment, but Kim wins public support early on for his effort to do something meaningful about systemic corruption.

The IAEA gives North Korea until March 31 to open its two suspected nuclear dumps to agency inspection.

On March 12, North Korea announces that it is exercising its option to withdraw from the Nuclear Nonproliferation Treaty it signed in 1985. If it carries through with this threat, it will be the first country ever to withdraw from the treaty, and it will effectively remove its nuclear program from any established international controls. There is consternation in the IAEA, United Nations, South Korea and Japan, and around the world as policymakers scramble to keep North Korea in the NPT community. On April 1, the IAEA vows to go to the U.N. Security Council to seek sanctions.

In May, North Korea test fires long-range nuclear-capable Scud-C missiles eastward into the East Sea (Sea of Japan).

On June 2, ten days before the North Korean withdrawal from the nuclear Nonproliferation Treaty is to take effect, North Korean vice foreign minister Kang Sok-ju and U.S. assistant secretary of state Robert Gallucci meet in New York amid further discussion of U.N. sanctions. They achieve no agreement. On June 10, however, Kang announces North Korea's decision to "suspend" its withdrawal, leaving the treaty and IAEA safeguards agreement intact for the indefinite future.

In July, after the G-7 meeting in Tokyo, President Bill Clinton visits South Korea to emphasize the continuing U.S. commitment to South Korean security and warns North Korea not to build nuclear weapons.

In mid-July, U.S. and North Korean officials meet in Geneva to discuss possible solutions to the standoff over Pyongyang's nuclear program. During three days of meetings, the North Koreans agree to (that is, demand) "full and impartial application of IAEA safeguards." They consent to further talks with the IAEA about implementing the "impartial" inspection regime—though they do not agree to open the two suspected nuclear sites of primary interest to the IAEA, nor do they agree to indefinite adherence to the NPT. They also agree to resume bilateral talks with South Korea on "denuclearization" of the Korean peninsula. The United States, for its part, agrees to consider helping North Korea replace its existing Chernobyl-style reactors with less dangerous models—ones that would also produce less weapons-grade plutonium. The two parties agree to meet again in two months.

Glossary

Agency for National Security Planning (ANSP). ROK foreign and domestic intelligence agency; replaced the Korean Central Intelligence Agency (KCIA) in the 1980s.

Agreement on Reconciliation, Nonaggression, and Exchanges and Cooperation Between the South and the North. A series of agreements signed by the prime ministers of North and South Korea at the height of progress in the 1990–92 high-level negotiations to ease tensions on the Korean peninsula. In the agreements the two sides resolved to settle disputes peacefully, set up communications, and exchange information. It was signed on December 13, 1991, and was followed at the end of the month by a six-point "denuclearization" declaration in which both sides agreed not to produce or possess nuclear weapons.

Armistice Agreement. An agreement to end the Korean War, signed at Panmunjom on July 27, 1953, by the United Nations Command (representing U.N., U.S., and South Korean forces), on the one side, and the supreme commander of the Korean People's Army and the commander of the Chinese People's Volunteers, on the other. The purpose of the agreement was to stop the fighting and prevent outbreaks of hostilities "until a peaceful settlement is achieved"; however, no permanent peace treaty replacing this supposedly temporary truce has yet been negotiated.

Blue House. Colloquial English term for the South Korean presidential establishment, derived from the blue-tile roof of the presidential residence, Chongwadae.

Bretton Woods Agreements (1945). The agreements that created the World Bank and the International Monetary Fund to help fund postwar reconstruction and support the international currency system.

Chaebol. Korean term for business groups such as Hyundai, Lucky–Gold Star, Samsung, Daewoo, and Sunkyong.

Cholla. Refers to North and South Cholla provinces in southwestern Korea. Also referred to as the Honam region. Home area of Kim Dae-jung. Kwangju is its main city.

Chung Ju-yung (Chong Chu-yong). Founder and honorary chairman of the Hyundai business group, he played a significant role in the Roh Tae-woo government's *Nordpolitik*, notably in creating commercial links to the former Soviet Union and attempting to take South Korean investment into North Korea. In 1991, after facing a tax investigation, he decided to enter politics and founded the Unification National Party (UNP). In the December 1992 election he placed third, with about 16 percent of the popular vote.

Chun Doo-hwan. (Chon Tu-hwan). President of the Fifth Republic of Korea, 1980–88. During Chun's term, the so-called Fifth Republic irregularities—for example, Chun's relatives' illegal economic activities—overshadowed his achievement in leading the nation to economic recovery. On December 31, 1989, Chun testified before the National Assembly on the Fifth Republic irregularities and the Kwangju incident of 1980. At the end of 1990, Chun completed a two-year period of contemplation at a remote temple in Kangwon province and returned to Seoul, where he lives in virtual seclusion.

Chungchong. Refers to North and South Chungchong provinces in west central Korea. Home area of Kim Jong-pil. Main city is Taejon.

Combined Forces Command (CFC). The military command structure created jointly by the United States and South Korea in 1978 to replace the outdated and unreliable United Nations Command structure dating from the Korean War. The mission of the CFC is to coordinate the use of military units in the defense of South Korea. Accordingly, the CFC embodies the arrangement whereby its commander in chief (CINC) commands U.S. and South Korean forces in wartime and, in effect, in peacetime for deterrence of any possible North Korean attack. Until now, the CINC of the CFC has always been the American general who is concurrently the CINC of the United Nations Command, U.S. Forces Korea, and the Eighth U.S. Army. The CFC structure is currently under review.

Defense Security Command. ROK military intelligence agency.

Demilitarized Zone (DMZ). An area of two kilometers on both sides of the Military Demarcation Line, 155 miles long, that is the border between South and North Korea. The DMZ was set aside by the Armistice Agreement of July 27, 1953, as a buffer zone to prevent an outbreak of hostilities.

Democratic Justice Party (DJP). Established in 1981 by President Chun Doo-hwan. Roh Tae-woo became its chairman in 1985. On January 22, 1990, under President Roh, the DJP merged with two of the three opposition parties to form the Democratic Liberal Party.

Democratic Liberal Party (DLP). Formed by the merger of the DJP and two opposition parties headed by Kim Young-sam and Kim Jong-pil in January 1990, it commanded more than a two-thirds majority in the ROK National Assembly until the Assembly election of March 24, 1992, from which it emerged with a total of 149 out of 299 seats, one vote short of a majority. In the December 1992 presidential election, DLP candidate Kim Young-sam won with a 42 percent plurality.

Democratic Party (DP). Established in early 1990 as an opposition party, after two of the three former opposition parties had merged with the ruling DJP to form the DLP. Its leader is Yi Ki-taek. In 1991 it merged with the Party for Peace and Democracy, headed by Kim Dae-jung, and in the March 24, 1992, National Assembly election it won a total of 97 of the 299 seats. In the December 1992 presidential election, DP candidate Kim Dae-jung drew 34 percent of the vote.

Democratic People's Republic of Korea (DPRK). Official name of North Korea since 1948.

Elections. The **13th presidential election of December 16, 1987**, was the first direct election for president in South Korea since 1971. DJP candidate Roh Tae-woo secured 36.6 percent of the vote, trailed by Kim Young-sam of the Reunification Democratic Party (RDP; 28 percent), Kim Dae-jung of the Party for Peace and Democracy (PPD; 27 percent), and Kim Jong-pil of the New Democratic Republican Party (NDRP; 8.1 percent).

On **January 22, 1990, the DJP, RDP, and NDRP merged** into the Democratic Liberal Party with a commanding majority of 216 seats in the Assembly.

Supreme People's Assembly elections took place in North Korea on April 22, 1990. Of the 687 seats, 601 (87.5 percent) were won by candidates of the ruling Korean Workers' Party (KWP).

On **March 26, 1991**, local elections were held for the first time since the military coup of 1961 to elect representatives to city, county, and district assemblies. Candidates ran ostensibly without party labels, but candidates supporting the ruling DLP were seen as having won a strong majority of the races.

On June 20, 1991, a second round of local elections was held for provincial and Special City (e.g., Seoul, Pusan) assemblies, in which declared party candidates ran and the DLP won 65.1 percent of the seats (564 out of 866), many more than most observers had predicted.

The 14th National Assembly election in South Korea was held on March 24, 1992. The ruling DLP emerged with 149 out of 299 seats in the national legislature, one short of a majority. The Democratic Party won 97, the new Unification National Party won 31, independents won 21, and a splinter party won the remaining seats.

The 14th presidential election of December 18, 1992, brought victory to Kim Young-sam of the Democratic Liberal Party. Kim is the first nonmilitary president to be elected in South Korea in more than 30 years.

Fifth Republic. The Chun Doo-hwan regime, 1980–88.

Guam Doctrine (Also the "Nixon Doctrine"). President Richard Nixon's 1969 declaration that the United States would avoid becoming entangled in Asian conflicts, but would continue to aid friendly states with technical and economic means. The doctrine set the stage for "Vietnamization," the policy leading to the U.S. withdrawal from Vietnam, and it raised questions in Korea about the resolve of the United States to keep its commitments under the 1953 U.S.-Korea Mutual Security Treaty.

Han Sung-joo (Han Song-ju). Foreign minister of the Republic of Korea, 1993–.

Hwang In-sung (Hwang In-song). Prime minister of the Republic of Korea, 1993–.

Juche (*Chuch'e*). Kim Il-sung's ideology, first articulated in 1955. Stresses self-reliance, nationalism, frugality, hard work, unity, and respect for North Korean revolutionary tradition. Ideological basis of the Kim Il-sung cult in North Korea. Basic texts include Kim Il-sung's collected works.

Kang Song-san. Prime minister of the DPRK, 1992–.

Kim Dae-jung (Kim Tae-jung). Coleader and 1992 presidential candidate of the main opposition Democratic Party. A native of South Cholla province, Kim's career in presidential politics goes back to 1971, when he mounted a surprisingly strong showing against then-president Park Chung-hee, winning 45.3 percent of the popular vote. After being subjected to various forms of pressure including incarceration during the 1970s, Kim was convicted of sedition in 1980, just before the start of Chun Doo-hwan's Fifth Republic, and sentenced to a 20-year prison term. Then–DJP chairman Roh Tae-woo's June 1987 Declaration restored Kim's civil rights and enabled him to establish a political party in time for the 13th presidential election of December 1987, in which he won 27 percent of the vote, as opposed to Roh Tae-woo's 36.6 percent. In 1990 he helped create the Democratic Party, and he ran as its candidate in the December 1992 presidential election, drawing 34 percent of the popular vote and coming in second to Kim Young-sam.

Kim Il-sung (Kim Il-song). Leader of the Democratic People's Republic of Korea since 1945.

Kim Jong-il (Kim Chong-il). The son of Kim Il-sung, now poised to succeed his father. He was appointed first vice-chairman of the National Defense Commission, his highest government post to date, in May 1990. On Christmas Eve 1991, he was appointed commander-in-chief of the DPRK's armed forces, a position normally reserved for the president under the North Korean constitution.

Kim Jong-pil (Kim Chong-p'il). Member of General Park Chung-hee's junta in the military coup of 1961 and founder of the Korean Central Intelligence Agency; architect of Park's ruling Democratic Republican Party (1963); key player in South Korea's normalization of diplomatic relations with Japan (1963–65); prime minister (1971–75); in semi-retirement after Park's assassination, reemerged as National Assembly member and founder of the New Democratic Republican Party. After winning only 35 of 299 seats in the National Assembly elections of April 1988, Kim merged his NDRP with parties led by Roh Tae-woo and Kim Young-sam to form the Democratic Liberal Party in January 1990.

Kim Yong-nam. Foreign minister of the DPRK.

Kim Young-sam (Kim Yong-sam). President of the ROK; formerly leader of the Reunification Democratic Party, which he represented in the presidential election of 1987 and later merged with President Roh Tae-woo's Democratic Justice Party in January 1990. Longtime opposition leader during the presidencies of Park Chung-hee and Chun Doo-hwan.

Kim Yong-sun. Secretary for International Affairs of the (North) Korean Workers' Party and a key player in North Korea's foreign relations.

Korean Workers' Party (KWP). The ruling party of North Korea, usually characterized as communist or "Kimilsungist."

Kwangju incident. A violent ten-day confrontation in May 1980 between ROK special forces troops and anti–martial law demonstrators in Kwangju, South Cholla province. The "incident," which involved a massacre in which at least 192 people died opposing Chun Doo-hwan's rise to power, opened wounds in the volatile Honam region that still fester today in the tension between the Cholla and Kyongsang provinces.

Kyongsang. Refers to North and South Kyongsang provinces in southeastern Korea. Also referred to as the Yongnam region. Home area of Roh Tae-woo, Chun Doo-hwan, and many other Fifth and Sixth Republic figures, as well as of Kim Young-sam. Pusan and Taegu are major cities.

March First (1919) Independence Movement. The spontaneous popular uprising against Japanese colonial rule that erupted with the reading of a Korean declaration of independence during preparations for the funeral of the fallen monarch, Emperor Kojong. The movement, planned in part by Korean students in Japan and by religious and community leaders in Korea, was the biggest outbreak of resistance to Japanese rule during the entire colonial period (1910–45). As it spread across the nation and continued into 1920, it provoked severe repression from the Japanese, who took an estimated 7,000 Korean lives in the process of quelling demonstrations. Most modern political movements in Korea claim some connection to the March First Movement.

National Security Law. Enacted in 1958 to control the activities of "anti-state" organizations. The law's ostensible purpose is to protect national security, but it has frequently been applied selectively to punish domestic dissidents. The law was amended in May 1991 to limit offenses to those that would "endanger the security of the nation or basic order of liberal democracy."

Nodong Sinmun (*Rodong Shinmun*). "Workers' Newspaper" in Pyongyang. The organ of the Korean Workers' Party.

Nordpolitik, or Northern Policy. A term to describe the Roh Tae-woo government's diplomatic strategy to initiate detente with North

Korea and to establish economic and diplomatic relationships with other countries of the former Soviet bloc when they were still under communist rule.

Panmunjom. Originally a village located south of Kaesong in what is now the DMZ; the site of the truce talks in the Korean War; since 1953 the primary point of contact between the United Nations (South Korean) side and North Korea.

Park Chung-hee. Leader of the military coup of 1961; President of the ROK from 1963 to 1979. In 1972 Park instituted the Yushin Constitution, under which he became the first indirectly elected president of South Korea, chosen by an electoral college, and ruled by decree through most of the 1970s. Park was assassinated by the Korean Central Intelligence Agency director Kim Chae-gyu on October 26, 1979.

Republic of Korea (ROK). The official name of South Korea since 1948.

Roh Tae-woo (No T'ae-u). President of the Republic of Korea, 1988–93. Having risen from the military with Chun Doo-hwan, he served as minister of home affairs, minister of sports, and chairman of the Seoul Olympics Organizing Committee under the Fifth Republic, and as chairman of the ruling Democratic Justice Party from 1985 to 1987, when he became the DJP's candidate for the presidency, which he won by a plurality of just under 37 percent in the December 1987 election.

As president, Roh worked to ease authoritarianism, open a dialogue with the former socialist bloc, and rectify the imbalances in the Korean economy. Though he was largely successful in setting the stage for "democratization" in South Korea, he never completely escaped the taint of association with Chun Doo-hwan and the Fifth Republic.

Status of Forces Agreement (SOFA). The agreement covering U.S. military facilities and jurisdiction over U.S. military personnel suspected of crimes committed in Korea, signed in 1966. In 1990 the SOFA was modified to give the Korean side more latitude in the arrest and prosecution of American military personnel charged with crimes in the ROK.

"Super 301" provision. Section 301 of the U.S. Omnibus Trade Act of 1988 designed to discourage unfair trading. Countries found to be trading unfairly or discriminating against American goods may have preferences canceled for their goods and restrictions such as special duties imposed, by way of retaliation.

Team Spirit. Annual ROK-U.S. joint military exercise between 1976 and 1991. In the 1980s it usually involved about 140,000 South Korean soldiers and 60,000 Americans, many of whom were flown in from outside Korea. In 1991 the exercise was scaled down in light of the Persian Gulf War and U.S. defense budget cuts, and in 1992 Team Spirit was canceled in the interests of promoting North Korean cooperation on nuclear inspections. However, with the impasse that was reached over the North Korean nuclear program, the exercises were resumed in March 1993.

Yang Hyong-sop. Chairman of the DPRK Supreme People's Assembly.

Yi Ki-taek (Lee Ki Taek). Cochairman, with Kim Dae-jung, of the Democratic Party.

Yi Sang-ok (Lee Sang-ock). ROK foreign minister, Dec. 1990–.

Yongbyon. City north of Pyongyang; location of North Korea's nuclear facility, which is suspected of being capable of producing nuclear weapons and to which, until June 1991, the DPRK refused to permit access for international inspection. In 1992 the Pyongyang facilities were opened to inspection by the International Atomic Energy Agency.

Suggestions for Further Study

South Korea's Politics Since Liberation

Clark, Donald N., ed. *The Kwangju Uprising*. Boulder: Westview Press, 1988.

Eckert, Carter J., et al. *Korea Old and New: A History*. Seoul: Ilchokak for Korea Institute, Harvard University, 1990.

Han, Sung-joo. *The Failure of Democracy in South Korea*. Berkeley: University of California Press, 1974.

Han, Sung-joo, and Robert J. Myers, eds. *Korea: The Year 2000*. Lanham, Md.: University Press of America for Carnegie Council on Ethics and International Affairs, 1987.

Kihl, Young Whan. *Politics and Policies in Divided Korea: Regimes in Contest*. Boulder: Westview Press, 1985.

Kim, Se-jin. *The Politics of Military Revolution in Korea*. Durham: University of North Carolina Press, 1971.

Lee, Manwoo. *The Odyssey of Korean Democracy*. New York: Praeger, 1990.

Macdonald, Donald S. *The Koreans: Contemporary Politics and Society* Boulder: Westview Press, 1990.

Oh, John Kie-chang. *Korea: Democracy on Trial*. Ithaca: Cornell University Press, 1968.

Sohn, Hak-kyu. *Authoritarianism and Opposition in South Korea*. London: Routledge, 1989.

Steinberg, David I. *The Republic of Korea*. Boulder: Westview Press, 1987.

The Transformation of the South Korean Economy

Amsden, Alice H. *Asia's Next Giant: South Korea and Late Industrialization*. New York: Oxford University Press, 1989.

Leipziger, D. M., et al. *The Distribution of Income and Wealth in Korea.* Washington, D.C.: Economic Development Institute of the World Bank, 1992.

Mason, Edward S., et al. *The Economic and Social Modernization of the Republic of Korea* (summary of a 10-volume study). Cambridge: Harvard University Press and the Korea Development Institute, 1979.

Wade, Robert. *Governing the Market: Economic Theory and the Role of Government in East Asian Industrialization.* Princeton: Princeton University Press, 1990.

SaKong, Il. *Korea in the World Economy.* Washington, D.C.: Institute for International Economics, 1993.

Woo, Jung-en. *Race to the Swift: State and Finance in Korean Industrialization.* New York: Columbia University Press, 1991.

U.S. Policy Toward South Korea

Asia Society. *Divided Korea II: Report of the Second Asia Society Study Mission.* New York: The Asia Society, 1993.

Gibney, Frank. *Korea's Quiet Revolution: From Garrison State to Democracy.* New York: Walker, 1992.

Lee, Chae-Jin. "U.S. Policy Toward North Korea in the 1990s." *Korean Studies* (1992).

Lee, Hong Yung. "South Korea in 1992: A Turning Point in Democratization." *Asian Survey* (January 1993).

Merrill, John. "North Korea in 1992: Steering Away from the Shoals." *Asian Survey* (January 1993).

Contemporary Literature in a Divided Land

Anthologies

Flowers of Fire, ed. Peter H. Lee. Honolulu: University of Hawaii Press, 1986.

Land of Exile: Contemporary Korean Fiction, trans. Marshall R. Pihl, Bruce Fulton, and Ju Chan Fulton. Armonk, N.Y.: M. E. Sharpe, 1993.

Listening to Korea, ed. Marshall R. Pihl. New York: Praeger, 1973.

Literature East and West (Korean literature issue), Vol. 14, no. 3 (September 1970).

Meetings and Farewells, ed. Chong-wha Chung. New York: St. Martin's, 1980.

Modern Korean Literature, ed. Peter H. Lee. Honolulu: University of Hawaii Press, 1990.

Modern Short Stories from Korea, trans. In-Sob Zong. Seoul: Mun-ho Publishing Co., 1958.

Postwar Korean Short Stories, trans. Chong-un Kim. Seoul: Seoul National University Press, 1983.

The Rainy Spell and Other Korean Stories, trans. Suh Ji Moon. London: Onyz Press, 1983.

Translation: The Journal of Literary Translation (Korean Feature Section), Vol. 13 (Fall 1984), pp. 1–129.

A Washed-Out Dream, trans. Kevin O'Rourke. Seoul: Korean Literature Foundation, 1980.

Words of Farewell: Stories by Korean Women Writers, trans. Bruce Fulton and Ju Chan Fulton. Seattle: Seal Press, 1989.

Authors

Ahn, Junghyo. *White Badge*. New York: Soho Press, 1989.

———. *Silver Stallion*. New York: Soho Press, 1990.

Ch-oe, In-hun. *The Square*, trans. Kevin O'Rourke. Devon, U.K.: Spindlewood, 1985.

Kang, Shin-jae. *The Waves*, trans. Tina L. Sallee. New York: Kegan Paul International, 1989.

Han, Mal-suk. *Hymn of the Spirit*, trans. Suzanne Crowder. Seoul: Korean Literature Foundation, 1983.

Hwang, Sun-won. *The Stars and Other Korean Short Stories*, trans. Edward Poitras. Hong Kong: Heinemann Asia, 1980.

———. *Trees on the Cliff*, trans. Wang-rok Chang. Seoul: Korean Literature Foundation, 1980.

———. *The Drizzle and Other Korean Short Stories*, trans. Kim et al. Seoul: Si-sa-yong-o-sa, 1983.

———. *The Moving Castle*, trans. Bruce Fulton and Ju Chan Fulton. Seoul: Si-sa-yong-o-sa, 1985.

_____. *The Book of Masks*, ed. J. Martin Holman. London: Readers International, 1989.

_____. *Shadows of a Sound*, ed. J. Martin Holman. San Francisco: Mercury House, 1990.

Oh, Yong-su. *The Good People*, trans. Marshall R. Pihl. Hong Kong: Heinemann Asia, 1985.

Yi, Ch-ong-jun. *This Paradise of Yours*, trans. Wang-rok Chang and Young-hee Chang. Seoul: Korean Literature Foundation, 1986.

Yi, Mun-yol. *Our Twisted Hero*, trans. Kevin O'Rourke. Seoul: Minumsa, 1988.

Yun, Heung-gil. *The House of Twilight*, ed. J. Martin Holman. London: Readers International, 1989.

The Many Faces of Korean Dance

Readings

Heyman, Alan C. *Dances of the Three-Thousand-League Land*. Seoul: Seoul Computer Press, 1981.

Kendall, Laurel. *Shamans, Housewives, and Other Restless Spirits: Women in Korean Ritual Life*. Honolulu: University of Hawaii Press, 1985.

Korean National Commission for UNESCO. *Korean Dance, Theater, and Cinema*. Arch Cape, Oreg.: Pace International Research, 1983.

Korean National Commission for UNESCO. *Traditional Performing Arts of Korea*. Seoul: Korean National Commission for UNESCO, 1975.

Van Zile, Judy. "*Ch'oyongmu*: An Ancient Dance Survives." *Korea Journal*, Vol. 8, no. 2 (Summer 1987), pp. 4–19.

Van Zile, Judy, "Dance in Contemporary Korea." *Korea Journal*, Vol. 12, no. 3 (Fall 1991), pp. 10–21.

Van Zile, Judy, "Korean Dance: An Introduction." *A Festival of Korea Humanities Guide*. Honolulu: University of Hawaii, 1992, pp. 13, 18.

Videotapes

Aak, Korean Court Music and Dance. New York: The Asia Society, 1979.

Buddhist Dances of Korea. Seattle: University of Washington Press, 1971.

Pongsan Masked-Dance Drama from Korea. New York: The Asia Society, 1977.

Shaman Ritual from Korea. New York: The Asia Society, 1983.

Sun Ock Lee: Korean Dancer. New York: The Asia Society, 1981.

Yangju Sandae Nori: Masked Drama of Korea. Seattle: University of Washington Archives of Ethnic Music and Dance, 1966.

Contemporary Korean Musical Cultures

Readings

Hwang, Byung-Ki. "Some Notes on Korean Music and Aspects of Its Aesthetics." *World of Music,* Vol. 27, no. 2. pp. 32–46.

Killick, Andrew. "Nationalism and Internationalism in New Music for Korean Instruments." *Korea Journal,* Vol. 31, no. 3 (Autumn 1991), pp. 104–16.

Lee, Byong Won. "Korea." *The New Grove Dictionary of Music and Musicians.* London: Macmillan, 1980.

———. "Improvisation in Korean Musics." *Music Educators Journal,* Vol. 66, no. 5 (January 1980), pp. 137–45.

Lee, Hey-Ku. *Essays on Korean Traditional Music,* trans. and ed. Robert C. Provine. Seoul: Royal Asiatic Society, 1981.

Provine, Robert C. "Korean Music in Historical Perspective." *World of Music,* Vol. 27, no. 2, pp. 3–13.

Discography (12″ 33 1/3 rpm discs)

Korean Buddhist Music. Recording and notes by John Levy. 1968. Bogue LVLX-253.

Korean Court Music. Recording and notes by John Levy. 1969. Lyrichord LL 7206.

Korean Social and Folk Music. Recording and notes by John Levy. 1969. Lyrichord LLST 7211.

P'ansori: Korean Epic Vocal Art and Instrumental Music. Produced by David Lewiston. 1972. Nonesuch H-72049.

Samul-nori: Drums and Voices of Korea. Produced by Herbert Harris. 1984. Nonesuch 72093–1.

The Korean American Community

Choy, Bong-Youn. *Koreans in America*. Chicago: Nelson-Hall, 1979.

Hurh, Won Moo, and Kwang Chung Kim. *Korean Immigrants in America: A Structural Analysis of Ethnic Confinement and Adhesive Adaptation*. Rutherford, N.J.: Fairleigh Dickinson University Press, 1984.

Kim, Hyung-chan, and Eun Ho Lee, eds. *Koreans in America: Dreams and Realities*. Seoul: Institute of Korean Studies, 1990.

Kim, Ilsoo. *New Urban Immigrants: The Korean Community in New York*. Princeton: Princeton University Press, 1981.

Kim, Ronyoung. *Clay Walls*. Seattle: University of Washington Press, 1987.

Koo, Hagen, and Eui-Young Yu. *Korean Immigration to the United States: Its Demographic Pattern and Social Implications for Both Countries*. Honolulu: Papers of the East-West Population Institute No. 74, 1981.

Lee, Mary Paik. *Quiet Odyssey: A Pioneer Korean Woman in America*. Seattle: University of Washington Press, 1990.

Light, Ivan, and Edna Bonacich. *Immigrant Entrepreneurs: Koreans in Los Angeles 1965–1982*. Berkeley: University of California Press, 1988.

Patterson, Wayne. *The Korean Frontier in America: Immigration to Hawaii, 1896–1910*. Honolulu: University of Hawaii Press, 1988.

Yu, Eui-Young. *Mekookeul Sanun Hanindul* (Koreans in the United States: A Collection of Columns). Los Angeles: Hankook Ilbo, 1992.

Yu, Eui-Young. *Korean Community Profile: Life and Consumer Patterns*. Los Angeles: Korea Times/Hankook Ilbo, 1990.

Yu, Eui-Young, and Earl H. Phillips, eds. *Korean Women in Transition: At Home and Abroad*. Los Angeles: Center for Korean-American and Korean Studies, California State University, Los Angeles, 1987.

Yu, Eui-Young, Earl H. Phillips, and Eun Sik Yang, eds. *Koreans in Los Angeles: Prospects and Promises*. Los Angeles: Koryo Research Institute and Center for Korean-American and Korean Studies, California State University, Los Angeles, 1982.

Korean Perceptions of America

Academy of Korean Studies and the Wilson Center. *Reflections on a Century of United States–Korea Relations*. Washington, D.C.: University Press of America, 1983.

Han, Sung-joo, ed. *After One Hundred Years: Continuity and Change in Korean-American Relations*. Seoul: Asiatic Research Center, Korea University, 1982.

Scalapino, Robert A., and Sung-joo Han, eds. *United States–Korea Relations*. Berkeley: Institute of East Asian Studies, University of California at Berkeley, 1986.

Yu, Eui-Young, and Terry Kandal, eds. *The Korean Peninsula in the Changing World Order*. Los Angeles: Center for Korean-American and Korean Studies, California State University, Los Angeles, 1992.

American Attitudes Toward Korea

Buruma, Ian. "Playing for Keeps." *New York Review of Books*, November 10, 1988, pp. 44–50.

Han, Sung-joo, ed. *After One Hundred Years: Continuity and Change in Korean-American Relations*. Seoul: Asiatic Research Center, Korea University, 1982.

Kwak, Tae-Hwan et al. *U.S.-Korean Relations, 1882–1982*. Seoul: Institute for Far Eastern Studies, Kyungnam University, 1982.

Underwood, Lilias Horton. *Fifteen Years among the Topknots*. Boston: American Tract Society, 1904.

About the Contributors

Donald N. Clark is Professor of History and Director of International Studies at Trinity University in San Antonio, Texas. The son of Presbyterian missionaries in Seoul, he began learning about Korea in the 1950s and went on to earn his Ph.D. in East Asian history at Harvard in 1978. His experience in Korea includes periods as a Peace Corps volunteer, Social Science Research Council dissertation fellow, and Fulbright scholar, most recently at Yonsei University in 1990. His publications include *Christianity in Modern Korea* (1986) and contributions to *The Kwangju Uprising* (1988), *Korea Briefing, 1991*, *The Cambridge History of China*, Volume 8, and a variety of specialized journals.

Kim Kyong-Dong is Professor of Sociology at the College of Social Sciences, Seoul National University, and Executive Director of the SNU Development Foundation. He has also taught at Seoul Women's University, North Carolina State University at Raleigh, and Ecole des Hautes Etudes en Sciences Sociales in Paris. Professor Kim is the author of several books in Korean and English, including *Rethinking Development: Theories and Experiences* (English, 1985). He edited the English-language volume *Asia in the 21st Century: Challenges and Prospects* (1990) with Su-Hoon Lee and has contributed articles to such journals as *Asian Survey* and *International Social Science Journal*.

Byongwon Lee is Head of the Ethnomusicology Program at the University of Hawaii at Manoa. He was educated at Seoul National University, where he majored in Korean music theory, and the University of Washington, where he received his Ph.D. in ethnomusicology in 1974. Professor Lee was a Fulbright scholar at Seoul National University in 1972 and 1980 and a Senior Scholar of the UNESCO-sponsored Silk Road Maritime Route Expedition team in 1991. He is the author of *Buddhist Music of Korea* (1987) and of an extensive article on Korea for *The New Grove Dictionary of Music and Musicians* (1980). Professor Lee is currently writing a book on the musical cultures of Korea and its people.

Chae-Jin Lee is Professor of Government and Director of the Keck Center for International and Strategic Studies at Claremont McKenna College. He received a B.A. from Seoul National University and a

Ph.D. from the University of California at Los Angeles. His publications include *U.S. Policy Toward Japan and Korea*, coauthored with Hideo Sato (1982); *Political Leadership in Korea*, coedited with Dae-Sook Suh (1976); *China's Korean Minority* (1986); *The Korean War: 40-Year Perspectives*, which he edited (1991); and *The Prospects for Korean Unification*, coedited with Jay Speakman (1993).

Donald S. Macdonald is a teacher and consultant in Washington, D.C. His career has included 20 years as a professor of political science, during which he has taught Korea studies at Georgetown University, and 20 years in U.S. government service. He lived in Korea for more than 10 years as military officer, diplomat, and scholar, most recently as a Fulbright scholar at Korea University (1990–91). He received his Ph.D. in political science from the George Washington University and is the author of *The Koreans: Contemporary Politics and Society* (1990) and *U.S.-Korea Relations from Liberation to Self-Reliance* (1992).

Marshall R. Pihl is Associate Professor of Korean Literature at the University of Hawaii at Manoa and serves as President of the International Korean Literature Association. He was born in Boston and educated at Harvard and Seoul National University. A pioneer in Korean studies, Pihl specializes in fiction but teaches all genres from all periods of Korean literature. He is the author of a work on traditional Korean oral narrative, *The Korean Singer of Tales* (forthcoming).

David I. Steinberg, Distinguished Professor of Korea Studies, School of Foreign Service, Georgetown University, is the author of *The Republic of Korea: Economic Transformation and Social Change* (1987) and many monographs and articles on Korea's political economy and development. He was a member of the Senior Foreign Service, Agency for International Development, Department of State, and a representative of the Asia Foundation in Korea. He was educated at Dartmouth College, Lingnan University (Canton, China), Harvard University, and the School of Oriental and African Studies, University of London.

Judy Van Zile is Professor of Dance at the University of Hawaii at Manoa, where she coordinates the dance ethnology program. Her publications include an annotated bibliography on dance in India, a monograph on Japanese *bon* dancing in Hawaii, and numerous articles on movement analysis and Asian dance. During four residencies in Korea from 1979 to 1990, she conducted the research on which her chapter in this volume is based.

Eui-Young Yu is Professor of Sociology and Director of the Institute for Asian American and Pacific Asian Studies at California State University, Los Angeles. He holds a B.A. degree from Seoul National University and a M.A. and Ph.D. from the University of Pennsylvania. He received an Outstanding Professor Award of CSULA in 1985. His published works include *The Korean Peninsula in the Changing World Order* (1992), *Korean Community Profile: Life and Consumer Patterns* (1990), *Juvenile Delinquency in the Korean Community of Los Angeles* (1987), *Korean Women in Transition: At Home and Abroad* (1987), and *Koreans in Los Angeles: Prospects and Promises* (1982).

About the Book

Published in conjunction with The Asia Society's Festival of Korea, this expanded issue of *Korea Briefing* provides historical insight into Korea, with retrospective chapters on politics and economics, and illuminates Korea's cultural heritage through chapters on music, dance, and literature. In addition, the political and economic chapters treat events of the past year, outlining the challenges and possibilities facing Kim Young-sam, the newly elected South Korean president. Another chapter examines the implications for U.S. policy toward Korea of Bill Clinton's election to the U.S. presidency. A chapter by the editor describing the U.S. outlook toward Korea is balanced by a chapter on the changes in Korean perspectives on the United States since the Korean War. The Korean American community's struggles in the United States are explored in a chapter that addresses the aftereffects of the Los Angeles riots in the broader context of issues facing the Korean American community.